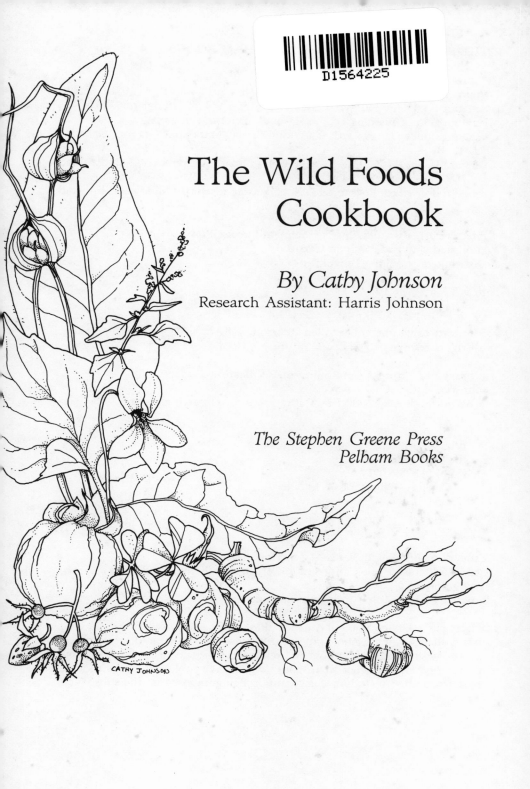

The Wild Foods Cookbook

By Cathy Johnson

Research Assistant: Harris Johnson

The Stephen Greene Press
Pelham Books

THE STEPHEN GREENE PRESS/PELHAM BOOKS

Published by Penguin Books USA, Inc.
Viking Penguin Inc., 40 West 23rd Street, New York, New York 10010, U.S.A.
Penguin Books Ltd, 27 Wrights Lane, London W8 5TZ, England
Penguin Books Australia Ltd, Ringwood, Victoria, Australia
Penguin Books Canada Ltd, 2801 John Street, Markham, Ontario, Canada
  L3R 1B4
Penguin Books (N.Z.) Ltd, 182–190 Wairau Road, Auckland 10, New Zealand

Penguin Books Ltd, Registered Offices: Harmondsworth, Middlesex, England

First published in 1989 by The Stephen Greene Press
Published simultaneously in Canada
Distributed by Viking Penguin Inc.

10 9 8 7 6 5 4 3 2 1

Library of Congress Cataloging-in-Publication Data
Johnson, Cathy (Cathy A.)
  Wild foods cookbook / by Cathy Johnson; research assistant,
  Harris Johnson.
     p.   cm.
  Bibliography: p.
  Includes index.
  ISBN 0-8289-0712-9
  1. Cookery (Wild foods) I. Title.
TX823.J54 1989
641.6—dc19   88-31906
                                                                          CIP

Printed in the United States of America
Set in Administer Book and Administer Light Italic by AccuComp
Typographers
Produced by Unicorn Production Services, Inc.

To Harris, who cares.

Spring
Beauty
(Claytonia
virginica)

edible corm or
tuber

Contents

Foreword

I have never been certain as to exactly when my interest in gathering edible wild plants began. This was not something my family did as I was growing up, nor any of my relatives as near as I can recall. And while my mother spent diligent hours tending a wonderful flower garden, we had no vegetable garden to get me used to the idea of gathering my own produce, domestic or otherwise. What we did have, however, were some delightful neighbors who not only had vegetable gardens full of exotic and unusual things but who even occasionally foraged in the wilds beyond. It was they who provided that initial spark for what became a lifelong pursuit.

On thinking back, it was probably the blueberries that did it—tall bushes that seemed to tower above my five-year-old self, laden with luscious blue-black berries. I had gone to the Rhode Island beaches with our neighbors, the Schaefers, and we had stopped to collect blueberries on the way home. Despite all the wonders of that day—immense sandy beaches, huge waves, and the like—something about those tall bushes and buckets filled to the brim with sweet, delicious fruit overshadowed all else and left an indelible impression. And, of course, the experience did not end there. In the days and weeks that followed there came a seemingly endless supply of jellies and syrups and pies to keep the memory fresh.

I have gathered blueberries and other wild edibles countless times since that day, but the essential wonder of it remains. Foraging satisfies my needs on so many different levels, both physical and spiritual. It has become my personal touchstone not only with my past but also with the natural world around me. Now, of course, I can and often do supply a litany of rationales as to why my pursuit is a desirable one—anything from personal survival, to improved nutrition, to even a heightened sense of environmental awareness. But all of these reasons come after the fact and serve only to justify what I am already doing. Basically, the reason why I gather wild foods now is the same one that applied when I was a child: it's fun.

One of the more remarkable aspects of collecting and preparing wild edibles is how much it still owes to the oral tradition. In a time when many activities have become the sole province of trained professionals, foraging remains essentially a populist endeavor. This is not to say that much new and valuable information is not being generated by the academic and professional communities; it is. On the other hand, an enormous amount of knowledge is still being passed along by word-of-mouth. From time to time, someone collects this information, adds their own interpretations and additions, and brings it alive for the rest of us. Cathy Johnson has done just that.

This is a delightfully written and illustrated book. If you have never gathered wild foods before, you can have no better introduction to its pleasures. If you are an old hand at foraging, it may suggest some new directions. Whichever it may be, this book will make an invaluable addition to your library.

—Lee Allen Peterson

Acknowledgments

A ny book is the product of many hands and minds. This one is no exception, and many people have helped me in its various stages. My heartfelt thanks go to Burt Wagenknecht, professor of botany at William Jewell College in Liberty, Missouri, for going through the book and checking my information entry by entry, as well as being so generous with his time when I had questions.

Similar thanks go to Dr. James Duke and to Lee Allen Peterson, who alerted me to the latest research on edibles and the nutritional values of wild foods.

Ann Zwinger is always there to encourage and empathize; there is no way to express my gratitude for that.

The Kansas City, Missouri, branch of the FDA, Health and Human Services Division, was extremely helpful in researching this book, as was the Missouri Department of Conservation.

My family and friends deserve thanks not only for their patience with me as I worked but in sharing a love of the outdoors and the wild foods found there.

My appreciation also goes to the *Mother Earth News*, for help with nutritional information.

Parts of this manuscript appeared first in other forms in the following periodicals: *Sports Afield*, *Early American Life*, and *Ford Times*. All kindly granted their permission to reuse parts of my articles for this book.

Thanks go to Mary Kennan for her steadfast encouragement and continued support in this project and to Thomas Begner of The Stephen Greene Press for finding it worthy of publication.

Moral support is always vital throughout any book project; Laura Helen and Wayne Wright and my sister, Yvonne Busey, provided plenty of that.

Recipes come to cooks in a variety of ways—as sheerest inspiration, as family favorites passed from generation to generation, from friends and acquaintances, from cookbooks and magazine articles. The recipes in this book have their genesis in all of these areas but have been made my own through experimentation and substitutions; in my thirty years of cooking, I've learned what I like. I hope you will, as well. My thanks go to all those sources that inspired my labors in the kitchen and the back roads, collecting basket in hand.

And very special thanks to my husband, Harris, who acted as research assistant, reader, taster, and artwork collater. His love and support were the glue that held it all together.

A Word of Caution

This book is not intended as a blanket endorsement of wild foods and should not be considered a final resource for identification. Be sure to positively identify any wild food you eat. Do not be misled by the fact that squirrels or birds are dining with impunity: squirrels eat nearly every mushroom and birds can eat plant seeds containing strychnine.

Individual plant allergies may affect your reaction even to commonly edible varieties; to begin with, go slow and taste only a bit of any new food.

Gather wildings only where chemical herbicides or fertilizers are not in use. Aside from surface pollution, plants are able to concentrate in their tissues nitrates and other chemicals that may be harmful in concentrations. For the same reasons, avoid collecting wildings near heavily trafficked areas. Heavy metals and asbestos contamination from automobile brakes and exhausts are a problem in these areas.

Cross-reference with a good field guide. In most cases, avoid plants with milky, orange, red, yellow, or soapy-tasting sap. Unless you have positively identified a plant as edible, avoid those resembling parsnip, dill, carrot, or parsley, as well as those resembling beans, melons, or cucumbers.

Eat only those parts of plants recommended. Like our familiar garden rhubarb, some parts may be edible while others are poisonous. In the case of plants requiring special handling to be safe, be sure to follow instructions carefully.

In the case of pokeweed, which has recently been discovered to cause possible birth defects if the juice is absorbed through skin abrasions in addition to the poisonous phytolaccin contained in the root, mature plant, and berries, or in the case of sassafras, which the FDA considers carcinogenic, use your discretion. The same is true for bracken ferns and sweet clovers: bracken ferns may be carcinogenic, and decaying sweet clover contains dicumarin, an anticoagulent. It is your decision in the end, and you may prefer to avoid them altogether.

Introduction—The Wild Foods Cookbook

W ild foods may not be as wild as they seem. To our hunter-gatherer forebears they were simply there, a part of life, an accepted and necessary component of survival—and the seeds of an infant civilization. Later, when we began to settle down, when we wanted our own fire and a place to call home, these same foods were planted and cultivated in communal gardens. Our supermarket vegetables began life as wildings; generations of crossbreeding and hybridization have produced the foods we know today. These foods may or may not be as flavorful as their wild ancestors; many are bred for color, size, ease of shipping, and a kind of visual perfection rather than for taste or nutritive value.

The ubiquitous pale-orange tennis ball of the common supermarket tomato springs to mind, but it is not alone in its overbred tastelessness. Why not explore a world closer to that known by earlier inhabitants of the earth, a world of "new" and satisfying flavors?

What could be more tempting than a salad just picked from the wild, fresh with dew and infused with energy and flavor? Try the well-known, milder greens to get started with wildings—greens like lamb's-quarter, plantain, curled dock, and very young, tender dandelion greens. You'll find them as good as their domestic counterparts but with a taste all of their own. The more adventuresome among us may try husk-tomatoes, maple key "beans," redbud pods, prickly pear cactus pads (*nopales*), and the delicious wild mushrooms. All the gourmet edibles in the market can't compare with this *most* gourmet fare—exclusively yours and fresh as morning, nouvelle cuisine at your fingertips.

If you've never tried wild foods before, go slowly; incorporate just a few into your diet at a time, perhaps as an adjunct to purchased salad ingredients. Their robust flavors—and sometimes more fibrous make-up—can startle an unprepared human digestive system. Introduce them to yourself and to your family a few at a time, if you are trying wild greens especially; healthful, hearty fare, too *many* the first time can give you an upset stomach. But let common sense be your guide. *Any* robust new food can upset your system, wild or not.

Why not combine a camping or backpacking trek with a foraging expedition? As far up as the timberline, climbers can find some wilding or another to complement their packed-in supplies or freshly caught mountain trout. Even *above* the timberline and on the arctic tundra, several varieties of lichen can provide survival rations for soups and stews or can be ground for a nutritious flour substitute.

Make a family outing a trip back in time, to a time when finding and collecting food together was a necessity instead of only the pure pleasure it can be today. Let the kids help you gather raspberries, hanging like amethyst globes, or tiny wild strawberries. If you are lucky, a few berries may make it beyond the berry pail and into your recipes!

Our grandparents knew more about the abundance of free edibles than most of us do today; Grandma's grits and greens were a springtime staple and only one of the wild foods my hill-country family knew and enjoyed. Poke salad, lamb's-quarter, dock, and nettles were mixed for a "mess of greens" that put spinach to shame, not only in taste and nutritional value but in the fact that they were both free for the picking and available much earlier than "garden sass," as Grandma called it. Pawpaws and persimmons were on Grandma's menu, as were the glowing jars of crab-apple butter, raspberry jam, and wild strawberry jelly. Great-grandpa was said to enjoy a tipple of wild elderberry wine for his digestion. It was put down in crocks to ferment just before the grapes were ripe—a favorite wild ingredient for autumn wines.

For anyone who enjoys the outdoors—and spends much time there—a rudimentary knowledge of edible wild plants is almost a must. Accidents *do* happen, and the unforeseeable could strand you in the wild for several days longer than you had originally planned. Unless you've packed in emergency rations, your inadvertent stay could prove unpleasant at best—no one enjoys hunger pangs. Get to know a few locally abundant, delicious, and easy-to-prepare wildings (some require only picking and eating out of hand), and your stay can seem like an extended vacation instead of a miserable inconvenience. You could even save your own life, with your wits alone.

A knowledge of wild food may literally *or* figuratively save your life under less dramatic circumstances, as well. During prolonged layoffs or periods of unemployment, such wildings are more than welcome gourmet touches—they can be necessity. At one period in my own life, and not so very long ago, my husband and I lived on $220 during one very difficult month's time—wild foods made all the difference, though I still lost ten pounds that month. Had I known it was coming, I could have canned, frozen, and dried enough wildings to have sailed through till things picked up; as it was, I remember standing out in front of the house, *willing* the mulberries to ripen so I could have fresh fruit. I am still grateful to that volunteer mulberry tree. Nothing has ever tasted so good. And every year, it still does.

During the Great Depression, when they were forced from relative to relative and job to job, my parents and older sister made good use of all the wildings they could harvest. My mother's upbringing stood her in good stead; she was able to recognize and collect a wide variety of edibles, and my sister remembers delicious meals of wild game, fish, and berry cobblers. It must have tasted as good as the mulberry breakfasts from my tree, nearly fifty years later.

The problems faced by the *new* homeless in America are far too complex to be solved by collecting a few wild greens and a handful of berries. But a bit of knowledge can help allay hunger pangs and keep one going for another day. Careful collecting and preparation can make the difference between nutritional disaster and a reasonably balanced diet.

During the sixties and early seventies, wild foods were popularized by such adventurous writers as Euell Gibbons, Bradford Angier, Ben Charles Harris, Grace Firth, and Nelson Coon. Gathering wildings became the province of back-to-the-landers, the militantly self-reliant, hippies, and others of a similar bent. But even then, interest in wild foods began to sift into the mainstream. Times were difficult, financially and physically, for a great many people, and we were looking for new ways to live. Gibbons even made it to national television in a series of commercials: "Ever eat a pine tree? Many parts are edible." Our diets were on the agenda of things we *could* control, if the world itself seemed frighteningly out of kilter. Some of us were dining and drinking quite well, thank you, on plants we had found growing in our own backyards, largely thanks to the writings of these pioneers in the field. This book carries on the tradition, updates it, and brings it into the odd mix society has become in these last years of the twentieth century. It speaks to our needs for recreation and quality of life as well as to basic necessities; the upwardly mobile that most of my counterculture friends have become should find it as satisfying as the hungry on a city street corner. And those of us happily in between will grin and say we knew it all along.

Most wild foods books address only the plant kingdom, and if we were a nation of vegetarians I would do likewise. But there's a wide world of fish and game to add savor to your meals, and I've included a main dish chapter of fish and poultry as well as a vegetarian chapter. Fish, frog legs, wild turkey, crayfish, quail, goose, and others can be found here; red meat recipes will not. We are a health-conscious nation, this latter half of the century, watching our intake of high-cholesterol, high-fat meats. It seemed simplest and best to leave them out; if you want, you can substitute meat in the dishes that call for poultry. I do, myself, on occasion.

If you don't hunt or fish, don't give up on these wild flavors; many of these wildings can be bought in specialty stores and some in your local market. Our grocer often carries catfish, crayfish, and rabbit (as well as an assortment of wild fruits and vegetables). Substitute domestic meats where you must, but try wildings if you can. There is a wonderful piquancy to wild foods that domestication smooths out.

Cranberries are a part of our winter holiday dinners; our forebears picked them from the wild, and those lucky enough to live in the Northeast still do. But if you don't live where you can visit a cranberry bog to gather these tart red berries for yourself, try for green gooseberries and red currants or any one of the wild bramble fruits.

There are wild flour substitutes, wild coffees, wild teas, wild wines, greens and potherbs, potatolike starches, and wild asparagus—as well as many wildings that can be prepared as you would the easily recognizable asparagus spears—all these will round out your menu and put new interest back in your meals. Provide a meat course with Cajun-style crayfish (''crawfish'' in bayou country, or ''crawdads'' where I live), heap your plate with tender panfish fillets or lemon-buttered rainbow trout, make up a coq au vin with game birds instead of chicken, and you will not only survive but live like pampered royalty.

How to Use This Book

To familiarize yourself with wild foods, look for a good edible-specific field guide like Lee Allen Peterson's *A Field Guide to Edible Wild Plants* or an earlier classic, *Edible Wild Plants of Eastern North America*, by Merrit Lyndon Fernald and Alfred Charles Kinsey (see bibliography for details). A good wildflower field guide can help you find many of these edibles but of course will lack information as to edible parts or seasons for collection. Nonetheless, the botanical drawings or color photographs in these books may be of help. Photographs can be an invaluable aid in final identification of plants you've found. And be *sure* you know what you are collecting. Some wild plants look edible and are not; some parts of edible plants may cause gastric distress or even death. Know your plants. (Peterson's guide is invaluable here.)

Then, browse through the cookbook. It is arranged as to subject—salads, vegetables, main dishes (both vegetarian and meat dishes), etc. If you have found a particular plant and don't know just how to use it, refer to the index for possible recipes. One plant, such as dandelion or cattail, may provide you with salads, main dishes, desserts, and beverages, either all at one time or seasonally—quite a wild supermarket.

Where to Look

Finding wild edibles depends largely on habitat and season; many of the greens are at their peak in early spring, but autumn rains may bring a reprise. Summer is a good time to look for edible flowers and fruits, autumn the time to find many of the nuts and seeds. Edible varieties of mushrooms may be found from early spring to late fall and occasionally into the winter. Some of the roots and tubers may be dug at almost any time of the year. A good edible-specific field guide should give you dates for the plants you've found, but common sense is a big part of it.

Keep an eye out in fields and meadows and in your own backyard for wild greens: most leafy plants are virtually ubiquitous through much of the continental U.S., once you know what you are looking for—and once you are thinking *edible* rather than *weed*. Many tuberous plants, like arrowhead and cattail, may be found close to a creek, in damp ditches, in ponds and bogs and swamps. Wild fruits—elderberry, gooseberry, and the bramble fruits—often grow along country roads or at the edge of the woods. Wild strawberries may grow on disturbed or burned-over land or in open meadows.

Look up to find grapes, pawpaws, crab apples, persimmons, and the nuts; down to locate greens and other wild vegetables that grow at ankle level. Damp woods are often prime mushroom habitat, as are abandoned orchards. Watch fencerows for a variety of wild plants, from wild asparagus to fruits and greens.

Refer to our *Concise Chart to Common Wild Edibles* for more specific information, and again, don't forget to take a well-illustrated field guide. I have found Peterson's *A Field Guide to Edible Wild Plants* to be most helpful, but one with good, clear color photographs is also a good diagnostic tool.

The edibles are all around us, if we know what we're looking for. Once, when we lived on a small farm, I counted thirty-two wild edibles just along our quarter-mile drive. I was delighted.

Wild Mushrooms

These most delectable treats take some study before we even *attempt* to collect them for consumption; some that look disconcertingly like common supermarket mushrooms are in fact deadly. Be sure you know what it is you are picking, and even if they are common edible species it is best to go slowly at first. Always cook your finds (wild mushrooms should never be consumed raw), eat only a bit the first time out, and don't mix wild mushrooms and alcohol—the chemical reaction can be toxic.

It may be best to take a guide with you until you know your way around the woods—either a human one, a naturalist or botanist, or a well-illustrated field guide, such as the *Audubon Society Field Guide to Wild Mushrooms*, from Alfred A. Knopf. It is illustrated with good color photographs as well as with information as to edibility, palatability, season, etc.

I gather only morels, giant puffballs, tree ears, inky caps, chanterelles, and sulphur shelf mushrooms, to be safe, and throw away any mushrooms that are discolored, dry, or beginning to decompose. Don't think that because a squirrel or bird has eaten a wild mushroom it is safe for human consumption; some are, some aren't, and it isn't worth taking the chance. Remember the old adage: "There are old mushroom hunters, and there are bold mushroom hunters, but there are no old, bold mushroom hunters!" Get to know the common, safe varieties and stick to them until you learn the ins and outs of mycology.

A Conservation Ethic

Of course it is essential that you know what you are harvesting for your own sake; a good field guide might well be supplemented with the presence of a trained naturalist, a knowledgeable old-timer, or an experienced friend. But it is also essential to know what you are doing for the sake of the world, as well.

Some plants are on endangered species lists; some are locally endangered or rare. Check with your state's conservation department for these lists. Even if you find endangered species in local abundance, they must still be left alone to propagate naturally. You will be acting responsibly, as a caretaker of the earth—and possibly avoiding a heavy fine if you should be caught with the plants in your possession.

Collect responsibly, in any case. A plant may be neither endangered nor rare, but if you harvest all that grow in a particular plant community, they soon could be. Leave some for next year, some for others, some for the birds and animals that depend heavily on these wild foodstuffs, and some for self-seeding. There are plenty of edibles out there—no matter how hungry we may be or how good they may taste, there's no need to feel we must pick them all simply because we've found them in great numbers.

Pick carefully, disturbing plants as little as possible. If you are collecting tubers, be sure to rebury what you don't take to ensure future foraging. Don't bruise or cut plants unnecessarily; an open injury can invite disease in plants just as in human beings. Leave your collecting area looking as if you were never there.

Pick your locale carefully, as well. If you forage on your own property, don't collect where you have used herbicides or pesticides or where other forms of pollution may contaminate your wildings—an open sewer or a leaching field may produce big, healthy-looking plants but will hardly be good for *your* health. I am careful not to collect too close to a street or road, as well, to avoid contamination by heavy metals and asbestos from automobiles.

If you forage in the country, remember that nearly everything is private property; this isn't the territories anymore. If you must trespass, ask permission. And if you collect wild edibles in a state or national park, be sure you know the rules governing such collection. In Watkins Mill State Park, near my home, it is permissible to collect wild fruits, nuts, or mushrooms but not to cut wildflowers or other plants.

It's a matter of what my husband calls native intelligence—common sense coupled with common courtesy. We take only what we need, cause no undue disturbance, and leave the rest for posterity.

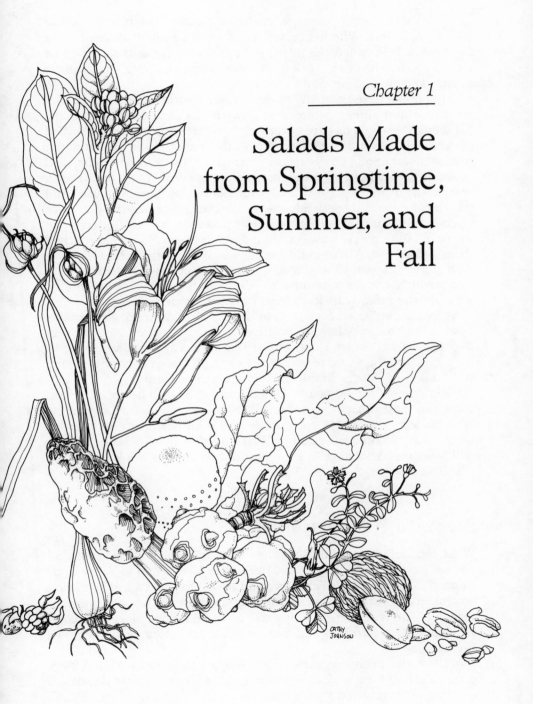

Chapter 1

Salads Made from Springtime, Summer, and Fall

Fresh, crisp, piquant; salads are a perfect complement to any meal. Whether served as an appetizer, first course, or as a hearty side dish, wild foods salads will pique your curiosity; satisfy your taste buds; boost your nutrition, mineral needs, and roughage requirements; and fill you up quite nicely.

Think of the freshest of ingredients: the crisp, fresh wildings you pick yourself only minutes before sitting down at the table (or the picnic blanket). These greens have never been irradiated, never been handled by strangers, never dusted with chemicals (that is, if you are careful to pick them far enough away from a chemical plant or areas where road crews, home owners, or crop dusters have sprayed. Look for strange, twisted plants in the area; this tells you herbicides have been used and if herbicides, possibly pesticides as well. Move on to a less-traveled place to collect.). The *wild* edibles were not picked hard and underripe to withstand the rigors of travel over hundreds of miles. *No one* has touched them before you. What could be fresher or more desirable?

Of course, as with all wild foods, you will want to wash them quickly under running water to remove any dirt, sand, or airborne pollutants; we'd do the same with food from our own gardens.

We've become salad conscious in the eighties. Aware of the benefits both to health and palate, we've discovered the salad bar. And the best of them are well worth discovering. The more adventurous among us have explored the world of garbanzo beans, alfalfa sprouts, endive, and sun chokes. Wildings simply add another dimension.

We love international salads: Greek fruit salads with honey and mint, Italian antipastos, taco salad. The salad aficionado—as opposed to one who just eats the lettuce and parsley and a bit of tomato because it's *there*—will welcome the addition of fresh wildings. The outdoor lover will welcome the chance to get out and discover this brave new world of edible nature.

Suggested Wild Ingredients

What your salad ingredients will be depends largely on the season, of course. No one grows lamb's-quarter in the San Fernando Valley to be shipped in for Vermont's February salad bowls. You won't find dandelion crowns in August or milkweed buds in November. But at almost every season of the year, some wilding will be there for the picking to complement your salad and add zest to your purchased or homegrown ingredients.

In the early spring—as early as late January in some areas, but more often March or early April—you may be able to harvest dandelion crowns, the unopened flower buds that wait, pale and blanched and delicate, just below the soil's surface. Just think, each time your salad boasts this gourmet treat—what sweet revenge on that pesky weed. (If you can't beat 'em—eat 'em.)

Wild mustard is tender and piquant at this season and on into May; later in the year its bite becomes almost vicious. You may want to harvest the seeds as they appear, though; fresh, they add a peppery bite to your salad bowl.

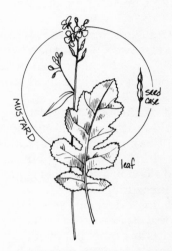

Asparagus may have long since escaped cultivation to grow in happy abundance along old roads, near abandoned farmsteads, or in fencerows. On our old farm there was a magnificent stand of this sought-after and expensive vegetable; the pale, tender shoots that sprouted each spring in the fencerow, planted there by wandering birds, were as big as a baby's forearm. I've never tasted better.

But even if you can't find asparagus (and try looking for the three-foot-tall, warm-colored ''ferns'' in the fall to locate them), poke or milkweed shoots make acceptable—and eminently available—substitutes with proper preparation.

Chickweed, the gardener's bane, is delicious in spring and summer salads, as are peppergrass, wood sorrel, wild onion, and dock.

Don't overlook the flowers in your search for wild salad ingredients. Violets are amazingly high in vitamin C—the young leaves provide nutrient-rich body to your salad while the flowers add a touch of color. Daylilies are a veritable supermarket of wild foods; in spring salads, try the young, pale green shoots. They're as tender as any lettuce in the market. Later, the buds and bright orange flowers make a festive—and delicious—salad bowl. Marinated milkweed buds are an Italian treat; a wild-foods addition to an antipasto platter.

After the first frosts have withered their tall, whispering tops, dig the crisp and crunchy tubers of the Jerusalem artichoke. These wild substitutes for water chestnuts can be dug any time you can get them out of the frosty soil until new growth starts in the spring; they're really a welcome addition to a season when there are all too few wildings.

Lightly cooked, Jerusalem artichokes can stand in for the starch in potato salad; their starch is in the form of inulin, easily digested by diabetics. (These are the sunchokes you may find in your neighborhood market—though usually somewhat smaller and more gnarled in the wild.)

Remember the wild fruits in summer and autumn salads. Crab apple and mint combine for a tart-sweet Greek salad; wild grapes are delicious for a kind of wild Waldorf—just be sure to remove the seeds. Wild plums, bramble fruits, cranberries, and rose hips all add their uncultivated goodness to salad bowls.

Don't forget the wild mushrooms as a salad ingredient. Steam them lightly and let cool; wild mushrooms should not be eaten raw. Some, like inky caps, shouldn't be consumed with alcohol—or within twenty-four hours of taking a drink—because of adverse chemical reactions between the fungus and alcohol; a good field guide of edible mushrooms should tell you these precautions.

Try marinated morels for a delicious side dish; they are so rich that just a few will satisfy you. Just as well, too—these mycologist's treasures are often as hard to find as any other pot of gold at the end of a rainbow.

In the fall, after summer's dormant period when many salad ingredients are too tough or too bitter, a new salad season comes with the late rains. Dandelions produce tender new leaves; dock, chickweed, and wood sorrel all mirror spring's bounty and extend your salad season into early winter.

And just because the snow is falling and the ground is like cement, don't think you must give up wildings in your salad. Plant a winter garden in your cellar (for directions, see Euell Gibbons' classic ''Stalking the Wild Asparagus''), and go down for some barbe de capuchin or witloof for the salad-hungry crew.

Our recipes will see you deliciously—and happily—through the seasons with something fresh and crunchy, tart, and refreshing for every palate. Mix and match with purchased or homegrown ingredients if you like.

Wilted Salad with Dock, Lamb's-Quarter, Sorrel, and Wild Onion

Serves 4-6

In the early spring, my family always looked forward to the first wilted lettuce salad made with leaf lettuce from the garden. This is a wild-food variation on a theme and one I've been able to enjoy even before the leaf lettuce is big enough to pick.

CURLY DOCK

Pick and wash enough young leaves of dock, lamb's-quarter, and wood or sheep sorrel to fill a large bowl. Cut out the midribs of the dock leaves if they are too heavy and tough.

4   strips bacon
3   T. red wine vinegar
1   T. sugar or 2 T. honey
½   t. salt
½   t. pepper (freshly ground is
      nice)

1   T. chives
½   C. chopped wild onion
4-5 cups mixed wild greens,
      well washed and drained

Fry bacon until crisp. Drain and reserve fat. Mix red wine vinegar, sugar or honey, salt, pepper, and chives in the bottom of a large bowl. Add washed and drained leaves and chopped onion and toss well. Crumble the bacon over the top. Then, heat 2 T. bacon fat until hot but not smoking. Pour over salad, stirring to distribute evenly. Leaves will wilt down to one-half or less in volume, depending on how hot the fat is. This is not low calorie, of course, nor low in fats, but it *is* wonderful. (If you want to cut cholesterol, use hot oil instead of bacon fat.)

"Potato" Salad with Jerusalem Artichokes and Wild Onions

Serves 6

Dig enough tubers to fill a 2-C. measure; more if you have a large family or are planning for a party. Wash with a stiff brush, but don't bother to peel—they are really too knobby, and the skins are rich in fiber and minerals.

2 C. artichokes
3 eggs, hard boiled
1 C. chopped wild onions
Wild dill
3 T. mayonnaise

2 T. apple cider vinegar
1 t. sugar
½ t. salt (or to taste)
Freshly ground black pepper
Celery seeds to taste

Cook artichokes till barely tender (about 5 minutes) and slice when cool. Peel and chop eggs coarsely; add chopped onions. Sprinkle with wild dill, if you can find it, and dress with mayonnaise, vinegar, sugar, salt, pepper, and celery seeds.

German "Potato" Salad

Serves 4

A hot alternative at our house is this old German treat with a wild-food twist; once again, Jerusalem artichokes stand in for potatoes, or try groundnuts (the walnut-sized tubers of *Apios americana*).

4 slices bacon
2 C. artichoke tubers (more for a larger group)
¾ C. chopped wild onions

¼ C. apple cider vinegar
2 T. brown or white sugar
1 t. salt
¼ t. pepper

Fry bacon until just crisp. Remove from skillet and drain. Boil washed artichokes until fork tender, then drain well. Sauté onions in 1 T. bacon fat until transparent and beginning to brown. Crumble bacon slices and return to the pan with onions; add drained artichokes and stir until slightly mushy. Dress with vinegar, sugar, salt, and pepper and serve hot with hasenpfeffer, sauerbraten—or just about anything else. (If you prefer to forgo the bacon fat, substitute 1 T. oil. To suggest a bacony flavor, add 1 drop liquid smoke and 1 t. brown sugar.)

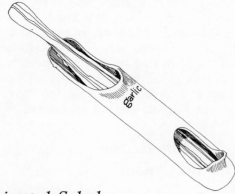

Italian Marinated Salad

Serves 6

This is made from husk-tomatoes, also known as ground-cherries. These small relatives of the garden tomato grow in small "Chinese lanterns" —the husk—and are sometimes raised in gardens for their edible fruit. I've seen them for sale in my neighborhood grocery store, though these domestic ones are much larger than the thumbnail-sized ones I find in the countryside. This fruit, incidentally, is often used to make jams and preserves and is popularly known as *Poha* in Hawaii.

This is a plant with many names; it's also called bladder cherry, strawberry tomato, and dwarf cape gooseberry. If nothing else these eminently edible names convince one that this is a plant to be tried in a number of ways.

1 pt. of husk-tomatoes, shelled
    free of their papery cover-
    ings and washed. Slice in
    half if you like.
1 or two cloves of wild garlic
½ C. chopped wild onion
¼ C. olive oil

4 T. red wine vinegar
1 T. sugar
1 t. salt
¼ t. pepper
1 T. wild marjoram or thyme
1 T. wild sage (pitcher sage)
1 T. basil leaves

Mix everything together in a quart jar; taste for proper balance of condiments and adjust if you like. Domestic or purchased herbs may be substituted if you can't find the wild ones; if you're using dried herbs, reduce the amounts by half.

Allow to marinate several hours or overnight for best flavor. This will keep for several days. I make a similar mixture with fresh tomatoes when they're in season, mixing the other wild ingredients as I can find them; it's a classic.

Poke Shoots Vinaigrette

Serves 8

Poke should be gathered in the early spring when no more than 6''–8'' tall (look for last year's bent-over stalks to help you locate these, or stake out a patch the year before. Their reddish green stems and beautiful— but toxic—blue-black berries help identify them.) Poke, like our domestic rhubarb, is a plant that has both edible and poisonous parts. Eat only the young shoots, properly prepared (see below) to remove any vestiges of phytolaccin, the cathartic and emetic contained in stronger concentrations in leaves, mature stalks, and berries.

20–30 young poke shoots (4''
    tall or smaller is best
    for this dish); wild
    asparagus or "Cossack
    asparagus" (cattail
    shoots) may be substi-
    tuted if you prefer.

1 head of wild garlic or two
    cloves
6 T. olive oil
2 T. red wine vinegar
½ t. salt
¼ t. pepper (or to taste)

Parboil young poke shoots until just tender and discard cooking water. Many people prefer to peel them first to further remove any taint of phytolaccin, but parboiling them should make them safe. Arrange shoots on a platter or casserole dish. Chop garlic very fine and sprinkle over poke shoots. Mix remaining ingredients to make vinaigrette dressing and pour over shoots. Refrigerate for 2 hours or less. This is a far cry from the poke greens my Dad brought home from his fishing trips, but it is a wonderful accompaniment to any meal.

MILK WEED BUDS

Marinated Milkweed Buds

Serves 4

You may have picked milkweed shoots earlier in the season to substitute for asparagus or poke; now, look for the tender green unopened buds on the tall plants. You should find them in midsummer.

Heavy, rounded leaves, thick stalks, and rounded flower umbels will help you identify these plants of fields and roadside. Milkweed is true to its name; it has a bitter, milky sap that permeates every part of the plant. Unless it is properly prepared, it is unpalatable in the extreme and may actually be toxic, but with preparation it is well worth the trouble.

Drop buds into already boiling water over high heat and return to a boil for 1 or 2 minutes. Drain off cooking water and repeat with fresh supplies of boiling water 2 more times. (Bringing to a boil in cold water only fixes the sap within the plant.) This basic recipe applies to all parts of the milkweed plant: young shoots, tender young leaves, buds, and pods.

1 pt. of milkweed buds, washed and prepared as above. Let cool.
1 T. capers
1 clove of wild garlic
½ C. olive oil

⅓ C. apple cider vinegar
1 T. fresh basil leaves or 1 t. dried herb
1 t. salt
⅛ t. pepper or to taste

Layer prepared milkweed buds, capers, and garlic in a quart jar. Pour olive oil/vinegar mixture over all, add seasonings, and allow to marinate overnight or for several days in the refrigerator.

Cold Artichoke Salad

Serves 6

Of course, this is the tuber of the Jerusalem artichoke, not the thistle-family variety we find at the greengrocer's. Cool, snappy-crisp, earthy, these sunchokes make a deliciously different salad.

3 small wild onions, sliced lengthwise	1 C. chopped nut meats (pecan, hickory, walnuts, hazelnuts, or any combination)
2 apples (I prefer Jonathans, usually in season when Jerusalem artichokes are at their best)	2 cloves of wild garlic
1½ C. raw artichoke tubers, well washed and sliced	3 T. mayonnaise
	1 T. prepared mustard
	Salt and pepper to taste

Chop onions fine. It isn't necessary to peel the apples, just slice them ¼" thick and discard core and seeds. Crush garlic, mix together with artichoke tubers and nut meats and the rest of the ingredients in a large bowl and dress with mayonnaise/mustard mixture.

Marinated Morels
Serves 4

If you can find enough of these succulent wild "sponge" mushrooms to spare for more exotic dishes (they are *so* good fried I usually eat them all up that way), try marinated morels.

1 C. morels, steamed, chilled, and sliced	½ C. red wine vinegar (malt vinegar is a good alternative)
1 or two cloves of wild garlic	1 t. crushed, dried basil
½ C. chopped wild onions	½ t. dried rosemary leaves
½ C. olive oil	1 t. salt or to taste

Prepare morels, garlic, and onions and place in a quart jar. Mix all the other ingredients together and pour over mushroom mixture. Allow to marinate in the refrigerator overnight, at least.

Dandelion Crown Salad
Serves 6

Dandelion crowns are one of my favorite vegetables; perhaps because I am so hungry for their fresh green taste by the time I can finally dig them from the frozen ground. This salad is a fine alternative to the crowns served hot with butter and vinegar.

Look for the rosettes of last year's dandelions; they're easy to find once the snow melts. Dig just under the soil surface (3" or so) or simply slice through the deep taproot at that level with a sharp knife and pull up the crown. You will be able to see the unopened flower heads among the blanched stems. Wash well; cut away the taproot and pull off any old dead leaves. Trim leaves and stems about an inch above ground level; the young stems and bud will hold together like a small crown.

Blanch briefly in hot water, then cool, if you prefer, to remove all traces of bitterness. Some people prefer the slight bite of the raw vegetable; take a nibble to see where you stand.

3   wild onions or ramps (these are also known as wild leeks; strong smelling but surprisingly mild, they can be substituted for garden leeks in any recipe. In West Virginia each spring they have a "Ramp Romp" to celebrate the return of these delicious wild onions.)

2–3 C. prepared dandelion crowns
½   C. olive oil
¼   C. apple cider vinegar
Salt and pepper to taste
3   hard-boiled eggs

Mix well-washed and prepared ramps (sliced or chopped) with dandelion crowns. Dress with oil and vinegar mixture and garnish with hard-boiled egg slices.

Primavera Salad

Serves 8

In the early spring in my woods, the tightly curled fiddleheads of young bracken and cinnamon ferns lift their tender, yellow-green heads in abundance. When I find a particularly thick stand, I can't resist a primavera salad.

The popular bracken fern, *Pteridium aquilinum*, is thought to be a carcinogen. Although there is no evidence against any other members of the fern family, it's best not to overindulge in this delicacy; let them be a special treat once or twice in the spring.

2 C. of fiddleheads, well washed and de-fuzzed by rubbing gently, if necessary. Drain well.
1 C. young, tender dandelion leaves
½ C. winter cress leaves (young mustard leaves may be used instead or in addition to these)
½ C. sliced morels or other edible mushrooms. (Check with a good mushroom field guide to see which are available at this time of year in your area.)

1 C. finely diced cooked ham, chicken, or turkey
½ C. mayonnaise
1 t. prepared mustard
¼ C. vinegar
¼ t. salt
¼ t. pepper
1 T. sugar or honey

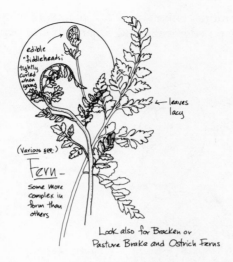

edible "fiddleheads" tightly curled when young

← leaves lacy

(Various spp.)

Fern -

Some more complex in form than others

Look also for Bracken or Pasture Brake and Ostrich Ferns

Wash, prepare, and drain wildings. Add ham, chicken, or turkey. Mix together mayonnaise, mustard, vinegar, salt, pepper, and sugar or honey to make a thickened dressing; pour over salad. Garnish with wild violets, if available.

Chickweed and Wood Sorrel with a Zesty Mayonnaise Dressing

Serves 6

Chickweed may seem to be an unprepossessing weed to add to your salad bowl; its tiny leaves and weak, trailing stems grow in waste places—and in our flower and vegetable gardens—over much of the country. In especially rich, shady areas, the leaves may grow to almost ½'' in length and look rich and glossy; I try to find such a stand to harvest my salad makings. Wood sorrel usually grows nearby, but you can substitute sheep sorrel if you find a good source. The flavor is nearly identical, tart and lemony.

1 C. chickweed leaves and stems, well washed, drained, and chopped

1 C. sorrel leaves, washed and drained

½ C. nut meats (you may have kept wild nuts in your freezer over the winter— these will still be fresh and moist)

½ C. wild onions, chopped (both white and green parts)

¼ C. chives, wild or fresh from your garden

½ C. mayonnaise

3 T. lemon juice

¼ t. curry powder

Sugar, salt, and pepper to taste

Toss leaves, onions, chives, and nut meats. Mix mayonnaise, lemon juice, and curry powder well. Add sugar, salt and pepper to taste, dress salad, and enjoy.

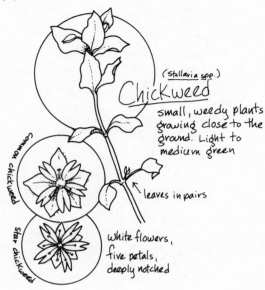

(Stellaria spp.)
Chickweed

small, weedy plants growing close to the ground. Light to medium green

common chickweed

star chickweed

leaves in pairs

white flowers, five petals, deeply notched

NOTE: Like domestic spinach, sorrel leaves contain oxalic acid and should not be consumed in huge quantities or continually, particularly by women. Oxalic acid interferes with the body's absorption of calcium.

Cranberry Relish/Salad

Serves 6

The fresh berries in this salad are tart-sweet and delicious; make it a few days ahead, if you like—it keeps well. I love the fresh, sprightly flavor of this one; it's a good side dish, appetizer, dessert, or snack—what more can you ask of one salad?

2 C. fresh cranberries, chopped
1 or two apples, coarsely chopped (skins can be left on)
1 or two oranges, peeled, sectioned, then chopped coarsely
1 or two ribs of celery, finely chopped (optional)
½ C. chopped walnuts, pecans, or hazelnuts

A few sprigs of fresh mint or sprinkling of dried leaves (even in December I find a few green mint sprigs under the protection of a blanket of dead leaves)
¼ C. honey
Juice of ½ lemon
1 t. fresh orange rind, grated

Mix all ingredients in a large bowl; chill well before serving. Garnish with a bit of fresh mint or lemon slices.

Wild Tossed Salad with Creamy Dressing *Serves 4*

The ingredients for this salad may be gathered at any season you are able to find wildings. In early spring, all of the traditional greens are tender and sweet enough for the salad bowl; later in the season, look for tender growing tips. After the autumn's late rains, dock, dandelion, sorrel, lamb's-quarter, winter cress, and even daylily may produce a fresh crop of young shoots. After winter's first frosts, look under a mitigating blanket of leaves, or mulch your own weeds for a protected supply. Or dig roots of chicory, dandelion, and others to plant in large pots indoors for a winter-long supply of fresh greens. (See appendix.)

3 C. mixed greens
1 clove of wild garlic, crushed
3 wild onions, sliced
½ C. Jerusalem artichoke
    tubers, if in season (wash
    and slice)
½ C. cattail shoots, daylily
    shoots or buds, arrowhead
    tubers—whatever is in
    season

¼ C. cottage cheese
2 T. oil
1 T. vinegar
1 t. sugar
Salt and pepper to taste
2 slices bacon, cooked crisp
    and crumbled

Toss greens well with shoots or tubers. Mix cottage cheese, oil, vinegar, sugar, and seasonings in a blender or food processor for a smooth, creamy dressing. Garnish with crumbled bacon.

pepper-
grass +
Seed case

Egg Salad with Wildings *Serves 4*

This hearty salad can serve as a light lunch, on a plate with greens, or on whole wheat bread as a sandwich filling.

4-5 hard-boiled eggs
¼ C. violet leaves, washed and drained
3-4 wild onions, chopped
2 stalks celery, diced
1 T. peppergrass seedpods
½ C. mayonnaise

3 T. red wine vinegar
1 t. sugar
¼ t. salt
¼ t. curry powder
½ C. wild lettuce, if young and sweet

Peel and slice hard-boiled eggs. Slice violet leaves into fine slivers. Chop onions fine. Toss with celery and peppergrass in a bowl. Mix mayonnaise, vinegar, sugar, salt, and curry powder in a cup until well blended. Toss into salad and serve garnished with wild lettuce.

Wild Waldorf
Serves 6

If you can find crab apples that aren't *too* tart, you'll want to use them in this recipe; if not, use domestic apples instead. This fresh, fruity salad is a wonderful summer cooler; wild ingredients add a bit of zest to an otherwise somewhat predictable classic.

2 C. chopped apples
½ C. diced celery
1-1½ C. coarsely chopped wild nut meats (pecan, hickory, black walnut, butternut, or a mixture of all of them, if you like)

1 C. washed and seeded wild grapes (fox grapes are tiny and sweet)
½ C. mayonnaise
3 T. honey
1 T. finely chopped wild mint leaves

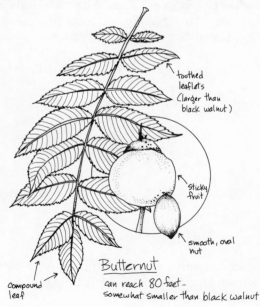

toothed leaflets (larger than black walnut)

sticky fruit

smooth, oval nut

compound leaf

Butternut
can reach 80 feet.
somewhat smaller than black walnut

Mix fruits, mint, vegetables, and nut meats well in your salad bowl; blend, mayonnaise and honey to dress the salad. This tastes best when flavors have had a chance to mellow a bit; chill for 2 hours or so.

Wild Potpourri Salad   *Serves 4–6 (or more, if you add more wildings)*

This simply means that you throw in whatever happens to be in season and abundant. In spring, use shoots and young leaves, fiddlehead fern shoots, or watercress if you live near an unpolluted, cold stream. In summer, cooked or blanched vegetables may be used, or fruits in season. Later in the year, nuts are abundant and add richness and protein. Whatever you find, put it in and dress with:

½ C. oil (use sesame oil for a different taste)

¼ C. red wine or apple cider vinegar (for fruit salads, try apple cider or juice instead of vinegar for a light, sweet taste)

Finely chopped wild mint leaves
1 T. sugar or honey
Salt and pepper to taste

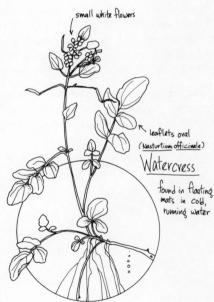

small white flowers

leaflets oval
(Nasturtiom officinale)

Watercress

found in floating mats in cold, running water

If you can't find enough wildings to make a salad at a given season, Wild Potpourri Salad is a great place to use up purchased vegetables spiked with a few of your wild finds. Shred carrots and throw in a handful of raisins. Use fresh or frozen peas, thawed but not cooked—or snow pea pods. Try garden tomatoes, cucumbers, peppers, lettuce, endive, parsley—whatever you have on hand. Then add whatever wild vegetables, herbs, flowers, or fruit you find in your yard, garden, nearby park, or countryside.

Greek Apple-Mint Salad
Serves 4

Made with wild mints and crab apples, this has a delightfully tart and refreshing taste. It *will* be different according to what variety of mint you find growing; wild spearmint grows near creeks and ponds and in moist woods, as does peppermint. Some of the more exotic mint-family members prefer open places—or even your backyard. Be brave; try some of these more unusual mints for a new taste. Look for the square stem typical of the mint family, and take a small taste of a leaf before adding it to your salad; some are almost overpowering. I like horsemint, for a change, but wild horehound, also a mint-family member, has a strong and bitter flavor—its fuzzy stem and leaves will help you identify it.

2 C. of crab apples, washed and sliced (leave the skins on for color; they're often too tiny to peel, anyway)
1 small handful of mint leaves, washed and chopped fine

3 T. honey
¼ C. lemon juice
Parsley and rosemary are optional. If desired, add 1 T. fresh or ½ t. dried and crushed herbs

Mix crab apples and mint leaves; dress with honey, lemon juice, and herbs. Add more honey if you like a sweeter taste. This may be eaten immediately or allowed to mellow for an hour or two to marry the flavors.

Chapter 2

Sauces, Butters, Dressings, and Spreads

CATHY
JOHNSON

There are times when these wonderful flavoring agents literally make the meal; a simple dish becomes a feast in seconds. It's wonderful to try something unexpected—we sit up and take notice.

Some of these wild additions are as close as your own back door; all are relatively easy to find throughout the contiguous United States, except in the desert regions or above the timberline, and even there you will find something to flavor your meals.

Some ingredients can even be bought in the local supermarket if it is well equipped. Here in Excelsior Springs, a small town some thirty miles from Kansas City, you can still find husk-tomatoes, persimmons, and locally harvested wild nuts. Fresh French sorrel is available in summer, as are gooseberries; cranberries are in seasonal abundance. If you can't find the time to forage—or the particular ingredient you want for your sauce or butter or spread—check the specialty section of your greengrocer's before giving up or try the farmer's market if you live in or near a city. It's worth the search and your palate will thank you for it.

Sauces add a special touch to ice cream, crêpes, pound cake—or even meat dishes. You can dress up an entire meal with the addition of only one exotic ingredient. Your family—and your guests—deserve the freshest and most delicious ingredients you can find. What's more, they may enjoy helping you harvest them!

Herb and fruit butters add special elegance to the humble soda cracker; just think what they can do for your homemade breads or elegant party snacks.

Some of the more exotic condiments are just great made with wild ingredients. You may have eaten chutneys before; they're spicy East Indian flavoring treats that have become a part of our vocabulary if not our everyday menu. But for a new twist try them made with husk-tomatoes or elderberries. They're easy, and you'll reap the compliments with your condiments.

And of course the salads from the last chapter can only be made more delicious when dressed—and dressed up—with our offerings.

Suggested Wild Ingredients

As with all wild-food dishes, the ingredients are seasonal—what you choose to fix will depend largely on what is available at the time. Some wildings can be frozen, canned, or dried for later use (gooseberries, elderberries, husk-tomatoes, etc.); others should be picked fresh and used immediately. Some you may even be able to keep on hand in pots in the house.

In the early spring, look for young wild peppergrass, watercress, shoots of wild onion and garlic, morel (and other) mushrooms for sauces and butters. Sheep sorrel and wood sorrel come up in the early spring and are available through the summer months.

Later in the summer, wild fruits come into season. Wild strawberries are usually first—you can add them to your cream cheese and wild-fruit spread with excellent results. Or wait a bit for spreads and sauces made with elderberries, mulberries, wild cherries, blackberries, may-apples, and—last of all—nicely frost-sweetened persimmons, all arranged in order of appearance.

Through the winter months, you may still be able to find, in a protected spot, on a south-facing bank or under a protective blanket of snow, the ingredients for wild dressings. The bulbs of wild garlic and onion may be harvested at any time, if you can dig them from the cold soil. Nuts left by neglectful squirrels may still be found and added to your *Black Walnut/Cream Cheese Spread*. Watercress, sorrel, and chickweed are usually to be found throughout the winter months. They are a delightful addition to herb butters and spreads.

A simple dish of plain vanilla ice cream or a rich but plain pound cake come alive with a dollop of homemade elderberry sauce. It's a family favorite on crêpes—not only a taste treat but a *visual* sensation poured slowly over a pale parfait dish full of homemade vanilla ice cream.

Afternoon tea—a graceful custom borrowed from Britain and becoming more popular all the time in this country—can't help but be sparked with the added excitement of wild-food sauces, spreads, and butters. A cracker is just that until you top it with a delightful spread of cream cheese and wild persimmon or watercress butter. Finger sandwiches of prettily sliced party breads are good with wild-herbed mayonnaise from this chapter.

Main dishes benefit from the offerings in this chapter, as well. Those chutneys add a special touch to an Indian dinner but also to roast beef or sliced pork. Wild plum sauce is good on meat or game. Or make nachos with a wild twist.

Not everything need be a production to be delicious, of course. Simple wild dressings are included here and my favorite, wild garlic butter. Garlic bread is popular in this country, not only with Italian dinners, where it is indispensable with pasta, but with seafood or a good Kansas City steak. One of my favorite snacks is a big slice of sourdough French bread, spread with *wild* garlic butter and toasted in the oven till golden brown.

Wild Mushroom Butter   *Serves 10*

Choose any single edible mushroom species; if you can't find enough of a single species, mix *judiciously*. This is particularly good on steaks, chops, and chicken, though a bit rich for fish. You may also use it to top a dish of steaming-hot vegetables.

¾ C. butter (or margarine)
1 C. finely diced wild mushrooms (morels or chanterelles are particularly good
   in this)
3 T. sour cream (substitute
   plain yogurt to conserve
   calories)

¼ t. salt
Pepper to taste
¼ C. good burgundy

Melt 2 T. of the butter in a heavy skillet and add drained mushrooms. Sauté until tender and beginning to turn golden. Cool and add the rest of the butter, sour cream or yogurt, salt, pepper, and burgundy to your food processor or blender; blend till smooth and chill until ready to use. (Use within 24 hours; some wild mushrooms do not keep well.)

Watercress Butter   *Serves 8–10*

This is a spicy, biting taste that just complements the cool smoothness of butter. It goes well with fancy snack crackers, seafood, or melted on a baked potato.

½ C. watercress leaves, well
   washed and picked over
¼ lb. butter (or margarine)

Pinch of salt
Pinch of pepper

Wash well to make sure your watercress leaves are free of any small passengers they may have picked up from the stream. Chop the leaves finely and cream with butter or margarine. If you like, add just a pinch of salt and pepper and roll into small individual balls. (A hint of lemon juice is not amiss here, either; use *fresh* lemon for best flavor.) If you don't live near a good, cold-water trout stream, you may substitute *winter* cress for watercress.

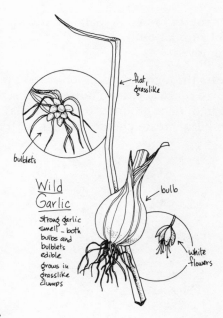

Wild Garlic

flat grasslike

bulblets

bulb

white flowers

Strong garlic smell - both bulbs and bulblets edible

grows in grasslike clumps

Garlic Butter

Serves 8

This is an all-time favorite at our house.

1 T. wild garlic (bulb, leaves, and all, chopped finely)
¼ lb. butter (or margarine)
¼ t. salt (omit if you are watching your salt intake; you won't miss it)

Pepper to taste
Pinch of curry powder (optional)

Chop garlic finely or bruise the bulbs with the back of a spoon or in a mortar and pestle. Cream with butter and seasonings; leave out curry powder if desired, but do try it both ways. Refrigerate to spread on thick hot toast or melt over a baked potato.

WALNUT

Black Walnut Butter

Serves 4–6

The rich oiliness of black walnuts makes them perfect on fancy tea breads. This butter is simple to make in your food processor or grinder; I have a small electric coffee and nut grinder that works well for small batches.

1 C. black walnut meats, well   Salt to taste
    cleaned (make sure all bits
    of shell are removed)

Run the nut meats through your grinder or food processor as many times as necessary to make a smooth butter, then season to taste with salt. Keep refrigerated, once ground, to avoid spoilage. Serve on bread or crackers with a bit of cream cheese; garnish with a fresh nut meat.

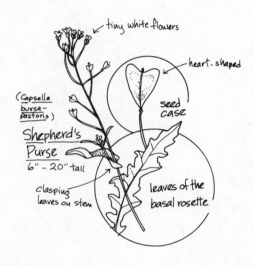

Wild Herb Butter

Yields 1 C.

This delightful addition to any bread or cracker can be made at virtually any season of the year. (But why stop there; let a dollop melt on a hot steak.) What you actually use in it depends on where you live and what you can find to add. Look for sheep or wood sorrel; peppergrass leaves (early spring) or seed (summer); shepherd's purse leaves (spring) or seeds (summer); any of the wild mints; young, tender violet leaves; orach (a slightly salty member of the spinach family found at the beach); wild sage or thyme; the fine leaves of wild carrot (Queen Anne's lace); winter cress; or even the ubiquitous backyard gill-over-the-ground. Any wilding, in other words, with a nice bite.

½ C. leaves or 3 T. seed   ½ lb. butter (margarine or the
    (peppergrass or shepherd's   margarine/butter mixes may
    purse—mix and match if   be substituted if you are
    you like; winter cress goes   trying to cut down on
    well with peppergrass   animal fats)
    leaves, and mints and
    sorrels mix well)

Chop the leaves finely. Cream with the butter or margarine and refrigerate at least 3 hours to allow the flavors to marry. If you like, make individual fancy molds for special occasions.

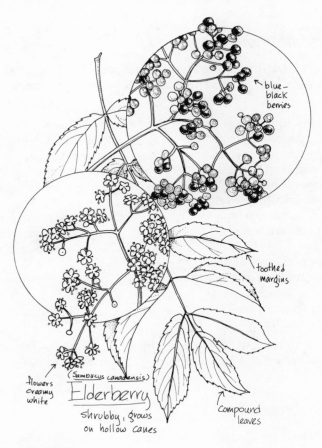

blue–black berries

toothed margins

flowers creamy white

(Sambucus canadensis)

Elderberry

shrubby, grows on hollow canes

compound leaves

Elderberry Chutney

Yields 3 pts.

This is an elegant and exotic chutney that will give a simple meal a gourmet edge. Make it when you have an abundance of dried elderberries — a simple enough trick, given the ease of gathering this prolific fruit.

3 C. dried elderberries
2 wild onions or 1 medium domestic onion, chopped
2 cloves of garlic (wild or domestic)
1 t. ground ginger
1 t. cayenne

1 chopped, seeded lemon
2¼ C. brown sugar (white can be substituted)
2 C. apple cider vinegar
1 T. mixed pickling spices (tie up in a cheesecloth bag)

Boil everything together until quite thick, stirring often to prevent sticking as the mixture thickens. Remove the bag of spices and pour into hot, sterilized half-pint jars. Seal immediately. Refrigerate to store. Try this with game as well as with more domestic fare.

Husk-Tomato Chutney
Yields 4 pts.

I have found these interesting little fruits in my local grocery store; look for them in the fall, or substitute an equal amount of green tomatoes or apples.

2   C. raisins (purchased or make your own from the wild—just be sure to seed the grapes first)
2   C. chopped husk-tomatoes (or substitute domestic green tomatoes or apples)
1   C. minced onions
1½ t. salt
2   C. chopped, tart apples (crab apples are good in this; no need to peel them, but do remove seeds and core)

3½ C. sugar (brown or white)
2   C. apple cider vinegar (or herb vinegar, if you like)
1   t. ground ginger or ½ C. fresh ground gingerroot
¼   t. cayenne
2   oz. dried mustard seed (use your own, if you've been able to forage this much)

Simmer all ingredients slowly until thick—2 or 3 hours. Stir often as it thickens and preserve as for Elderberry Chutney. Store in the refrigerator.

Spicy Mushroom Spread
Yields 2½ C.

This is delicious on canapés or tea breads. It will make that afternoon tea a memorable experience.

1½ C. finely sliced mushrooms (morels, chanterelles, or meadow mushrooms are good for this; you can also substitute store-bought)
2   C. water, boiling
½   t. salt
1   small onion, wild or domestic, finely chopped
1   small cucumber, peeled and chopped

2   T. chives (wild or domestic) chopped finely
1   t. Dijon mustard
Dash of nutmeg, freshly ground if desired
¼   t. curry powder (substitute paprika for a milder taste)
¼   C. mayonnaise

Cover sliced mushrooms with boiling water and simmer with the salt until tender (8–10 minutes). Drain well and reserve the stock for soup. Cool. Mix in remaining ingredients and refrigerate till needed (at least 1 hour before serving).

Wild Fruit/Cream Cheese Spread

Yields 2 C.

I had a variation of this at a friend's home and have since made it with a number of wild fruits, depending on the season. Try it on steamed breads, cookies, or crackers.

1 8-oz. package of cream cheese (or Neufchâtel)
2 T. mayonnaise
¼ C. sugar (more to taste if tart fruits such as cranberries or rose hips are used)

1 C. wild fruit (mulberries, strawberries, chopped mayapples or persimmons, blackberries, cranberries, wild currants, chokecherries, ground-cherries, or even rose hips) washed, chopped fine

Stir cream cheese and mayonnaise until light and fluffy; add sugar and fruits and mix well. Refrigerate until needed. This is tart and sweet all at the same time; a nice surprise on the tongue.

SHEPHERD'S
PURSE

Peppergrass or Shepherd's Purse Spread

Yields 1½ C.

You can use either the fresh chopped leaves in the early spring or the seedpods of peppergrass or shepherd's purse in midsummer.

½ C. finely chopped leaves or
   ¼ C. chopped seedpods
8 oz. softened cream cheese
2 T. mayonnaise (substitute
   plain yogurt if desired)

1 clove garlic
Salt to taste

Stir leaves or chopped pods into softened cream cheese and add mayonnaise. Chop 1 clove of garlic very finely and add to mixture. Salt if desired, although it is spicy enough that you could do without the extra sodium if you prefer. If you are watching your calories, substitute Neufchâtel or well-blended cottage cheese for the cream cheese.

Black Walnut/Cream Cheese Spread
Yields 2 C.

This couldn't be simpler or more elegant. It's also quite rich, so you may want to substitute Neufchâtel for real cream cheese.

¾ C. finely chopped black
   walnut meats (you can use
   pecans, English walnuts,
   filberts, or whatever is
   available—except peanuts!)

1 8-oz. package of cream
   cheese, softened at room
   temperature
¼ C. mayonnaise

Stir nut meats into cream cheese and mayonnaise; if the resulting mixture is still hard to spread, add just a splash of herb vinegar or sherry to the blend.

Wild Onion/Sour Cream Dressing
Yields 1¼ C.

This is delightfully simple to make and good on green salads, potato-type salads, fruit salads, or even as a topping on vegetables. You can't go wrong. If you find yourself short of dips for your chips, bring this one out.

¼ C. finely diced wild onions or
   chives
½ t. salt
1 C. sour cream (you can use
   yogurt or blended cottage
   cheese if desired)

1 T. lemon juice (fresh, please)
Dash of curry powder (optional)
Pepper to taste (optional)

Stir ingredients together cold for one taste possibility; sauté onions until just transparent and stir sour cream, etc., into pan until just warmed for an entirely different taste from the same ingredients. Serve warm or cold; try it on warm Jerusalem artichoke salad.

Wild French Dressing

This is a lovely continental dressing that proves *wild* is not necessarily synonymous with *uncultivated*.

4 T. olive oil
2 T. red wine vinegar
1 clove wild garlic, crushed
1 T. shepherd's purse seeds, chopped

1 T. finely chopped sorrel leaves
¼ t. dry mustard
¼ t. salt
Pepper to taste

Mix all ingredients thoroughly to blend oil and vinegar.

Wild Italian Dressing

The success of this dressing depends on the freshness of your ingredients.

½ C. olive (or other vegetable) oil
½ C. red wine vinegar
1 t. fresh diced wild chives
1 t. fresh diced thyme

1 clove garlic, diced
½ t. salt
Pepper to taste

Shake ingredients well and refrigerate until needed. (To make a creamy Italian, use mayonnaise instead of oil.)

Bleu Cheese "Wild" Dressing

For serious fans of bleu cheese dressings—and I am one—this recipe is a delight.

¼ t. salt
¼ t. peppergrass seeds or finely chopped leaves
4 T. olive oil

2 T. vinegar or lemon juice
¼ t. dry mustard
1 clove wild garlic, crushed
¼ C. crumbled bleu cheese

Mix salt, peppergrass seeds or leaves, garlic, 1 T. of the olive oil, 1 T. vinegar or lemon juice, and the dry mustard. Add additional lemon juice or vinegar alternately with 3 T. of olive oil, stirring constantly. Add the bleu cheese.

Grandma's Wild Herb Mayonnaise

Of course, Grandma never owned a blender or food processor—she made this the hard way, with a mortar and pestle and a whisk.

BASIC MAYONNAISE

1 egg, room temperature	½ t. salt
2 T. lemon juice or cider vinegar	Dash of pepper
1 t. each powdered mustard and sugar	1 pint vegetable or olive oil

Mix first 5 ingredients together in blender bowl, then *slowly* pour in oil until thick. It should be little more than a trickle.

For herbed mayonnaise add to blender container:

2 garlic cloves	2 T. sorrel leaves (use winter cress in early spring when the leaves are not too spicy)
2 T. chopped chives	

Blend until green—this is great on salads, sandwiches, boiled potatoes, steamed artichokes—you name it.

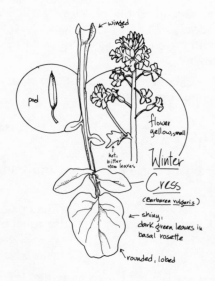

Herbed Mayonnaise

Serves 8

Depending on the season, pick spicy or tart-flavored herbs—peppergrass, shepherd's purse, wood sorrel, French sorrel, wild onions or chives, mint, water- or winter cress.

¼ C. finely chopped, washed, and drained leaves	½ t. Dijon mustard
½ C. mayonnaise	Curry powder to taste (optional)

Mix ingredients well and refrigerate till needed.

Mushroom Sauce

Serves 6–8

If mushroom butter doesn't suit your fancy, try this special sauce—it's really a rich gravy, but it's too elegant for that appellation.

1	large domestic onion or 4 wild onion bulbs, chopped	½	t. wild or domestic thyme
¼–½	C. finely sliced wild mushrooms	½	t. fresh basil leaves, chopped finely
2	T. butter (or margarine)	Salt and pepper to taste	
1	T. wild or domestic chives, chopped finely	¼	t. Tabasco (optional)
		1	C. sour cream

Sauté onions in butter or margarine until they begin to turn golden and transparent—not brown. Remove from pan and add a bit of butter if necessary. Brown mushroom pieces until just tender; add herbs and seasonings; if you prefer a milder sauce, leave out the Tabasco. Stir in sour cream and heat gently. (Again, you may substitute plain yogurt if you wish.) Serve over meat or fowl.

Sorrel Sauce

Serves 6

Use either wood sorrel or sheep sorrel in this delightfully tart sauce; it's especially good on baked fish or steamed potatoes.

½	C. wild (or domestic) onion, chopped	½	C. water
2	C. sorrel leaves, washed and drained, then chopped finely	1	C. basic white sauce
		½	t. salt or to taste
		¼	t. white pepper

Sauté onion until tender. Add sorrel leaves to pot and cover with water; simmer gently for 20 minutes or so. Drain, mix with basic white sauce, season to taste, and serve.

WOOD SORREL

BASIC WHITE SAUCE

Makes 1 Cup

This is a quick and basic version of the classic white sauce used in a number of recipes.

| 2 T. butter (or margarine, if you prefer) | 1 C. milk or milk and light stock (perhaps that mushroom stock you saved?) |
| 1½–2 T. flour | Salt and pepper to taste |

Melt butter over low heat and stir in flour. Stir 3–4 minutes until flour begins to brown lightly and look somewhat translucent. Slowly stir in milk or milk and stock mixture, and whisk constantly until thickened.

If desired, flavor further with 1 t. lemon juice, 1 t. Worcestershire sauce, 1 t. sherry, a light grating of nutmeg, 1 T. chives, or 1 T. parsley.

There's nothing wild about this sauce at all, of course — it's just a handy base for other things.

Mint Sauce for Meats

Yields 2½ C.

Many of the wild mints are good in this; taste first to see which flavor you'd prefer. Spearmint is traditional, but wild peppermint or wood mint have a nice and unusual bite. Try it with lamb, of course, but also with game.

1 C. water	½ C. *dried* mint leaves or 1½ C. fresh, washed, and finely chopped leaves.
½ C. sugar	
1 C. apple cider vinegar	

Heat water and add sugar; stir to dissolve. Remove from heat and add cider vinegar and chopped mint leaves. For best flavor, allow to stand at least ½ hour before serving. This makes rather a lot — about 2½ C. or so. It will keep well in your refrigerator, though, so you will no doubt use it up.

Green Chili Sauce

Serves 4–6

This is an authentic American Indian recipe from the desert Southwest. Our Indian forebears were premier wild-food gatherers — they were extremely good cooks, as well, as the recipes handed down to the present attest. Try this sauce with your own garden-grown or purchased green chilis for a hot bite.

| 4 or 5 mashed green chili peppers, freshly cooked or canned | 1 clove of garlic (wild or domestic) |
| 1 large domestic or two small wild onions | 1 t. wild thyme |

Combine all ingredients well and serve with any of your favorite Mexican or Indian dishes.

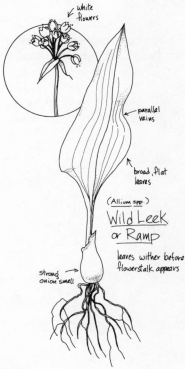

white flowers

parallel veins

broad, flat leaves

(Allium spp.)
Wild Leek
or Ramp

leaves wither before flowerstalk appears

strong onion smell

Wild Nacho Sauce

Serves 6

Here is another recipe that may have its roots planted deep in our past.

½ C. wild onion, ramps, or garlic, finely chopped
1 T. butter or margarine
2 medium tomatoes, peeled and chopped

1 t. wild thyme
1 4-oz. jar of green chili peppers
Dash of salt
1½ C. shredded cheddar cheese

Cook onion, ramp, or garlic in butter until just transparent. Stir in tomatoes, thyme, chilis, and salt and simmer for 10 minutes. Add cheese a little at a time until melted; keep stirring to ensure smoothness and use as a dip for tortilla chips or pour over a plate of them for nachos.

Wild Plum Sauce

Serves 4-6

Try this with venison, buffalo, or wild fowl. It's equally good, of course, with beef roast, chicken, pork, or turkey; the wild flavor just seems to complement the gamey flavor of the wild meats.

Sauces, Butters, Dressings / 31

½ C. juice or drippings from your roasting meat ½ C. stewed or cooked wild plums	2 T. sugar ½ T. dry mustard Salt to taste ¼ t. dried rosemary

Remove all possible fat from drippings and stir in soft, cooked plums. Add mustard, sugar, and salt, and stir until well mixed. Add rosemary.

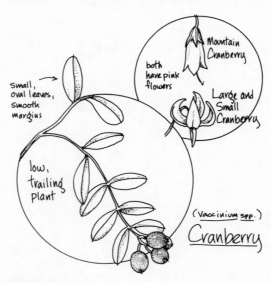

Traditional Cranberry Sauce

Serves 12

If you live in the Northeast section of the country, you will be able to find cranberries growing in the wild; if not, you can certainly substitute fresh ones from your grocer's! This is extremely simple and quick.

1 qt. fresh berries
2 C. sugar
1 C. water

Wash and drain cranberries, making sure to remove any bits of stem or debris. Put in a heavy pot with sugar and water and boil till the berries pop open; should take about 10 minutes.

This may be served hot immediately or kept in the refrigerator for up to a week.

Anyberry Sauce

Serves 4

Depending on what is in season in your area, you can make this sauce to complement game, pour over ice cream or pancakes, or even to flavor plain yogurt. Try it with wild raspberries, strawberries, mulberries, gooseberries, cranberries, huckleberries, or ground-cherries.

1 C. fresh berries, depending   ¾ C. water
      on what is in season   ½ C. sugar
1 T. cornstarch

Wash and mash berries slightly. Mix cornstarch in a little cold water, and pour into berries; add sugar and the rest of the water. Stir over medium heat until thickened. Serve hot or cold; it's delicious.

If you use gooseberries before they turn red-purple, you may need to add a bit more sugar—they are *tart*.

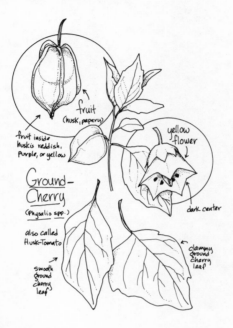

fruit
(husk, papery)

fruit inside
husks reddish,
purple, or yellow

yellow
flower

Ground-
Cherry
(Physalis spp.)

also called
Husk-Tomato

dark center

clammy
Ground
Cherry
leaf

smooth
Ground
Cherry
leaf

Elderberry Sauce

Serves 6–8

To strip the berries from their umbeled heads, try *combing* them off with a clean pocket comb.

2 C. fresh elderberries   ¼ C. lemon juice (fresh)
1 t. cornstarch   ½ C. sugar or to taste
¼ C. water   Water to thin

Put berries, cornstarch, water, and the lemon juice in a saucepan; simmer gently until done—about 15 minutes. Add sugar, continuing to stir. If sauce is a bit thick, add water to proper consistency.

As elderberries are a bit bland in taste, the lemon juice will help add some zest.

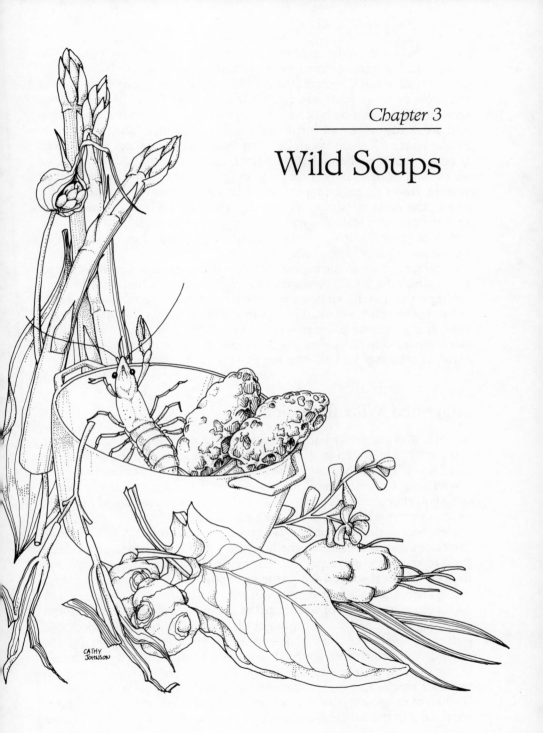

Chapter 3

Wild Soups

Soups can be comforting and warming, cold and elegant, rich or light, or even sweet or sour (have you ever had Scandinavian fruit soup?). Your mother made soup to send you off to play in the snow or when you were sick with a cold; the finest of restaurants serve delightfully smooth or hearty offerings. Backpackers tote trail soups and stews to warm and fortify after a long day of hiking.

Take your pick—soups can be quick and easy to concoct or you may choose to simmer them all day on the back of your woodstove. Choose an all-American soup or a rich and tangy ethnic blend—but whatever you do, don't forget about soups when creating your wild meals. It's one of the most satisfying ways to make use of the bits and pieces we find on our wanderings—you may not forage enough wild sorrel for a dish of greens, but you can certainly add a handful or two to a nice mixed soup for a tangy bite.

In my family, when the ingredients were diced small or pureed, we had soup; when the bowl swam with hearty chunks we called it stew—not, perhaps, the line drawn by an epicure but a handy enough designation. Whatever *you* choose to call it, it is much more than a thin and meager bowl of anonymous liquid to serve as a prelude to the "real" meal. With our recipes, soup can be the meal in itself, served complete with a crisp salad of wildings and an offering of your own homemade bread.

Suggested Wild Ingredients

Sorrel is a wonderfully continental soup ingredient. In fact, in Europe it is commonly grown in gardens to be handy to the soup pot and the salad bowl. The oxalic acid in the leaves has a lemony tartness that gives a wild tang to Greek *avgolemono sopa*—and a delightful savor to any soup you choose to toss it into. (Note, though, that oxalic acid may also block calcium absorption, so use only occasionally.)

Members of the wild onion family are as good in soups and stews as their domestic cousins and sometimes more so. Ramps have a particularly good reputation in some parts of the country for adding the perfect touch to French onion soup. Wild garlic is strong and tangy, but the leaves are available for a slightly milder flavor, if you like.

Of course, the array of wonderful wild mushrooms make mushroom soups like Campbell's never thought of; morels, chanterelles, inky caps, puffballs, chicken of the woods—whatever you can find in season will extend your mushroom soup all year-round—especially if you choose to dry a good supply for winter use. They are easily reconstituted in water or stock, and on those serendipitous days when you discover a landfall of fungi, it's wise to stock up. (Keep in mind, though, that over-harvesting in the Pacific Northwest for the gourmet food-import market has made several species quite rare. Know what you are picking, and always leave some to resow by means of spores.)

I am particularly fond of soups made with Jerusalem artichokes—so much so that I moved a few tubers to the south side of my house where I can "forage" at my convenience. You may wish to do the same—or ask for sun chokes in your local supermarket. These, and cattail, ground-nuts, and arrowhead tubers, stand in for the starch in many a wild soup and give potatoes and pasta some stiff competition.

Purslane Soup is as rich and thick as gumbo—and speaking of gumbo, we've included an authentic Louisiana gumbo using crayfish you catch yourself.

We couldn't begin to overlook the meats and fish and shellfish that give such tasty protein to our soup pots; even one small bird will flavor a nice stew. I still remember the wonderful dove stews, quail soups, and coq au vin I made from the day's bag when I was young and my father was as much hunter as naturalist. Supper was an adventure, and I was forced to give up my childhood prejudices for hamburgers and hot dogs.

A wild meal well worth having is a tasty soup or chowder made with freshwater clams or fish fillets. If you live near the coast, you'll have clams and oysters available for the picking.

If you have trouble procuring game, or if you don't fish, check your local supermarket. Mine stocks catfish, clams and oysters, ducks and geese (though domestic) near the holidays, and crayfish on occasion.

If you are fond of camping, consider making a soup of wildings and fresh-caught fish for one evening on the trail—you'll feel an affinity with the earth you can get in no other way. Our Indian forebears knew this and offered a prayer before taking the life of any creature.

French Wild Onion Soup   *Serves 4*

This soup could not be beat in Paris.

1 C. wild ramps (or other wild onions), cleaned and sliced
2 T. butter or margarine
4 C. strong beef broth or consommé
1 t. salt

Ground pepper to taste
3 T. sherry (optional)
1 thick slice of French bread for each bowl of soup
¼ C. freshly grated Parmesan cheese

In a heavy skillet at medium heat sauté onions in butter until just beginning to turn soft and golden. Add broth or consommé and simmer 20 minutes. Add seasonings and sherry.

Dip into individual bowls and top each with a slice of lightly toasted French bread. Pile freshly grated Parmesan thickly on each toast round, and put bowls under the broiler until the cheese just begins to bubble.

Wildfowl au Vin

This is a favorite at our house, for just the two of us or when we have guests in for an elegant dinner. Wildfowl gives this a special taste, similar to coq au vin, but quite unique. This and the next recipe are made with bacon. It may seem that I start all my soups with cholesterol-rich bacon; I really don't, but these two seem to benefit most from that smoky saltiness.

6	strips of bacon	1	clove wild garlic, crushed
1	C. wild onions, tops and all	1	t. salt
2½	lb. quail, pheasant, wild turkey, or domestic chicken, cut up in serving pieces	¼	t. peppergrass seeds (or ground pepper)
½	lb. wild mushrooms, sliced	½	C. broth (chicken, mushroom, or broth made from necks, backs, and feet of wild fowl)
8–9	Jerusalem artichoke tubers, cattail, or arrowhead tubers (or small new potatoes may be substituted)	½	t. dried wild thyme
		½	C. burgundy wine

Sauté bacon until crisp; break it into coarse pieces. Remove and drain on a paper towel, reserving 2 T. of fat. Sauté onion in reserved fat; remove when translucent. Add fowl to skillet and brown lightly on all sides. Remove and set aside. Sauté mushrooms.

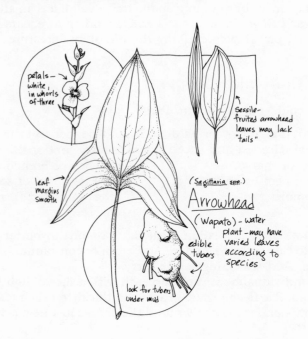

petals—white, in whorls of three

Sessile-fruited arrowhead leaves may lack "tails"

leaf margins smooth

(*Sagittaria* spp.)

Arrowhead

(Wapato) - water plant - may have varied leaves according to species

edible tubers

look for tubers under mud

Put tubers (or potatoes), mushrooms, and garlic in soup pot, add browned pieces of meat, bacon, and green onions. Add salt and peppergrass seeds or pepper, plus broth. Add thyme.

Cover and cook over low heat 1 hour; add burgundy and simmer another half hour.

(Omit bacon and use 2 T. of vegetable oil to sauté, if you prefer.)

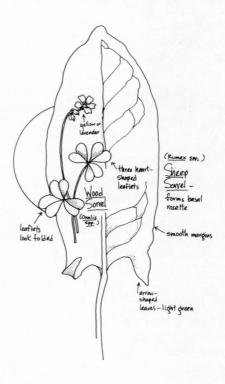

yellow or lavender

three heart-shaped leaflets

(Rumex spp.)

Sheep Sorrel – forms basal rosette

Wood Sorrel

(Oxalis spp.)

leaflets look folded

smooth margins

arrow-shaped leaves – light green

Sorrel Soup
Serves 4

This is a tart-light soup well suited for a summer meal.

3 strips bacon
½ C. wild onions, tops and all
2 C. wood sorrel or sheep
   sorrel leaves

3 C. wild fowl, chicken, or
   mushroom broth
Grating of fresh nutmeg
Salt and pepper to taste

Fry bacon until just crisp; crumble and drain, reserving 1 T. of fat. Sauté onions in same skillet, with reserved fat, and while they and the grease are hot, drop in washed sorrel leaves. Lower heat and put a lid on the skillet to just wilt sorrel. Then put everything in the soup pot with the broth; simmer 20 minutes. Use a vegetable oil substitute for the bacon, if desired.

Creamy Cheese and Ramp Soup (Quick)

Serves 4

I like this rich soup on days when I don't have time for a lot of preparation—and when I've neglected to save a broth in the refrigerator!

1   C. finely chopped ramps or other wild onions
2   T. butter or margarine
1   11½-oz. can cream of chicken soup, prepared according to package directions
1¼ C. water or milk
1   C. freshly shredded cheddar cheese (you can use less; I like mine quite cheesy)
Splash of sherry (optional)

Sauté onions (ramps) in butter and add to canned soup. Stir in water or milk according to directions on soup can, cheese, and sherry. Stir until well blended. Sprinkle with nutmeg, if desired.

Golden Mushroom Soup

Serves 4

Try this when you don't care *how* rich it is; it is wonderful. Also very, very filling; you won't need much more, even after a hard day outdoors.

1   C. washed, sliced mushrooms (morels, chanterelles, puffballs, chicken of the woods, etc.)
¼ C. butter
2   C. rich chicken broth
1   C. light cream
1   t. salt or to taste
¼ t. peppergrass seeds or ground pepper
¼ t. curry powder (optional)
1   egg

Sauté mushrooms in butter until golden brown. Add chicken broth and cream with the other seasonings and simmer 20–30 minutes.

With a wire whisk, beat egg in a small bowl, then drizzle over hot soup to form "instant noodles." The egg is optional as well, but it adds a bit of protein.

Artichoke Vichyssoise

Serves 6

This pale soup is as elegant as its domestic counterpart and perhaps more interesting.

½ C. finely chopped wild onions or ramps (bulbs only)
6   C. chicken broth
3   C. Jerusalem artichoke tubers, peeled, washed, and boiled
2   C. light cream or half-and-half
½ t. salt
¼ t. ground white pepper

Simmer onions in broth until tender; add artichoke tubers. Cook until well done—15 minutes or so, then blend till smooth in your food processor or blender (if you have neither, a simple sieve will do). Add cream and seasonings. Serve cold with a garnish of chopped chives.

This soup is every bit as good served hot—I like it with a garnish of crumbled bacon, chopped chives, or parsley, if this is the case.

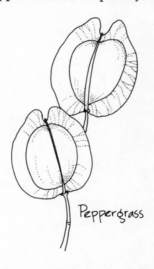

Peppergrass

Chicken Soup with Wild Vegetables and Herbs

Serves 6-8

Grandmother's chicken soup may have gone something like this one; my grandmother, at least, was fond of adding wildings to her home-style cuisine—for taste as well as necessity.

1 stewing chicken (if you can find one—a broiler or fryer will substitute, if not)	½ C. celery, finely diced
	1 garlic clove
	4 medium-sized carrots, peeled and sliced
2 pairs of chicken feet for rich coloring (optional)	½ C. poke shoots
3 wild onions	½ C. fresh celery leaves
½ C. wild mushrooms, washed and sliced	¼ t. curry powder (optional)
	7-8 Jerusalem artichoke tubers
1 T. butter or margarine	

Boil chicken until meat falls from the bone—about 1½–2 hours. Include well-washed chicken feet, if you have been lucky enough to find them—they add immeasurably to the rich golden color of the final soup, not to mention a true chicken-y flavor. Remove from pot and pick remaining meat from the bones, being careful to remove all small bones.

Sauté onions, garlic, and mushrooms in 1 T. of butter or margarine, and add to the pot with celery, carrots, poke, and seasonings.

Fifteen minutes before soup is to be served, return meat to the stock and add sliced Jerusalem artichoke tubers; the tubers will retain a bit of their crispiness and give a delightful texture to your soup pot.

Garnish with a bit of spring winter cress, watercress, or parsley.

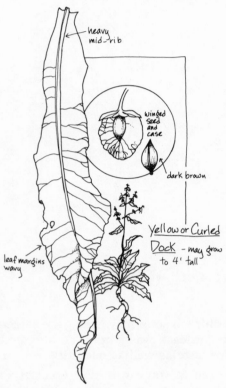

heavy mid-rib

winged seed and case

dark brown

Yellow or Curled Dock - may grow to 4' tall

leaf margins wavy

Mixed Greens and Ham Broth

Serves 4–6

You can make this hearty broth with whatever you find in abundance, or mix and match. I like it with dock leaves, lamb's-quarter, tender spring winter cress, violet greens, or mustard greens if they are picked early enough.

1 T. butter or margarine
3 wild onions, chopped
2 smoked ham hocks
4 C. water

2 C. washed and chopped greens
1 clove garlic (optional)
Salt and pepper to taste
1 C. beer

Melt butter in a heavy pan and sauté onions until golden. Simmer ham hocks in water until tender, about an hour; then add greens and seasonings to taste. For a robust flavor, add a cup of flat beer in the last half hour of cooking.

The beer in this recipe is really optional as well; I just like the hearty flavor it imparts to a light broth. You may wish to omit the ham hocks and rely on beer alone.

Wild Bouillabaisse

Serves 6–8

This is often called *the* fisherman's stew; with our wild additions it is even better.

¼ C. olive oil
½ C. wild (or domestic) onion, chopped
2 chunks of dried orange peel
1 clove garlic
½ C. chopped celery stalks
1 14½-oz. can of tomatoes or 4–5 fresh, chopped tomatoes
2 8-oz. cans of tomato sauce (or a 15-oz. jar of Italian-style sauce)

1 t. salt
2 t. paprika
½ C. sherry or dry white wine
2 C. water
1 bay leaf
1 lb. bluegill, bass, or catfish fillets
1 lb. cleaned crayfish tails (shrimp can be substituted)
1 lb. freshwater clams (purchased mussels can be substituted)

Throw everything into the pot except the fish and crayfish; simmer 1 hour. Then add fish fillets, crayfish tails, and freshwater clams or mussels; simmer a few minutes until barely cooked.

In any bouillabaisse, the most important ingredient is freshness; if you are making your own from wildings, this ingredient is assured.

Clam Chowder

Serves 4

If you are fortunate enough to live where you can dig your own clams, this recipe is an epicurean delight.

1 qt. clams
1 pt. water
½ C. celery leaves
1½ C. wild onions, cut into chunks

½ lb. wild mushrooms
1 C. light cream
2 T. butter
1 t. salt
½ t. pepper

First, clean the clams of sand and grit. Cover them with cold water and 1 t. salt; add a pinch of cornmeal and soak for 1 hour.

Steam clams in water until all the shells are open. Pour broth into a soup pot, being careful not to disturb any leftover sand that may have settled to the bottom of your steamer. Add celery and onion to broth and simmer for 5 minutes. Strain.

Sauté mushrooms, dice, and add to the broth. Mince clams and add; pour in 1 C. light cream or half-and-half. Float a dot of butter on top, season with salt and pepper, and serve hot with oyster crackers.

Crayfish Gumbo

We tend to think of eating crayfish (or "crawdads" as we called them when I was young) as quite adventurous and almost unheard of. Down Louisiana way, however, they are an everyday delicacy. A friend brought back orders of great, fat tails. I've never seen them that big in the creek near my home, but that doesn't stop me from enjoying their mild, shrimplike flavor in a number of dishes.

This gumbo filé is a classic in New Orleans; a bit of trouble to make, but once tasted you'll know why every restaurant in New Orleans serves a variation on this theme.

Sassafras and Filé Powder

Filé powder, called for in a number of creole recipes, is simply dried powdered sassafras leaves; any forager in the southern part of our country, from the Ozarks southward, should be able to pick a year's supply in just minutes. Otherwise, it's available in specialty shops, delis, and some fish markets.

3	C. wild onions, chopped finely	1	t. wild dried thyme
3	cloves wild garlic	1	t. basil
1½	C. celery stalks, chopped	3	bay laurel leaves
2	T. oil	4	qts. stock (fish, mushroom, or light vegetable)
2	lb. fresh okra, sliced (or 1½ lbs. frozen)	2	lbs. crayfish tails (shrimp can be substituted)
2	T. flour		Salt and pepper to taste
4–5	fresh tomatoes, peeled and chopped, or 1 16-oz. can	1	T. filé powder
½	C. diced ham		Dash of Worcestershire sauce
		3	C. cooked brown or wild rice

Sauté the onion, garlic, and celery in 1 T. oil. In a separate skillet, sauté the sliced okra until soft; the mucilaginous texture will be gone at this time.

In another frying pan, make a roux of 1 T. oil and 2 T. flour. (To make a roux, melt butter in a heavy skillet and stir in flour. Stir until golden brown and add to your broth.) Add tomatoes and cook to a paste. Add ham and herbs and cook 5 more minutes. Then add the stock and cook until it begins to thicken. Simmer for an hour, and when it is almost time to eat, add the crayfish tails or shrimp; cook another 15 minutes or so, with salt and pepper, then add filé powder and a dash of Worcestershire sauce at the end, just before serving. (If you like it hotter, add a dash of Tabasco as well.)

Serve with cooked rice.

Dove Stew with Wild Onions
Serves 6

One of the last times I went hunting with my father—over twenty years ago—we brought home these tiny succulent birds. Although I couldn't bear to shoot one now, I still remember this rich stew.

2	slices bacon	1	C. well-washed groundnuts
5–8	dove breasts (other parts		or Jerusalem artichokes
	may be included but they	2	carrots, peeled and sliced
	are very small)	1	bay laurel leaf
3	wild onions, white parts	1–2	cloves wild garlic
	only	¼	t. rosemary
4	medium potatoes, peeled	½	t. black peppercorns or
	and cubed		peppergrass seeds

Cook bacon in a heavy skillet until crisp, then remove from pan, drain on paper towels, and break into coarse pieces. Brown dove in the bacon fat, then put in stew pot. Add onions, potatoes, groundnuts or Jerusalem artichokes, and carrots. Just cover with water or broth.

Tie up bay leaf, garlic, rosemary, and peppercorns or peppergrass seeds in a small cheesecloth bag and drop into the pot. Simmer gently 30–45 minutes or until birds are tender. Thicken broth with a roux of 1 T. butter and 2 T. flour.

Nettle Soup
Serves 6

Most people seem intent only on getting *rid* of nettles; my favorite way is to eat them. According to an elderly friend who knows homeopathic medicine, these greens serve to thin the blood in the spring. I'm not sure about that, but they are quite good and extremely good *for* you. They contain vitamins C and A, valuable trace minerals including iron,

SPINY STINGING NETTLE

and protein. Pick carefully or wear gloves, though; the sting in stinging nettles is no joke.

2 C. nettle greens, washed (be careful—use metal tongs)
6 C. beef, mushroom, or vegetable broth (or water)
½ C. chopped wild onion
¼ C. diced ham or 2 slices of bacon, chopped
1 C. beer (can be flat)

Amazingly enough, the poison in nettles that makes them sting you in the woods is eliminated by cooking—don't worry, you won't feel as if you ate poison-ivy salad. Cook everything together over low heat, about 30 minutes. Blend until smooth, if you like, and garnish with a dollop of sour cream.

Purslane Soup

Serves 4

Purslane is slightly viscous, like okra—but very, very good. It grows well in disturbed ground; you may find it in your backyard garden, as I do.

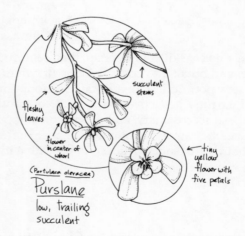

succulent stems

fleshy leaves

flower in center of whorl

(Portulaca oleracea)
Purslane
low, trailing succulent

tiny yellow flower with five petals

This immigrant from southern Asia has done well in the New World; you'll find it nearly everywhere. Wash the tips and stems well, since they tend to retain grit.

½ C. diced ham
4 C. beef broth or wild greens broth
¼ C. uncooked brown or wild rice

Salt and pepper to taste
⅛ t. Cajun seasoning (optional)
2 C. well-cleaned purslane tips

Simmer all ingredients except purslane gently, covered, approximately 40 minutes or until rice is tender; add purslane and cook another 10 minutes or so. (Omit ham if you prefer a vegetarian soup.)

Purslane Gumbo

Serves 4

This recipe takes advantage of purslane's passing resemblance to okra; it's hearty fare. Cooked without meat, it's a delicious vegetable soup; add chicken or beef and it's a meal.

1 T. oil
1½ C. purslane tips
2 C. chopped, skinned tomatoes
1 pkg. frozen corn or 1½ C. fresh, cut from the cob
2 small green peppers
½ C. chopped wild onion (white parts only)

¼ C. uncooked rice
1 T. lemon juice
3 C. beef broth (if you are planning to add chicken, use a chicken-based broth
1 bay laurel leaf

Heat oil in skillet and cook purslane until just tender; this will reduce the mucilaginous nature of the beast. Put in the soup pot with the other ingredients and simmer gently or until rice is tender. Remove bay leaf, if desired.

NOTE: To make this soup stick to your ribs a bit more, add 1 C. diced chicken or beef and cook as before.

Scandinavian Fruit Soup with Wildings

Serves 4

This icy fruit soup tastes great as a light summer luncheon or dessert. So refreshing! Make it with whatever fruit is in season to extend your enjoyment; the kids will eat it up. Try it with wild cherries, for a traditional taste, or use raspberries, elderberries, ripe (purple) gooseberries, strawberries, pawpaws, or even crab apples.

1 lb. wild fruits, mixed or a single flavor
2 C. water
1 C. red wine

½ C. sugar
½ t. grated fresh orange rind
1 t. arrowroot powder
Sprig of wild mint

Boil fruit and liquids together until fruit is tender, about 10 minutes. Strain to remove seeds, if any, or blend until smooth. Add sugar, orange rind, and arrowroot powder to thicken the juice slightly, and simmer 5 more minutes. Chill ice cold and garnish with a sprig of wild mint.

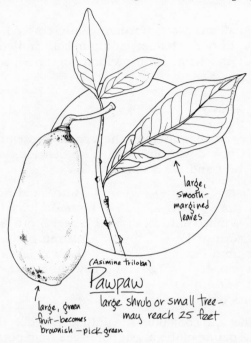

large,
smooth-
margined
leaves

(Asimina triloba)

Pawpaw

large shrub or small tree—
may reach 25 feet

large, green
fruit—becomes
brownish—pick green

NOTE: This can be served as a prelude to the entrée, German-style, or as a dessert, as they do in Scandinavia; you can even serve it hot for a winter treat. One recipe calls for 2 T. of tapioca stirred in and cooked for about 20 minutes for thickening.

Chapter 4

The
Vegetable
Course

CATHY
JOHNSON

Vegetables are too often underrated, added to our menu almost as an afterthought. Fortunately, the best chefs, home cooks, and even the producers of frozen entrées available at our supermarkets have seen the light of day. Vegetables have become exciting additions to our diets.

Our markets are filled with exciting *new* vegetables, crowding up to the familiar old favorites, and we're all in an adventurous mood. Those who sample the best of wild vegetables have even more to choose from, and we have the added incentive—as I did as a child—of fresh air and the beauty of nature all around us.

These wild vegetables may be just the spark you need to kindle a fresh interest on the home front. In my family, vegetables were always a great treat: not only because you weren't sure just what was on the agenda for the night, but because the choices were so often delicious. I loved Jerusalem artichokes, even as a child—their crispy crunch made them great fun to eat. And I was quite impressed by the preparations my parents took to render poke "safe." The fact that I was often allowed to gather the evening's vegetable course on my own made them doubly delicious.

I've picked the vegetable course in my own backyard—growing wild between my cultivated plants, along the gravel lane, or by the back fence. I've found them along city alleyways or railroad rights-of-way (I didn't realize I was trespassing!) and pushing up between cracks in an inner-city sidewalk (although I'd be cautious about picking them too close to sources of automobile exhaust or possible asbestos pollution). I've found them in small-town parks and in state parks and, where regulations permit, I've harvested there. I've picked wildings beside a quiet country road, and although I'd not pick them beside a superhighway for fear of pollution, I've seen them growing there.

The discovery of a bulldozer-denuded patch in my favorite woods is tempered somewhat by the observation that the disturbed ground is now a perfect wild farmer's market of purslane, nettles, dock, and the best stand of poke I've seen in a long time (my father would have been delighted).

Look around you; the vegetable course is free for the picking, with ordinary caution. These recipes will give you fresh ideas to go with your fresh-as-spring-rain vegetables.

Suggested Wild Ingredients

As always, your vegetable course depends on season and weather; it puts us in touch with the life outside our own small boundaries, with the seasons of nature. Spring greens are the best known of wild foods. Autumn rains often bring a second spring, with new and tender shoots of nettle, dock, sorrel, dandelion, and even daylily. If you look carefully, you may find a stand of winter cress that has been cut over the summer and has sprouted again in August or September—or even as late as November in a good year. These second-growth shoots are tender and mild once again; summer's fiery bite is gentled. Fall greens are never as abundant as the bounty of spring, but they are still succulent and fresh.

My favorite wild vegetable is the ubiquitous dandelion. I eat them from late fall (fresh, new sprouts, crowns) through the winter months (crowns, roots) and on into the spring; until, in fact, the blooming of those lovely yellow flowers tells me the leaves are too bitter to eat. (Then I turn the flower heads into wine, but that's another chapter.)

Nettles are eagerly awaited in the early spring; on a south-facing bank in a protected area I may find them as early as late February.

My family's favorite, poke shoots, are a spring-only treat; later in the season the stalks, leaves, and berries develop a strong narcotic, cathartic, and sometimes slow-acting emetic (phytolaccin) that, taken in large doses, can prove fatal. Always cook in at least two changes of water; latest research suggests picking with rubber gloves.

In the summer you may find milkweed shoots or buds; arrowhead tubers; cattail ''sweet corn''; daylily shoots, buds, or spent flowers. Wild onions, ramps, leeks, garlic, chives—these wild members of the *allium* family are available early spring through late winter. Be sure to check for the distinctive onion-family odor—some *alliums* are toxic.

Mushrooms can be found at nearly every season of the year and add their gourmet touch to your meals without adding undue calories (until you batter-fry them in bacon drippings, of course).

Our American Indian forebears used prickly pear cactus as a vegetable; I've included a delicious recipe or two to tempt you to take the chance of an errant needle. Careful handling, as with nettles, makes this possibility a remote one in any case.

Some of these wild vegetables are abundant. Others must be picked only in case of real need or transplanted if their habitat is to be destroyed for development. I could never bring myself to eat spring beauty tubers, for instance, unless I knew I'd die without them—even though they are occasionally abundant in our park. They are simply too beautiful to destroy.

Choose what looks best to you; what is easily available or abundant. You may even enjoy ''revenge on the lawn'' by eating your weeds—I do.

Dandelion Crowns Vinaigrette
Serves 4

This recipe comes first because it is, hands down, my favorite wild vegetable recipe: simple but sophisticated, I look forward to it all winter.

(Dandelion crowns are the small, crown-shaped bundle of preemerged leaves and buds just beneath the ground.)

2–3 C. dandelion crowns (harvest by cutting the plants just an inch or so below the surface of the ground. Leave ¼''–½'' of the root attached; cut off old leaves or those that have gotten too strongly flavored. I usually leave only about 1'' of leaf stems and the unopened buds that hide just below the ground).

2 T. olive oil
1 T. finely chopped chives
Salt and pepper to taste
Splash of herb or wine vinegar
   or the juice of ½ lemon

Wash crowns well, making sure to get all the dirt or sand out from between the leaves still attached to the root. Steam lightly until just tender. Drizzle with olive oil, add chives, salt, and pepper, and pour on vinegar or lemon juice to taste. (If you prefer, serve these with butter and vinegar.)

Sautéed Dandelion Buds
Serves 4–6

I am often too busy to catch my dandelions at the right season for dandelion crowns. Don't despair if this happens to you; it's not too late to enjoy this delightful dish. You can still enjoy the unopened buds in this recipe.

¼ C. butter or margarine
2–3 C. unopened dandelion
   buds (leave on ¼'' of stem)

Pinch of saffron (optional)
Salt and pepper to taste

Melt butter or margarine in a heavy saucepan and drop in dandelion buds; they will burst open and display their yellow petals. Cook until just beginning to turn golden brown, and season with saffron and salt and pepper. These will go fast!

Spring Greens
Serves 4

What you make this dish with depends on what grows in your area. I am fond of dock, lamb's-quarter, and a bit of winter cress for bite. Others like mustard greens and chicory mixed with dandelions. You may even want to try a bit of purslane and daylily shoots. Lamb's-quarter is mild, like spinach; so is dock. Some of the others turn awfully strong very early in the season for my taste. At any rate, any of the greens cook

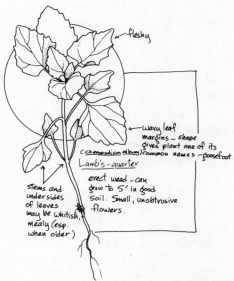

fleshy

wavy leaf
margins – shape
gives plant one of its
(*chenopodium album*) common names – goosefoot.

Lamb's-quarter

erect weed – can
grow to 5' in good
soil. Small, unobtrusive
flowers.

stems and
undersides
of leaves
may be whitish,
mealy (esp.
when older)

down considerably, so pick more than you can imagine you'll use. If you've gardened you are familiar with how much greens reduce in the cooking; wildings are no exception.

6 C. fresh-picked greens, well   ¼ C. water
   washed

Cover and steam greens until tender, then season with butter, salt and pepper, and red wine or balsamic vinegar; can't be beat!

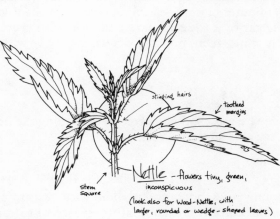

stinging hairs

toothed
margins

Nettle – flowers tiny, green,
inconspicuous

stem
square

(look also for Wood-Nettle, with
larger, rounded or wedge-shaped leaves)

Nettle Greens

Serves 4

These can be mixed with your other greens, of course, but I like them so well I eat them alone. Gather carefully and carry home in a paper bag. Rinse under running water, turning with metal tongs; since they often grow at streamside, you may have to wash off quite a bit of fine silt.

2 slices bacon	Splash of herb vinegar
4 C. nettle greens	Butter, if desired
Salt and pepper to taste	Nutmeg (optional)

Render bacon slices and remove from pan (use a heavy iron skillet). Drop washed greens into hot grease and stir until just coated. Add a bit of water, turn down heat, and simmer, covered, about 10–15 minutes. Season with salt and pepper and splash with vinegar (or lemon juice, if you prefer). This is good with just a sprinkle of nutmeg.

Poke Shoots
Serves 4

Find a patch of very young poke; you can mark them the year before or learn to recognize them from last year's stalks. Pick or cut when no more than 8" tall. Make sure the stalks are green; once they have begun to change color, the natural chemical has begun to build up in them. If you have any doubts, wear rubber gloves and peel outer skin from stalks. Leave the small, tender leaves furled at the top of the stalk; they're good.

2 C. poke sprouts; cut in 2"–3" lengths	2 slices bacon

Boil poke sprouts in water to cover for 10 minutes. Throw out this first water and reboil in second water. Meanwhile, render bacon slices in a heavy skillet. Put drained poke sprouts into skillet with drippings and stir well to coat thoroughly. Cover again with water and cook an additional 20 minutes or until seasoning permeates the vegetable. Serve with hops vinegar or a squeeze of lemon. Top with crumbled bacon.

If you prefer, omit bacon, boil in 2 waters, and serve with butter, salt, and pepper.

Fried Poke Shoots
Serves 4

Gather and prepare poke shoots as before, discarding the first 2 cooking waters, then try this southern recipe.

2 C. poke shoots	¼ C. bran
½ C. cornmeal	Salt and pepper to taste

Peel thick young poke shoots and parboil twice, discarding this water. Roll shoots in the cornmeal/bran mixture, seasoned to your taste. Fry in bacon drippings (or vegetable oil if you are watching your cholesterol intake).

Poke Shoots Oriental

This is really just a classic stir-fry, but poke shoots are so good any way you fix them—as long as you follow safety directions—I couldn't resist adding it with the others.

½ C. fresh wild mushrooms
2 C. poke shoots, sliced diagonally *(prepare as before in
   2 changes of water)*
1 C. wild onions, sliced
½ C. sliced fresh Jerusalem artichokes (you may substitute
   canned water chestnuts if
   the artichokes are out of
   season)

¼ C. cooking oil
1 clove garlic
Salt and pepper to taste
Soy sauce to taste
3 C. chow mein noodles or
   cooked rice

Slice mushrooms, poke, onions, and Jerusalem artichokes; keep artichokes separate. Heat oil and stir-fry mushrooms, prepared poke, and onions; add garlic, well diced. Cook until just beginning to soften; approximately 15 minutes. Drop in sliced Jerusalem artichokes or water chestnuts and stir until they are just warm through to preserve crispness. Season with salt and pepper; add soy sauce to taste.

Serve these greens on a bed of noodles or rice; the most ordinary meal will be enhanced.

Creamed Poke Shoots

Many people find poke shoots reminiscent of asparagus; as fond as I am of the latter, I enjoy poke more. This recipe will especially remind you of the domestic delicacy. Gather the poke when only 3''–4'' tall.

2 C. poke shoots, cut in 1''
   pieces. Boil in slightly salted
   water for 10 minutes or
   until barely tender; pour
   off water. Boil again and
   discard water.
2 T. butter or margarine

2 T. flour
1 C. whole milk or half-and-half
½ t. sugar
Salt and pepper to taste
Squeeze of fresh lemon juice
   (optional)

Prepare poke. Melt butter in a heavy pan and stir in flour to make a roux. Cook to a light golden brown, then slowly pour in milk until thickened. Season to taste; add lemon if desired. Pour over hot poke shoots and cook together until done—10 minutes or so.

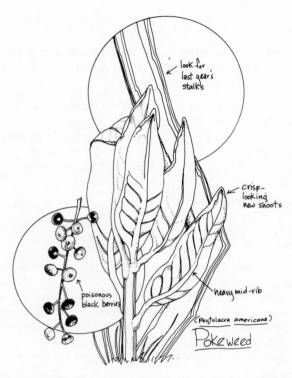

look for last year's stalk's

crisp-looking new shoots

poisonous black berries

heavy mid-rib

(Phytolacca americana)

Pokeweed

NOTE: You may use poke shoots in any recipe you normally would use asparagus in; just remember to parboil and discard the two waters. Some experts suggest you peel the outer layer to remove the phytolaccin; I prefer to follow the safety instructions that require boiling in two water baths. It's a bit of extra trouble but well worth the time for the flavor *and* the margin of safety.

Milkweed Shoots with Tart Sorrel Sauce

Serves 6

Milkweed has a bitter juice that must be processed out before it can be eaten, but once that is done it is really a wonderful vegetable; it rivals any in our backyard gardens.

BASIC MILKWEED PROCESSING

To get rid of the bitter, milky sap, the plant must be placed in *boiling* water—never cold water that is brought to the boil. (Cold water seems to set the sap in the plant rather than removing it.) No matter which of the milkweed vegetables you use, the processing principle is the same, so if you are using shoots, leaves, buds, or young, tender pods, be sure to follow these directions. Boil 1 minute, drain, and replace water 3 times;

taste after 2 blanchings, though—sometimes that's enough.

You may complain that you are throwing all the nutrients down the sink—but as bitter as they are in their milky state, you wouldn't want them anyway.

3 C. milkweed shoots, prepared   Salt and pepper to taste
  as above

SAUCE

1 C. dairy sour cream   ¼ C. milk or buttermilk
1 C. fresh sorrel greens,   ¼ C. chopped wild chives
  chopped fine   (optional)

Heat sour cream and sorrel gently over low heat until sorrel leaves are tender; pour remaining ingredients over milkweed shoots and serve immediately.

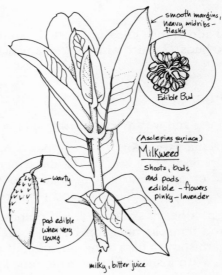

smooth margins,
heavy midribs—
fleshy

Edible Bud

(Asclepias syriaca)
Milkweed
Shoots, buds
and pods
edible—flowers
pinky—lavender

warty

pod edible
when very
young

milky, bitter juice

Mexican Milkweed Pods

Serves 6

This one is *hot*; be ready with an icy drink nearby.

3 C. prepared milkweed pods   ¼ C. oil
  (see basic milkweed   Salt and pepper to taste
  processing, page 56)   Dash of cumin powder
2 wild garlic cloves, finely diced
½ C. chopped wild onions
1 dried hot pepper (whole) or a
  sprinkling of prepared
  crushed red pepper

Vegetables / 57

Fry vegetables in oil over medium heat until they just *begin* to brown, about 10 minutes. Cover and steam until tender. Add seasonings and cumin. Serve with fluffy cooked rice, if you like.

Milkweed Buds and Butter Sauce
Serves 4

Prepare the buds as before to rid them of the milky sap; it's this same bitter sap that protects the monarch butterflies that feed on this plant from preying birds.

2 C. prepared milkweed buds (see basic milkweed processing, p. 56)
¼ C. clarified butter (clarify by melting and skimming away foam)

2 T. fresh orange juice
Grating of fresh orange rind
Salt and pepper to taste

Melt butter and add orange juice and peel. Season to taste and pour over hot milkweed buds. Garnish with a sprinkling of slivered almonds.

Fried Wild Onions
Serves 4-6

For lovers of onions—and we are legion—this simple dish is ambrosia.

¼ C. oil, butter, margarine, or bacon drippings
2-3 C. sliced wild onions (white parts only)

1 egg per person
½ C. diced ham or crumbled bacon (optional)
Salt and pepper to taste

Put shortening in a heavy skillet and add onions. Fry gently until tender, golden, and transparent. Drop 1 egg for each person directly into the onions, garnish with ham or bacon, and put a lid on the skillet until the eggs set. With a slice of homemade bread and a salad, this is a wonderful winter's meal.

WILD ONION

German Apples and Wild Onions

Serves 6

I like this recipe with pork; if you want, add potatoes to the skillet for a hearty dish. It's tart and sweet all at the same time.

1 C. sliced wild onions (white parts only)
3 tart domestic apples (I use Jonathans) or 5–6 good-sized wild crab apples
1 C. diced potatoes (optional)
¼ C. oil or drippings
¼ C. finely diced wild chives

Sauté onions, apples, and potatoes together in oil in a heavy skillet; garnish with chives and enjoy hot and steaming.

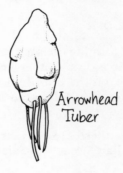

Arrowhead
Tuber

Baked Arrowhead Tubers

Serves 6

The American Indians called these starchy tubers *wapatoo*. Gather them any time in fall, winter, or early spring; they must be dredged off the bottom of a pond or creek edge with your hands, a pitchfork, or other tool. They average about an inch in diameter, but if you are lucky you may find chicken-egg-sized ones.

3 C. arrowhead tubers, peeled
¼ C. chopped onions
6 soda crackers, pulverized
3 T. butter or margarine
¼ C. half-and-half or cream
Salt and pepper to taste
Sprinkling of paprika

Peel and slice arrowhead tubers. Mix well with onions and cracker crumbs and place in a shallow, well-buttered casserole dish. Top with dots of butter and a splash of cream or half-and-half; season to taste and sprinkle with paprika. Bake in 350° oven for a half hour or until tubers are tender.

Comfrey and Bacon

Serves 4

Comfrey is generally considered a medicinal herb or tea, though with its mild flavor it's a shame to overlook its value as a vegetable. Its young leaves have a slightly cucumberlike flavor that adds a nice touch to spring salads, or they can be enjoyed as this rich greens dish.

4   slices bacon
3–4 C. washed young comfrey
       leaves, midrib removed

Malt vinegar to taste
Salt and pepper to taste

Render bacon and remove from pan to drain. Reserve 1 T. bacon fat and drop comfrey leaves into the pan; stir rapidly to coat, then cover the pan and cook till tender. Garnish with crumbled bacon and season to taste. (Substitute butter, margarine, or olive oil and omit bacon, if desired.)

Cattail "Sweet Corn"

Serves 4

When cattails are just forming their tender new bloom spikes, you might try this easy and delicious dish. Gather while still green, before the yellow pollen begins to show on the outside of the spikes, or you will feel as if you are eating a mouthful of cotton fibers. Plan on 6–8 spikes per person.

24 cattail bud spikes (these are
       much smaller than sweet
       corn)

Lots of butter or margarine
Salt and pepper to taste

Pick cattail spikes when they are tender and green; remove the husk as you would sweet corn's. Boil and douse with butter or margarine to overcome the slight dryness, and salt and pepper to taste. Eat the granules off the hard, wiry stem and discard as you would a corncob.

Cattail and Cheese Casserole

Serves 6

If you like cattail "sweet corn," try this recipe; it's filling and tasty and could double as an entrée.

1   egg
3   C. steamed cattail buds,
       scraped from the stalks
½ C. milk
1   C. soft bread crumbs

Salt and pepper to taste
¼ t. nutmeg
1 C. freshly grated cheddar
       cheese (or your favorite)

Beat egg; add cattail buds, milk, bread crumbs, salt, pepper, and nutmeg. Put a layer of this mixture into a well-greased shallow casserole; sprinkle with cheese, add another layer of cattail mixture, then one of cheese, and so forth until you run out. Top with grated cheese and bake at 350° for 35–45 minutes or until set and browned lightly on top. This is a hearty dish indeed.

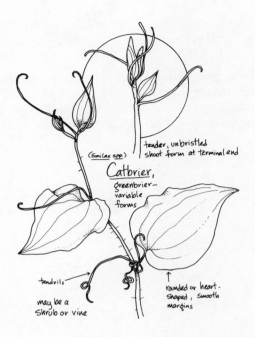

(Smilax spp.)

tender, unbristled shoot form at terminal end

Catbrier,
greenbrier—
variable
forms

tendrils

may be a shrub or vine

rounded or heart-shaped, smooth margins

Catbrier with Orange Sauce

Serves 4

Try this elegant dish with a simple meal; it will really dress it up. Catbriers, members of the *Smilax* spp., are also known as greenbriers.

¼ C. butter or margarine
½ C. chopped wild onions
2 C. tender catbrier tips (be
    sure to discard the lower,
    woody, thorny portions)
3 T. orange juice concentrate or
    6 T. fresh juice

1 T. fresh orange zests (cut tiny
    strips from the orange part
    of the peel; discard the
    pithy white portions)

Melt butter in a heavy skillet; sauté onions until translucent and just beginning to brown. Remove and add catbrier tips. Cover and cook until just tender, 3–5 minutes; replace onion and stir together until hot through. Stir in orange juice and garnish with fresh orange zests.

Home-fried Jerusalem Artichokes

Serves 6

Try this delicious alternative to potatoes; it tastes different but still very good—wild foods never taste just like their domestic alternatives but have a flavor all their own to be cultivated and appreciated.

¼ C. oil, butter, or drippings
4 C. Jerusalem artichokes,
    sliced but not peeled

½ C. chopped wild onions or
    leeks—white parts only
Salt and pepper to taste

Melt butter or drippings in a heavy skillet; add artichokes and onions and fry until tender on the inside and brown outside (Jerusalem artichokes do not cook just like potatoes; they tend to get quite soft in the process). Season to taste and serve hot. Garnish with paprika or chives, if desired.

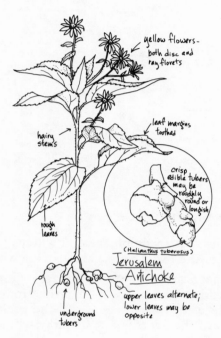

yellow flowers—
both disc and
ray florets

leaf margins
toothed

hairy
stems

crisp
edible tubers
may be
roughly
round or
longish

rough
leaves

(*Helianthus tuberosus*)
Jerusalem
Artichoke

upper leaves alternate;
lower leaves may be
opposite

underground
tubers

Artichokes au Gratin

Serves 6

I like the rich earthy flavor of artichokes in this adaptation from my mother's recipe for potatoes au gratin.

3 C. Jerusalem artichokes,
    sliced but not peeled
½ C. flour
½ t. salt
Pepper to taste

¼ C. bran or wheat germ
1 C. shredded cheddar or your
    favorite cheese
½ C. milk or light cream

Grease a shallow casserole dish well, and add a layer of sliced artichokes. Mix flour, salt, pepper, and wheat germ or bran in a small bowl and sprinkle a layer over the 'chokes. Add a layer of cheese. Pour a little milk over, and add another layer of artichokes, then more flour mixture, then more cheese, until all the ingredients are used. Bake in a 375° oven for 40 minutes. Even the kids in the family will like this one—if you don't tell them what it is.

Escalloped Artichokes
Serves 6

You can substitute arrowhead tubers, groundnuts, or cattail tubers for the artichokes in this recipe, depending on season and what you have been able to find.

Fix just as the preceding recipe but omit cheese. Bake until brown and bubbly on top; dot with butter before you put it in the oven.

Daylily Shoots and Butter Sauce
Serves 4-6

You may not have realized the daylilies in your backyard were also a delightful and very available vegetable. They are so prolific in many places that they escape cultivation and fill whole hillsides with their lovely orange blooms later in the year. If you find such a spot, mark it well in your memory; it will provide you with a number of wild dishes. Cut shoots just above the root in early spring and discard the larger outer leaves for this dish.

NOTE: This wild vegetable has a laxative effect on some people; try only a bit at first.

2-3 C. of tender young daylily shoots
¼ C. butter or margarine
Dash of prepared mustard

2 T. orange juice concentrate or orange juice with 1 t. fresh grated rind
Salt and pepper to taste

Steam daylily shoots until just tender. Mix all the other ingredients in small pan and pour over vegetables just before serving. (If you prefer a simpler taste, omit orange juice and mustard, and just add butter, salt, and pepper to your steamed shoots.)

Daylily Buds Oriental
Serves 4-6

The unopened buds of the daylilies themselves make a fine vegetable, with butter and salt or as we've suggested here; they are a staple in Asian markets and mild enough to agree with Western tastes as well. Try the buds sparingly, at first; they may be cathartic.

¼ C. oil
2-3 C. unopened flower buds— can be young and green or orange and just ready to flower

1 clove garlic
½ C. wild onions, chopped
Soy sauce or tamari to taste
Grating of fresh ginger (optional)

Heat oil very hot in a heavy skillet. Add all ingredients and stir-fry until just tender. Season with soy or tamari to taste. Serve over rice, if you like.

Daylily Tempura

Serves 4

This rich eggy dish is wonderful with or without an Oriental flavor; use or omit soy sauce as you wish.

2 eggs, well beaten
½ C. flour or enough to thicken
    eggs
Dash of soy sauce, if desired, *or*
    salt and pepper to taste

2 C. (or more) daylily buds or
    fully opened flowers
1 C. vegetable or peanut oil

Mix egg and flour to form a rich batter; add soy sauce or salt and pepper as desired. Dip buds into batter and drop immediately into hot oil; deep fry until golden brown and drain on paper towels.

The daylilies have a slightly gelatinous texture like okra; and like okra, they are quite delicious.

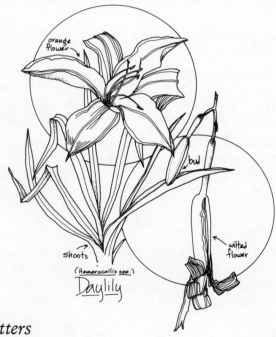

orange flower

bud

shoots

wilted flower

(*Hemerocallis* spp.)
Daylily

Daylily Fritters

Serves 4–6

With salt and pepper and a bit of onion, these fritters are a vegetable side dish; omit those flavorings and dust with powdered sugar or drizzle with honey or syrup and you have dessert.

2	eggs	Salt and pepper to taste
½	C. flour	2–3 C. fully opened flower heads
¼	C. finely chopped wild onions	2 C. cooking oil for deep frying

Mix egg and flour to form a thin batter. Add finely chopped onion, salt, and pepper. Dip flowers into batter, coating evenly.

Fry a few at a time in hot oil until golden brown and drain well on paper towels. Serve *hot*.

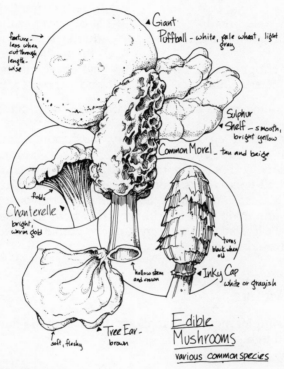

texture-less when cut through lengthwise

▲ *Giant*
Puffball – white, pale wheat, light gray

Sulphur
◄ *Shelf – smooth, bright yellow*

Common Morel – tan and beige

folds
Chanterelle ▼
bright, warm gold

turns black when old

hollow stem and crown

◄ *Inky Cap*
white or grayish

▲ *Tree Ear – brown*
soft, fleshy

Edible
Mushrooms
various common species

Batter-fried Morels

Serves 4

It is hardly necessary to batter a morel; of all the wild mushrooms they are probably the best known and most sought after for their rich flavor, at least in the Midwest. You may prefer simply to fry them in butter or a light oil (or bacon drippings) and serve with a touch of salt and pepper. Nonetheless, many people do like them battered; I'm including a simple recipe.

1½ C. morels	½ C. flour
2 T. milk	Salt and pepper to taste
1 egg	½ C. hot oil, butter, or drippings

Wash and drain morels carefully and slice lengthwise. Make a thin batter of the milk and egg; dip your morels in this batter and roll in seasoned flour. Fry in hot oil or butter until golden brown.

Stuffed Morels

Serves 4-6

This is good *and* festive; it will make a meal. Try it when you have found large-crowned mushrooms.

2 C. morels
2 C. cubed stale bread
½ C. mushroom or chicken broth
1 egg
½ C. finely chopped wild onions
½ C. diced celery stalks

½ t. dried, crumbled pitcher
    sage leaves (substitute
    domestic sage, if you wish)
¼ C. finely diced, cooked
    oysters or clams (optional)
Salt and pepper to taste

Remove hollow stems from morels and dice them. Slice caps in half lengthwise.

Mix bread, broth, egg, onions, celery, mushroom stems, and herbs; if mixture is too thin, add a bit more bread. Mix in diced oysters or clams if desired and season to taste. Stuff morels with this mixture and place in a well-greased casserole dish and bake 30 minutes at 375°.

This is a nice side dish for a festive meal—Thanksgiving or otherwise—or a fine main dish for dinner for two with a good bread and a salad. (You can also use this recipe for any edible capped mushroom; fix as you would morels.)

Sautéed Morels

Serves 4

I prefer the simpler method that allows the taste of the mushroom itself to come through.

1½-2 C. morels
¼ C. oil, butter, margarine,
    or drippings

1 clove minced garlic

Split morels lengthwise and wash well to remove any small insects that may be inside their hollow stems and crowns. Some people soak them in saltwater to remove any impurities, but I find a good hard stream of water does the job.

Heat oil until it is almost smoking. Drop in washed, well-drained morels (you may wish to pat them dry with paper toweling to keep them from popping too much when placing them in the hot oil). Sauté with minced garlic until just golden.

Butter-fried Puffballs

Puffballs are one of my favorite wild mushrooms, perhaps because they are relatively easy to identify and there are a number of edible species. If you find a *giant* puffball you need only one for a feast. Make sure they are fresh by slicing through the fungus from top to bottom; meat should be white and firm throughout. If there is any discoloration or dryness, discard the entire mushroom.

These easy-to-identify mushrooms are good in casseroles, soups, or with any meat dish; look for one of the many varieties nearly year-round, but be sure to use only the white-skinned varieties and identify them carefully, as with all mushrooms. Slicing through the mushroom will also tell you if there is an undeveloped stem or gills; if so, discard it unless you can identify it positively as edible. Puffballs are featureless when sliced.

¼ C. butter
1 small clove of wild garlic
  Puffballs to feed the number
  of people you have on
  hand; plan on about ½–1
  C. per person

Salt and pepper to taste

Peel and slice the puffballs. Melt the butter in a heavy skillet; dice garlic into pan and sauté mushroom slices until golden, then stand back as the crowd beats its way to your kitchen—the smell of frying puffballs is heavenly.

Herb-baked Mushrooms

For this recipe you can use whatever mushrooms you find, first making sure the mushrooms are compatible. (If you are using wild mushrooms, though, don't serve or drink alcohol for 24 hours before or after eating mushrooms.)

1 C. chopped wild mushrooms
3 C. cooked brown rice or brown
  and wild-rice combination
½ C. chopped wild onion
2 eggs, beaten
½ C. chopped broccoli
¼ C. diced wild chives

½ t. dried wild thyme (substitute domestic, if desired)
1 C. shredded cheddar cheese
Dash of Worcestershire sauce
¼ t. curry powder
Salt and pepper to taste

Mix ingredients together in a large bowl; spread in a shallow, well-greased baking pan and bake for 40 minutes at 350° or until casserole is set.

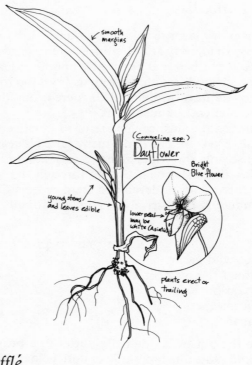

smooth margins

(Commelina spp.)
Dayflower

Bright Blue flower

young stems and leaves edible

lower petal may be white (Asiatic)

plants erect or trailing

Spring Soufflé

Serves 4

Try this in the early spring for a light luncheon dish or as a side dish with an elegant dinner.

2 T. butter or margarine	2 *more* T. butter or margarine
½ C. diced wild onions (white parts only)	2 T. flour
	½ C. milk or cream
2 C. mixed wild greens (dandelion, lamb's-quarter, mustard, winter cress, dock, dayflower, etc.), cooked and drained	½ C. evaporated milk
	3 beaten egg yolks
	Salt and pepper to taste
	Nutmeg to taste
	3 egg whites, stiffly beaten

Melt butter or margarine in a heavy pan and sauté onions until just tender. Remove and drain on a paper towel. Rinse and drain the prepared greens, then chop finely.

Melt additional butter in a saucepan and stir in flour until well blended. Combine and stir in milk and evaporated milk. Stir in the greens and onions. Add 3 beaten egg yolks.

Season with salt and pepper and a dash of nutmeg, then carefully fold in the 3 stiffly beaten egg whites. Bake at 325° for approximately 30 minutes until set.

Lamb's-Quarter in Sour Cream Sauce

Lamb's-quarter is one of the mildest of wild greens; the sour cream in this recipe makes just the right piquant statement.

3 C. lamb's-quarter, washed
    and drained
¼ C. water
1 C. dairy sour cream

¼ C. milk
2 T. dry white wine (optional)
Wild chives, diced (optional)

Steam lamb's-quarter greens until just tender; drain well. Meanwhile, gently heat sour cream and milk; add wine after taking the sauce off the heat, if you wish. Pour over greens and top with a garnish of chopped chives.

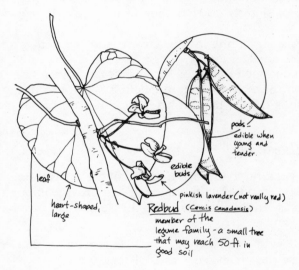

pods —
edible when young and tender.

edible buds

leaf

heart-shaped, large

pinkish lavender (not really red)

Redbud (Cercis canadensis)
member of the legume family - a small tree that may reach 50 ft. in good soil

Redbud Pods

You may have played "green beans" with these pods when you were a child, but it may surprise you to know that you can eat them, properly prepared and picked at the young and tender stage. (Redbuds are small, flowering trees of the understory, *Cercis canadensis*. Their reddish flowers develop into beanlike pods.)

2 C. young seedpods, washed
    and well drained
1 clove wild garlic, sliced

¼ C. oil
Soy sauce to taste

Stir-fry seedpods and garlic in hot oil for 10 minutes or until they begin to brown just lightly. Sprinkle with as much soy sauce as you like; serve over brown rice. These go well with a bluegill tempura dinner.

Onion Pie

This is one of my favorite vegetable dishes, although with its rich eggy filling and crisp crust, it's really more of a light main dish. Whatever you choose to call it, however you want to *use* it, you'll enjoy onion pie.

2 C. sliced wild onions, ramps, or leeks (white parts only)
3 T. butter
3 eggs
1 C. sour cream
1 t. salt

1 pie shell (see our recipe in the dessert section, page 155, or use a purchased shell)
4 strips bacon or 2 sliced sausages (optional)

Sauté onions in butter until they are soft and just beginning to turn golden. Cool slightly so that they won't cook the egg when mixed together.

Beat eggs slightly, mix in sour cream; add seasonings and pour into unbaked pie shell.

Top with chopped bacon or sliced sausage, if you wish to make this a main dish. Bake 30 or 40 minutes in a 375° oven until the filling is set (the pie is done when an inserted knife comes out clean).

Onion Shortcake

For a nice, peasant-style meal, rich and filling, try this one when you've found a good stand of wild onions. It can provide enough protein for a main dish with its abundance of cheese and egg; we have it with a salad.

4 C. sliced wild onions (you can use the green parts as well as the white), ramps, or leeks
3 T. butter or margarine
½ t. salt
Biscuit dough (see below)

1 C. cream sauce (see below)
1 egg
1 C. grated cheddar cheese (or other favorite)
¼ t. paprika
½ C. diced ham (optional)

BISCUIT DOUGH

1 C. flour
1¼ t. baking powder
½ t. salt

⅛ C. butter or margarine
⅓ C. milk

Sift flour; measure and sift again with baking powder and salt. Cut butter into the flour mixture until it is slightly crumbly. Pour in milk and stir quickly and lightly.

CREAM SAUCE

2 T. butter or margarine   1 C. milk
2 T. flour

Melt butter in a heavy pan. Stir in flour and cook 2–3 minutes, then slowly pour in milk and stir until mixture thickens. Add cheese and egg for onion shortcake.

Sauté onions in butter until transparent. Cool well. Spread biscuit dough in the bottom of a deep, well-greased casserole dish and cover with the onions.

Prepare a cream sauce; stir in egg and cheese and keep stirring over a low heat until the cheese melts. Add salt and paprika and pour over the onions (if you are using diced ham, spread it over onions first). Bake in 425° oven for about 20–25 minutes or until biscuit dough is done. This is good the second night if you have leftovers!

Fried Prickly Pear Pads   *Serves 4*

These are the green pads of the common cactus, *Opuntia humifusa*; the inner flesh is succulent. Use tongs to collect only the very young prickly pear pads in the spring (1–3'' size is best). (These are called *nopales*, by the way, by the Mexican Indians.)

¼ C. oil, butter, or drippings   Salt and pepper to taste
16 pads, prepared (see page 72)

Heat oil or drippings in a heavy skillet; sauté prickly pear pads until golden brown. Season to taste, and enjoy their crispness.

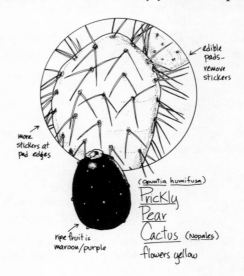

edible
pads—
remove
stickers

more
stickers at
pad edges

(opuntia humifusa)
Prickly
Pear
Cactus (Nopales)
flowers yellow

ripe fruit is
maroon/purple

Boil pads for 20 minutes, then scrape off skins and stickers or roast and remove skins; trim away the edge of the pad—there are simply too many small prickly thorns there. Rinse each pad well under water—look over each one well before setting aside—better to have a bristle in your finger now than in your tongue later.

An alternative is to bake in a 375° oven for 45 minutes. The skin will split and can be peeled off, stickers and all. Slice and store in water in the refrigerator to add to Mexican dishes, mix into omelets, or use as suggested in our recipes.

Sweet and Sour Nopales (Prickly pear pads)
Serves 4

It was hard to imagine eating these when I first heard of them; my earliest memory of prickly pear cactus was having to go home from a swimming jaunt at the lake and pick the painfully imbedded prickles out of a small behind! They are quite good, though, when prepared according to directions.

4 strips bacon
2 C. prepared *nopales*, sliced
    lengthwise about ¼" wide
3 T. chopped wild onion (white
    parts only)

3 T. white wine or wild herb
    vinegar
3 T. brown sugar

Render bacon in a heavy skillet; remove and add *nopales* and onions to 1 T. of the hot drippings. Stir until just golden brown. Add vinegar and sugar; salt to taste. Crumble bacon over the top of the dish for a nice taste surprise. (Omit bacon if you like and substitute oil for sautéing.)

Oyster Plant á Blanc
Serves 6

Salsify (or oyster plant) has a tendency to discolor on exposure to air. Cook it unpeeled or try this recipe.

1 T. flour
½ t. salt
2 t. lemon juice
3 C. water

2 C. peeled, sliced oyster plant
    roots
1 C. cream sauce (see page 71)
Salt and pepper to taste

Dissolve flour, salt, and lemon juice in water and bring to a boil. Drop in salsify and cook 7–10 minutes or until tender. Drain and top with cream sauce or butter, salt, and pepper.

Salsify or Oyster Plant

Alice's Escalloped Oyster Plant

Serves 6–8

A friend makes this hot and hearty dish and says her family can't tell it from real scalloped oysters.

3 C. cleaned and sliced oyster plant roots
5 C. water
1 C. soda cracker crumbs

¼ C. butter
¾ C. milk or cream
Salt and pepper to taste

Boil oyster plant in water until it is tender; drain well and slice.

Butter an ovenproof casserole dish and put in a layer of oyster plant slices, then a layer of crumbs. Dot with butter. Add another layer of oyster plant, another of crumbs, etc. End with a layer of crumbs. Pour milk over the whole until milk just shows. Top with butter and bake at 350° for an hour or until top is browned.

Asparagus Stir-Fry

Serves 4

We are often lucky enough to come across a stand of ''wild'' asparagus (asparagus that has escaped from cultivation and become naturalized). When we lived on a farm there was a clump of wonderfully tender stalks that would get as big around as my husband's thumb! Watch for the feathery bushlike asparagus ''ferns'' in the autumn and remember where you saw them come spring; you won't be sorry.

You can use these wild asparagus stalks in any way you normally would use domestic ones—with hollandaise sauce, in a pie, etc., but here's a recipe with an Oriental tang.

¼ C. oil (peanut oil is good)
2 C. asparagus stalks, cut diagonally
½ C. wild onions, sliced lengthwise
1 clove wild garlic

1 t. sliced gingerroot (use wild, if you can find it)
½ C. sliced wild mushrooms— whatever variety is in season —or use reconstituted dry ones

Heat oil until hot but not smoking; stir-fry other ingredients until tender-crisp. If you like, serve with a dash of tamari or soy sauce.

Wild Rice Dressing with Crab Apples   *Serves 6*

This dressing is particularly good with game, but you may like it as a side dish with fish, fowl, or pork. You could even use it to stuff mushrooms; anything this good has just got to be versatile.

4 C. stock or water
1 t. salt
½ C. meat scraps, giblets, wings, or necks (remove meat from bones)
1 C. wild rice
¼ C. butter
2 T. chopped wild onions
¼ C. diced wild mushrooms (you may use dried ones, if it is too late in the season for fresh—reconstitute by soaking in water to cover until they are soft. Use that soaking water as part of the broth, though—don't throw it away!)

1 T. chopped green pepper
¼ C. diced celery
½ C. chopped crab apples (it isn't necessary to peel them, but do remove stems and cores)

Bring salted stock to a boil with meat scraps, giblets, or wings and necks; simmer until they are tender. Remove from pot and pick the meat from the bones. Dice, if necessary.

Cook the rice in broth until tender—about 30 minutes.

Melt ¼ C. butter in a skillet and sauté onions, mushrooms, peppers, and celery; add chopped crab apples and barely cook. Add the hot drained rice and the reserved meat. Serve hot with meat or use to stuff a bird or mushrooms.

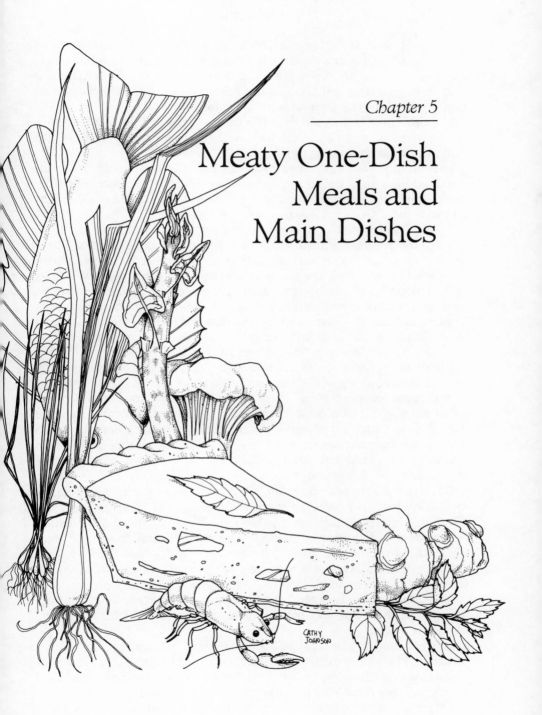

Chapter 5

Meaty One-Dish Meals and Main Dishes

The fishing is good. Sleek, fat rainbow trout turn slowly to gold over a sagebrush fire; the aromatic smoke blends with the fresh evening smells of pine and of the oncoming night. The fire and an old sweater feel good in the mountain air; the dinner soon to come will make the contentment complete.

Lemon butter is drizzled over the trouts' sides as they broil, adding a tang that fills the air like a promise. A day spent in fresh air and activity adds the final seasoning to the meal.

Last night's feast was just as good: the culmination of a day's careful marination, a slow cooking to perfection—*Pheasant au Vin*. The burgundy-garlic marinade permeated the tender pheasant; one could expect no finer meal from a Parisian chef.

Americans appreciate meat; we were raised on its savory juices. There are fast-food hamburger restaurants in every American town, doing brisk business; we also love the flavor of chicken and other fowl. Wildings only make it better. Although we can live quite well on meatless soups and grains and vegetable casseroles—and there are some delicious choices for just this sort of recipe in chapter 6—there are times when at day's end a dish rich with animal protein is as comforting and as fulfilling to our Western sensibilities as it is delicious.

Elaborate preparation is not necessary. I have included some quite simple choices along with those requiring a number of ingredients and a time spent for marination. There are dishes from many cultures, some of which require a bit of preparation; if you prefer, however, a simple baked quail with a bit of butter and salt and pepper is celebration and plenty. You may like your crayfish simply boiled and served with lemon butter or simmered with commercial crab boiling spices (pickling spice works as well); it is enough.

But if you are ready to do more, to experiment, to explore the delights of the kitchen and combine them with the joys of foraging, read on. Camping, hiking, or at home, try these wild-food-enhanced main dishes. Many are one-dish simple, making them excellent trail foods—or great dishes for a tired executive to whip up after work. They'll enrich your culinary vocabulary and amaze you at the range of nature's bounty. They can complement your store-bought groceries or provide you with a fascinating look at how our Native American predecessors ate. Wildings give us a chance to explore the cuisine of other cultures—with a distinctly American twist.

Crayfish (crawfish or crawdads) are an integral part of Creole and Cajun cuisine and are supremely edible. Although the biggest of these delicious crustaceans seem to live only in Louisiana's bayous, your own backyard creek or farm pond can provide good, if small, eating.

Or perhaps you live where clams or oysters are readily available; many recipes are easily adaptable to these wonderful shellfish—or substitute freshwater mussels, if they are plentiful.

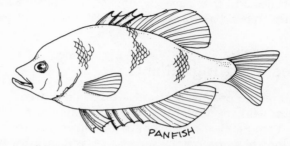

PANFISH

Where I live, fishing is good and provides us with a variety of freshwater fillets: trout, bluegill, bass, crappie, catfish, and a number of less well-known but equally edible varieties.

Wildfowl meets the modern criteria for healthful, nonred meat protein; if you have quail, grouse, pheasant, or other game birds available to you, don't hesitate to try them in any recipe that calls for chicken. A Thanksgiving bird can as easily be a *wild* turkey or goose; our ancestors would have felt at home at our board.

What this chapter does *not* contain are great numbers of red meat recipes. We are becoming more and more aware of the high-fat, high-cholesterol content of these meats, and more of us tend to avoid them in our everyday fare or use them as treats or condiments only. This book reflects that trend, for your health's sake—and for another reason as well. Red meats from the wild require specialized preparation in skinning, cleaning, and storing that are beyond the scope of a book of this sort; there are musk glands to avoid in venison and muskrat as well as in other mammals; some meats require hanging the meat to age and to allow the animal to bleed.

And, I must admit, there's a very personal reason as well. My father was the hunter in our family. I often accompanied him when I was young and even developed into a pretty fair shot in my own right. But with age—and increasing care for the animals I now study and sketch—I've lost the heart to hunt. Why be hypocritical and suggest you do something I am not willing to do myself?

There *are* recipes for quail and pheasant and other wildfowl, it's true; cleaning game birds is a fairly standard procedure, with few of the complications posed by game mammals. And truth be told, I buy or trade for my game birds; I'm no more comfortable shooting them than I am rabbits, squirrels, or deer. But still, a wild savor adds immeasurably to our main dishes—and to our enjoyment of the necessity of eating. It goes far deeper than survival.

We are put in touch with ourselves as well as with nature when we prepare these wild entrées. I feel humbled and blessed by the astounding bounty I pass by on my way to the supermarket. I am grateful for these offerings, free for the taking, that have seen my family through hard economic times and that have given us so much cause for celebration in *good* times. When I am most truly myself, I stop and accept the gift.

Suggested Wild Ingredients

In addition to the protein portion of our wild entrées, look for fresh and different wild vegetables to give your dinner zest. Wild onions are more than a simple flavoring agent in an entrée; use them as the main ingredient for a piquant, oniony surprise. Substitute arrowhead, ground-nut, or cattail tubers for potatoes in steaming dishes for a different and intriguing taste. Combine all the wildings you can find in an elegant but simple *Peasant Pot Pie* and serve it with a good red wine. And of course, wild mushrooms form the base of any number of delicious dinners, perfectly complementing the flavor of the meat.

My favorite meal—wild *or* domestic—is a fresh and crunchy stir-fry, with ingredients from my backyard, garden, and the park down the road. When camping, I've made a version of this endlessly varied dinner over a crackling fire, with meat brought from home. What *else* I throw into the wok depends on what I can find; after summer rains in August bring out the delicate, apricot-scented chanterelles, I may add those mushrooms to the pan; in early spring the dish is heavy on mixed greens so abundant after the warming of spring. Later, I may use crunchy Jerusalem artichokes in place of water chestnuts, adding them at the last minute to retain their snap; Japanese knotweed stands in for asparagus; dock greens that have entered a second season after fall rains stand in for garden spinach.

JAPANESE
KNOTWEED

Try ethnic dishes with your wild-foods ingredients; Greek dishes can use wild mints as well as cultivated ones, and many Mexican and American Indian dishes actually started out wild and got tamer as we turned more and more to the supermarket and backyard gardens.

Keep your eyes open—and your mind, as well, for fresh new combinations of ingredients—and your main dishes will surprise even the cook with their unique goodness.

HOW TO FILLET FISH

Remove the head with a sharp knife. Then cut down along the backbone until you hit the rib cage; you'll be able to feel it with the tip of your knife. Slide the point of the knife parallel to the ribs and along the rib cage until you reach the tail section, then continue the width of the fish, cutting till you free the fillet at the tail. If you are working with the smaller panfish, these are tiny pieces of meat but as sweet and succulent as any of the larger game fish.

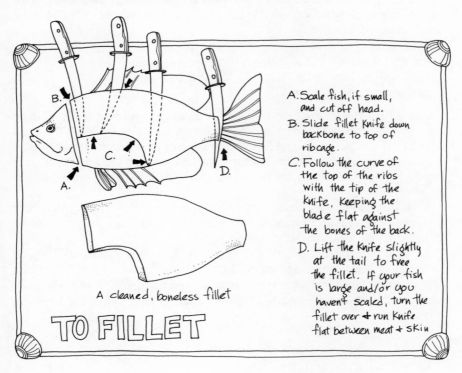

A. Scale fish, if small, and cut off head.

B. Slide fillet knife down backbone to top of ribcage.

C. Follow the curve of the top of the ribs with the tip of the knife, keeping the blade flat against the bones of the back.

D. Lift the knife slightly at the tail to free the fillet. If your fish is large and/or you haven't scaled, turn the fillet over & run knife flat between meat + skin

A cleaned, boneless fillet

TO FILLET

Poached Salmon

Serves 4

This member of the trout family makes some excellent eating.

1½ C. fresh watercress
4   salmon steaks
1   clove wild garlic, diced

1   C. dry white wine
1   T. butter or margarine
     (optional)

Make a bed of watercress in a flat, open pan. Lay on the salmon steaks and sprinkle with diced garlic. Pour the wine over all, and dot each steak with a bit of butter or margarine if you wish. Simmer for 5–7 minutes or until fish flakes with a fork. Season to taste at the table; you may find this needs no additional seasoning.

Rainbow Trout à la Chuck
Serves 2–3

My father invented this recipe in the mountains of Colorado; it was incredible and incredibly simple—but the best food often is, isn't it?

This recipe can use any member of the trout family, of course—I've just come to depend on rainbows since that's what we seem to have most of in Missouri.

½ C. butter
Juice of 1 lemon (this is quite tart; adjust lemon to your preference)

½ t. salt
Pepper to taste
2–3 fat trout

Get a nice fire going and let it burn down to glowing coals. Throw on a few handfuls of green sagebrush to make a savory, sage-flavored smoke. (If you're not in the Rockies and can't find sagebrush, try wild sage, hickory leaves, mesquite chips, apple twigs, or wild mint on your coals. Experiment with flavors—you can't go far wrong with broiled trout.)

Melt butter in a small saucepan and squeeze in the lemon juice. Salt and pepper to taste. I go heavy on the pepper on this one; it seems to bring out the sparkle of lemon.

Drizzle over both sides of the fish to help keep it from sticking to your grill, then continue to baste the trout as it broils until tender-flaky (check with your fork). Remove carefully from the grill; it has a tendency to fall into the coals—enough to make strong men cry, after smelling that aroma.

Cornmeal-breaded Catfish
Serves 4

I fillet these meaty bottom-feeders as I do bluegill. They are much larger and you will require fewer fillets per person.

1½ lbs. skinned catfish fillets, cut to serving pieces
½ C. flour
1 C. cornmeal
¼ C. wheat germ (optional)
1 t. salt
Pepper to taste
1 clove wild garlic or 1 t. garlic powder

1 C. oil or drippings (My father swore by bacon drippings and it *is* good, but if you prefer a dish lower in cholesterol, try peanut oil instead. It cooks hot without smoking.)

Fillet fish and dredge in flour, cornmeal, wheat germ, salt, and pepper mixture. Rub the inside of your frying pan with the bruised garlic clove or add garlic powder to your dredging mixture.

Heat skillet with oil or drippings until almost smoking hot. Carefully place fillets in hot oil and cook until crisp and tender on both sides — it doesn't take long. Serve with lemon juice or vinegar.

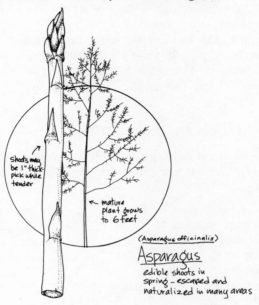

shoots may be 1" thick - pick while tender

← mature plant grows to 6 feet

(Asparagus officinalis)

Asparagus

edible shoots in spring - escaped and naturalized in many areas

Oriental One-Dish Stir-Fry with Fish, Shellfish, or Chicken

Serves 4

There is a growing interest in one-dish meals and lighter cooking methods. This recipe satisfies both.

¼ C. peanut oil
½ C. sliced green peppers
½ C. thinly sliced wild onions
2 cloves wild garlic, diced
2 carrots, sliced diagonally
6–8 stalks of wild asparagus, sliced diagonally
1 C. diced or chopped meat from crayfish, freshwater mussels, oysters, or sliced fillets from your catch of the day (chicken may substitute)

½ C. Jerusalem artichokes, well scrubbed and sliced
2 C. cooked rice (use a mixture of wild and brown rice for a special flavor or substitute Oriental noodles)

Heat oil almost to smoking in a wok or skillet; peanut oil works well for this since it resists smoking even at high temperatures. This not only makes for a more pleasant kitchen but it is better for your health. Add all the vegetables except Jerusalem artichokes and stir-fry quickly.

Add the meat 2–3 minutes before the end of cooking time; slightly longer if you use chicken. Stir quickly to coat with oil.

At the last minute, add Jerusalem artichokes. They will stay pleasantly crunchy if not overcooked.

Season with salt and pepper, soy or tamari sauce, or for a very different and unexpected pleasure, use a light, rice-wine vinegar from your store's Oriental section. This adds a delicate tang without overpowering the fine flavors of the fish or shellfish. Serve over rice.

Panfish Fillets in Beer Batter
Serves 4

My favorite panfish is the bluegill, often plentiful and easy to catch here in Missouri. If you catch crappie or rock bass they are admirable substitutes.

½ can of beer (may be flat)
Salt and pepper to taste
1 finely diced wild garlic
   clove or ½ t. garlic
   powder
Flour to make a smooth, pan-
   cakelike batter

2 T. cornmeal (optional)
20–25 bluegill, crappie, etc.,
   filleted
¾ C. oil or drippings, hot

Mix batter using a half can of beer, salt, pepper, diced garlic or garlic powder, and enough flour to make a smooth batter. Add a little corn-meal, if you like. Don't get the batter too thick (it won't stick to the fillets) or too thin (it will run right off). Try a single fillet to check the consistency, then adjust the flour or liquid content as necessary. Dip each fillet into the batter and drop into hot oil. They cook rapidly; turn as they become golden brown. The fillets will be done when the batter on both sides is crisp and brown. Remove to a paper towel and drain. Serve with malt vinegar, lemon juice, or a seafood sauce made of ketchup mixed with lemon juice and a little garlic and horseradish.

Braised Frog Legs
Serves 4

Frog legs are said to taste like chicken; they are certainly as mild, but I find they have a wonderful, rich taste all their own. They are notoriously active in the pan—they kick as if protesting their fate! Chill well before cooking or be sure to cover the pan to minimize the action.

If you buy your frog legs they will most likely come skinned and ready

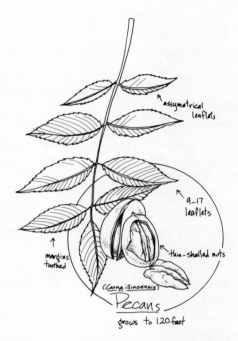

asymmetrical
leaflets

9–17
leaflets

thin-shelled nuts

margins
toothed

(Carya illinoensis)
Pecans
grows to 120 feet

to cook. If not, you will need to prepare them yourself. Only the hind legs are eaten; cut them away from the frog's body and discard it. Remove the feet, then strip skin off from the tops as if you were taking off a pair of gloves.

My father used to bring home huge, tender bullfrog legs; it was a staple in bullfrog season. Little did I know then that the finest French restaurants are never without their own special version of a frog leg dinner!

8 large frog legs
¾ C. flour
Salt and pepper to taste
¾ C. butter or margarine
½ C. chopped wild onions
¾ C. chicken or fish stock
1½ C. bread crumbs

½ t. dried crumbled sage (domestic may be substituted)
¾ C. finely chopped wild pecans, black walnuts, or hazelnuts
1 t. lemon juice

Roll cleaned frog legs in flour seasoned with salt and pepper. Melt 6 T. of butter or margarine in a saucepan and skim off the foam, then use it to sauté onions and frog legs together until just brown. Reduce the heat under the skillet and add the stock, simmering the frog legs and onions until tender, about 10 minutes.

In a separate pan, melt another 6 T. of butter or margarine and stir in the bread crumbs, sage, chopped nuts, and lemon juice. Roll the frog legs in the buttered crumbs and serve with steaming hot potatoes, groundnuts, or arrowhead tubers.

Fried Frog Legs

A simpler recipe and closer to what my father used to make.

8 large frog legs, cleaned
Beer batter (see *Panfish Fillets in Beer Batter*, page 82) or *Egg Breading* (recipe follows)

¾ C. oil or drippings or a combination of the two

Clean and dry frog legs well. Dip in batter or egg breading and allow to dry for about an hour. Fry in hot oil or drippings until brown, and drain on paper toweling.

EGG BREADING

1 C. seasoned flour (salt and pepper to taste)

1 egg, diluted with 1 T. water or milk

Dip frog legs in seasoned flour, then into egg mixture, then again into the flour mixture. Allow to dry 1–2 hours; this will assure the breading will stay put during cooking.

Fancy Frog Legs

Serves 6

This recipe is quite elegant, though simple to prepare.

12 frog legs, cleaned
¼ C. brandy
4 T. butter or margarine
½ C. thinly sliced mushrooms (wild or domestic)

¼ C. chopped fresh parsley
Juice of 1 lemon
Salt and pepper to taste

Sprinkle the frog legs with brandy and marinate about 2 hours. Sauté in melted butter or margarine until just beginning to brown, then add the rest of the ingredients to the pan. Sauté until the mushrooms become limp. Serve immediately.

Crawfish Etouffée

Serves 4–6

A friend from New Orleans tells me that what gives this dish its special richness is the fat from the cooked crawfish's brains. If you want the true Creole flavor, use this part of the small crustacean as well as the tails (to use, simply crack the shell of the cooked crawfish and scoop out the brains).

By the way, the difference in spelling for this dish and the one that follows is a respectful nod to the popular spelling among fine bayou chefs.

A spicy cooking sauce is traditional for crawfish and other seafoods in New Orleans; try it with your own home-caught crawdads.

To clean crawfish: If your small crustaceans are fresh-caught and haven't been cleaned, put them in a large pot of heavily salted water to purge them. Let them rest for 30 minutes or so, then change to fresh water and allow to soak another 10 minutes.

It takes about 6 lbs. of live crawfish to make 1 lb. of cleaned tail meat; allow ½–1 lb. per person.

1 C. brown or brown and wild
   rice mixed
2 C. water
2 lbs. of crawfish tails, cleaned
   and shelled
3 T. butter
½ t. salt
½ t. pepper
¼ t. paprika

1 C. chopped onions
2 cloves wild garlic, diced
2 t. flour
2 t. lemon juice
2 T. brandy or rum
¾ C. water
Tabasco to taste
1 T. chopped parsley

Bring rice and water to a boil, reduce heat, and cook for 30–40 minutes or until fluffy.

Sauté crawfish in melted butter; add salt, pepper, and paprika. Cook for 2 minutes, then add garlic and onions. Continue to cook until onions are golden and translucent. Sprinkle the flour over all and stir until well coated; then add lemon juice, brandy or rum, water, and Tabasco.

Serve over fluffy hot rice; garnish with parsley.

Boiled Crawfish Creole   *Serves 4–6*

Like shrimp, crawfish are wonderful boiled with shrimp spice (or crawfish spice available in the Cajun-cooking section of your grocery). It's traditional to serve these little morsels with red and white potatoes, sweet corn, and onions; if you prefer, substitute wildings such as arrowhead tubers or groundnuts, wild onions, cattail bloom spikes, etc.

4 lbs. cleaned crawfish	1 large onion, sliced
5 qts. of water (more if you are serving a large crowd)	3-4 cloves garlic
1 lemon, sliced	2 stalks of celery, sliced
2 T. shrimp or crawfish boiling spice	5 small red potatoes
1 T. salt	5 small white potatoes
	4-5 ears of corn, cut into quarters

Put crawfish into a large pot with water, lemon slices, spices, salt, onion, garlic, and sliced celery. Bring to a boil over high heat. Meanwhile, scrub potatoes and prepare corn. Add to boiling mixture, cover, and cook until potatoes are nearly tender—10-15 minutes. Remove vegetables to a hot platter. Add crawfish to stock and cook over high heat for 5 minutes. Only the tail meat is eaten; break off and de-vein.

Crayfish Piccata

Serves 4-6

Piccata means "sharp" in Italian; I think I'd be more inclined to think of this dish as piquant—and delicious.

1 C. chopped wild onion	2 T. butter or margarine
3 cloves wild garlic, diced	2 T. dry sherry
2 T. olive oil	2 T. fresh lemon juice
3 C. cleaned and shelled cray-fish tails (you can substitute shrimp—or chicken breasts, cut in strips)	2 T. chicken stock
	1 T. capers
	2 T. chopped parsley (optional)

Sauté the onion and garlic in olive oil and set aside. Sauté the crayfish tails (shrimp, chicken) in butter until tender; add the onions and garlic. Pour in sherry, lemon juice, and chicken stock; add capers. Stir until hot and serve over fluffy cooked rice. Garnish with chopped parsley.

Crayfish Tempura

Serves 6

This is another wonderful dinner with an Oriental flair (use bluegill or other panfish fillets, if you prefer). The batter puffs up and turns a crisp golden brown, helping sometimes meager catches go further to feed a hungry crowd.

2 eggs, separated	4 C. crayfish tails, well cleaned
3 T. water	and patted dry with paper
1 C. flour	toweling (substitute bluegill
Salt to taste	or other panfish fillets or
	larger fish fillets cut into
	1'' x 3'' pieces for uniform
	cooking)

Separate eggs; beat yolks very well—until lemon-colored and smooth. Stir in water, flour, and salt. Beat egg whites until light, and fold into the batter. Dip crayfish tails or fillets into the batter and fry in deep fat (or oil) until puffed and brown.

Serve with soy sauce, sweet-and-sour sauce, or hot mustard. A vegetable stir-fry goes well with this, or use the same batter to coat vegetables and cook them tempura-style as well.

Crayfish Oriental

Serves 4

This is nicely spicy; we love it with wild or domestic vegetables.

1 C. sake or gin (or a mixture of ½ C. water and ½ C. vinegar)
1 t. grated wild gingerroot (or purchased fresh ginger)
1 clove wild garlic, crushed
1 C. sliced wild onions, ramps, or leeks
2 carrots, sliced
¼ C. oil

½ C. sliced wild mushrooms
2 C. cleaned crayfish tails
½ C. daylily shoots, buds, or flowers, depending on the season
2 C. wild greens, sliced ½" wide; chicory is delicious in this
½ C. Jerusalem artichokes or water chestnuts

Marinate crayfish tails for 2 hours in a mixture of sake or gin (or water and vinegar), grated ginger, and crushed garlic.

Drain well. Sauté onions and carrots in oil. Add mushrooms. Add crayfish tails, stirring well to coat with oil. Stir in daylilies and add greens; stir-fry until greens are just wilted. Add Jerusalem artichokes or water chestnuts. Remember, daylilies may be cathartic to sensitive individuals; know your guests and your own tolerance here, or omit.

Serve over rice; splash with soy sauce or tamari, if you like.

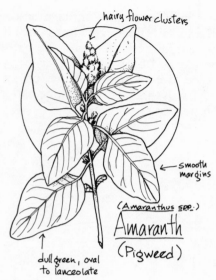

hairy flower clusters

← smooth margins

(*Amaranthus* spp.)

Amaranth
(Pigweed)

↑ dull green, oval to lanceolate

Stir-Fry Dinner

Serves 4

Of course, you needn't stick only with seafood or fowl from the wild. A delicious dinner can be made using edible wild plants and your own chicken, pork, or beef.

¼ C. oil
3 carrots, sliced diagonally
1 C. wild onions, sliced
2 cloves wild garlic, sliced very thin
Young cattail heads, still green —cut from the spike
1½ C. thin-sliced meat (if fowl, remove from the bone and slice ¼" thick; discard skin)

1 C. dock greens
1 C. lamb's-quarter or amaranth greens
½ C. chicory, if in season (early)
Soy sauce to taste

Heat oil to almost smoking; drop in carrots and stir-fry until edges just begin to brown. Add onions, garlic, young cattail head granules, and stir until almost tender. Add meat and continue to stir-fry; the thin slices will cook very rapidly (even pork), so don't let it get overdone. Drop in greens and stir to coat with oil; cover briefly and season with soy sauce to taste.

Serve over rice you have cooked in water or stock for a special treat any time of the year that you can find wildings. Use your personal favorites; I have used daylily shoots, buds, and flowers (remember possible cathartic effect), Jerusalem artichokes, groundnuts, catbrier shoots, chickweed, and any or all of the wild greens. In early spring, mustard or cress, chicory, and the first leaves of dock are delicious; you can't go far wrong with a one-dish stir-fry.

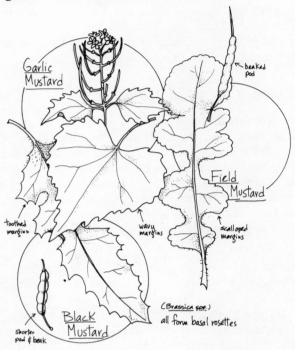

Roast Duck (or Quail, Pheasant, or Goose)

Serves 2–4

I served this one for Thanksgiving, and we were thankful indeed! If you have skinned the fowl, as some people do, you will need to place bacon strips over the breast and place the bird under the broiler for 10–15 minutes just before serving.

1 C. vermouth
½ C. brandy or rum
½ C. oil (sesame oil is wonderful for this)
3 T. fresh lemon juice
1 bay leaf
2 C. or more water

1 larger duck, goose, pheasant, or 2 mallards or 6 quail
Salt and pepper to taste
3–4 chopped medium potatoes
3 chopped apples
3 chopped carrots

Mix a marinade with vermouth, brandy or rum, oil, lemon juice, crumbled bay leaf, and water to cover game. Soak the bird(s) overnight in the refrigerator. Remove and season inside and out with salt and pepper. Brown in lightly oiled skillet, then stuff each cavity with a mixture of chopped potatoes, apples, and carrots. This stuffing is later discarded; its purpose is to absorb fat and reduce an overly wild flavor.

Place bird(s) in a well-greased casserole, add ½ C. water or vermouth, and bake, covered, at 375° for 2 hours.

Serve on a bed of fluffy wild and brown rice that you've drizzled with the pan drippings from the casserole.

Curried Duck with Wild Honey

Serves 2

Wild honey, of course, simply means you've been brave enough to collect your own. It seems to have a special flavor imparted by courage, stamina, and good old foolhardiness. All honey is wild; bees collect the ingredients like the little bandits they are. Some honeys, however, have flavors imparted by whatever is blooming at the time; you can taste the wonderfully subtle differences between wildflower honey and white clover honey, for instance. Your duck can be domestic, too, if you like—I've made this both ways and you can't go far wrong.

1 duck	5 T. honey
Salt and pepper	1½ T. curry powder
1 C. wild onions, whole	1 clove wild garlic, crushed
2 cloves	

Wash and dry the duck thoroughly, then salt and pepper inside and out. Stick the cloves into one of the onions and stuff them into the bird's cavity. Bake at 325° for an hour (cooking time will vary with the size of your duck; figure on 20 minutes per pound), then baste with a mixture of honey, curry, and garlic every 10 minutes or so for another 30 minutes.

Braised Quail and Wild Mushrooms

Serves 2

There's almost no way to go wrong with quail except by overcooking; they are delicious no matter what you do with them. This is a particularly rich and filling dish. You can also use dove (or even rock dove or pigeons) in this dish.

6 quail	2 T. flour
1 T. chopped wild onion	½ C. stock or water
1 T. chopped parsley	1 C. sherry or burgundy
1 T. butter or margarine	Salt and pepper to taste
1 C. wild mushrooms, sliced	

Preheat oven to 350°. Brown quail in a separate pan. Make sauce by browning onion and parsley in butter; add mushrooms and cook until just tender. Thicken with flour, then add stock or water and wine. Season to taste. Place quail breast down in this sauce, cover, and simmer until tender; inserted fork should come out easily. Fifteen or 20 minutes should be sufficient cooking time. Do not overcook any small game or domestic bird.

Pheasant (or Other Game Bird) au Vin

This is an elegant dish, worthy of celebration with your family and friends.

1 pheasant or other game bird
3 T. butter or margarine
2 C. red wine (preferably burgundy)
3 slices of bacon, rendered till crisp (reserve drippings)
1 C. chopped wild onions
1 carrot, sliced
2 small cloves of wild garlic, diced

2 T. flour
½ t. thyme
1 t. salt
Pepper to taste
2 T. fresh minced parsley
1 small bay leaf
2 C. sliced mushrooms (wild or domestic)

Brown pheasant lightly in butter or margarine and marinate 4–6 hours in red wine; reserve wine.

Fry bacon until crisp and sauté the vegetables in 1 T. of the drippings. (Substitute butter or oil if desired.) Add to the pot with the bird. Mix a thin batter of the flour, seasonings, and herbs with a bit of the reserved wine, then mix it with the whole to thicken. Add to the pot. Cook until done over low heat—about 1 hour. Add mushrooms for the last 5 minutes of cooking. (If you prefer, simmer this one all day in a low-heat crock; it is delicious after a long winter's day.)

Chicken with Wild Ramps and Cream

This is a rich dish; with the wonderful flavor of the wild ramps you won't mind a bit. You can use a game fowl instead of chicken if you have one; it would be good with any of the milder-flavored birds.

5–6 wild ramps or other wild onions
1 clove wild garlic, diced
1 T. oil
3–4 lbs. deboned and cubed raw meat

Dash of nutmeg
Salt and pepper to taste
½ C. heavy cream

Clean the ramps well, then slice lengthwise and sauté with the garlic in oil, until transparent but not brown. Add the cubed chicken; cook gently 15 minutes. Add nutmeg, salt, and pepper to taste. Stir in cream and garnish with a sprig of wild mint, if you like.

Dove Poached in Wine

This is extremely elegant fare; if you have grouse or pheasant or other wildfowl, they make excellent substitutes (as does chicken).

8   breasts of dove (or serving
      size pieces of other fowl)
1½ C. water
½   C. white or burgundy wine
      (I've even used champagne
      that had gone flat with
      good results)

4   cloves wild garlic and tops,
      diced
½   t. rosemary
½   t. thyme
½   t. tarragon
Salt and pepper to taste

Put meat breast side up in a saucepan with a tight-fitting lid. Add other ingredients; cover and simmer until just done, about 15 minutes for small pieces of meat, 25 for larger.

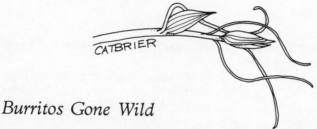

CATBRIER

Burritos Gone Wild

Serves 4

Almost everyone loves Mexican food, and I'm certainly no exception. Try these wild burritos for a new twist on an old favorite.

1   C. chopped wild onions
1   can of refried beans
½   lb. chicken or wildfowl,
      steamed lightly and diced
1   T. cumin powder or 2 T.
      chili powder (or both)
1–2 flour tortillas per person
1½ C. shredded cheddar cheese
1   C. mild, medium, or hot
      taco sauce or Mexican
      salsa

1   C. catbrier shoots, wild
      asparagus, or mild greens
      (lamb's-quarter, dock,
      amaranth, etc.)
¼   C. prepared, chilled *nopales*
      (optional) sliced ¼'' wide
      (see directions for basic
      preparation, page 72)

Mix chopped onions, refried beans, and steamed meat in a bowl; stir in cumin and/or chili powder. Put ¼ C. or so of this mixture in the center of each flour tortilla. Top with cheese and taco sauce and roll up. Place seam side down in a greased casserole and top with more sauce and cheese.

Heat in a 350° oven for 20 minutes or so, then remove and top with shredded cheese, chopped greens, and *nopales*. Serve hot.

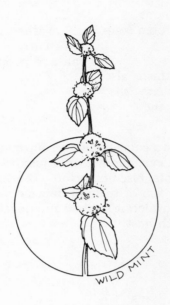

WILD MINT

Wild-stuffed Pita Bread

Serves 4

Pitas may be stuffed with any combination of ingredients. I like a meaty salad for a filling main dish. One pita usually is enough per person.

¼–½ C. meat per person—use sliced chicken, turkey, or ham, or what have you
2 C. wild greens (choose the milder ones)
1 C. Jerusalem artichoke tubers, steamed or raw
½ C. chopped wild onions
¼ C. chopped wild mint
¼ C. olive oil
¼ C. lemon juice or vinegar
Salt and pepper to taste
1 pita for each person, sliced across the circle to make two pockets

Cook and slice meat. Mix with chopped greens, sliced artichoke tubers, onions, and mint. Dress the whole with olive oil and lemon juice and season to taste. Stuff this mixture into pitas and enjoy!

Quick Poultry Hash

Serves 4

There are times when we want a fast and easy meal; this recipe is both delicious and as simple as one could ask.

1 C. chopped wild onions
1 can cream of mushroom soup concentrate
¼ C. milk
1 C. diced wildfowl (this is also good with fish or crayfish tails if you adjust the seasonings)

½ C. diced sheep sorrel or washed wood sorrel leaves
¼ C. curry powder
Salt and pepper to taste

Sauté onions; stir into a pan containing soup concentrate. Stir in milk and remaining ingredients; simmer until just hot.

Serve over toast points, biscuits, or hot corn bread.

If you choose to use fish or seafood, replace milk with ¼ C. white wine and omit curry powder; it's subtle and delicious. (The alcohol in the wine cooks off with heat.)

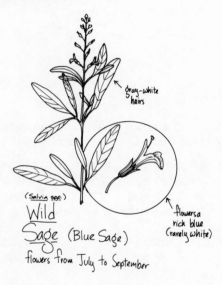

(Salvia spp.)
Wild Sage (Blue Sage)
flowers from July to September

gray-white hairs

flowers a rich blue (rarely white)

Quick Peasant Pot Pie

Serves 6

This simple dish takes advantage of leftover cooked fowl; use pheasant, quail, grouse, wild turkey, what have you. The recipe calls for precooked pie shells, as well, so the time involved is little more than that required to heat the dish through.

1 C. cooked, diced wildfowl
1 C. lightly steamed Jerusalem artichokes, diced
1 C. chopped wild onions, steamed until just transparent
½ C. cooked sausage, cut into bite sizes (optional; adds a nice, hearty flavor)

½ t. thyme
Salt and pepper to taste
1 C. prepared white sauce (make a roux of 1 T. butter, 1 T. flour, and add enough milk to thicken)
1 prebaked pie shell (see dessert chapter for recipe or use your own favorite)

Mix all ingredients and fill your precooked pie shell. Top with another prepared crust, baked flat, or spooned-on biscuit dough. Bake at 400° until heated through, about 20 minutes, or until biscuit topping is browned.

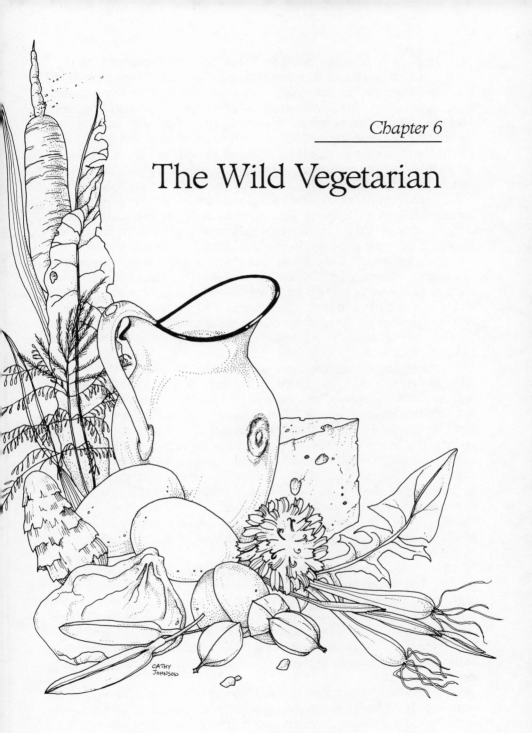

The Wild Vegetarian

By now, nearly everyone has at least experimented with vegetarian cooking, many on a full-time basis. Some have found it a viable choice to be completely vegetarian. Others choose vegetarianism as a several-times-a-week alternative, as we do—to help cut down on red meats, as an economic measure, and to provide variety.

Vegetable proteins, carefully combined, can give us a high-quality substitute for meats—and a delicious choice, as well. You'll never miss the meat. When we use wildings in our vegetarian dishes, we enhance flavor and nutrition while enjoying an added panache; we go wild in style.

Wild grains, nuts, seeds, and pollens are rich in nutrients, which help maintain a healthful balance. Sunflower seeds, for example, are not only delicious, but they'll generously provide you with protein, calcium, phosphorus, and potassium while you munch; a nutritional bargain.

Did you know that many of the wild greens are also important sources of proteins, vitamins, and minerals, as well? Nettle greens, for instance, are a good source of protein and an excellent source of vitamins A and C. Dock is rich in vitamin C, phosphorus, and potassium; it has 2 milligrams of protein per 100 grams and 3,000 International Units of vitamin A. The common dandelion tops even that, nutritionally, with 14,000 I.U.s of vitamin A.

You may wish to combine these nutrient-rich wildings with the vegetable proteins in domestic beans and grains. A wild foods cookbook, in fact, could be centered around a vegetarian diet; after all, wild plants are certainly easier to come by than meats. There's no need to catch them by stealth or cunning (although hunters of morel mushrooms might argue with me about that—my father always swore they saw him coming and waited until he had passed to shoulder aside their blanket of leaves). Unlike many of the meat dishes featured in the last chapter, we need no hunting or fishing license to hunt wild vegetables. If you observe the rules of common sense, good stewardship, and common courtesy (asking before you collect on private property), and if you've made sure you're within the law when you collect on state or national lands, these wildings are free for the taking.

I've included what are called ovo-lacto vegetarian dishes among the straight vegetarian fare. If you prefer meatless meals but don't mind eggs, milk, or cheese, you'll find plenty of suggestions here.

The basic ingredients pack well and can be taken into the field to supplement the wildings you forage on the spot with protein from home. Mix these nonmeat proteins with vegetable wildings and the staples of flour, cornmeal, shortening, and dried beans and you can live a rich, well-rounded life.

Again, in this chapter, I've adapted international dishes as well as old family recipes handed down from my mother and grandmother. Many of the world's cultures have survived quite well for centuries on dishes very much like these; more than likely, they originally included wild plants among their ingredients.

Suggested Wild Ingredients

If you are planning to go totally wild, you'll need to gather good sources of protein as well as the wildings that usually come to mind. Although rich in fat and therefore not as desirable in some cases, the wild nuts can give us plenty of protein for our effort. Seeds are also a good choice; try amaranth, sunflower, or wild rice (really a grass seed rather than a true rice plant). These can give us *vegetable* proteins, especially when combined with other incomplete proteins such as legumes (again, if you're going wild, you can opt for one of the edible wild "beans"—redbud, for instance).

Wild pollens would appear to be good choices to supplement a vegetarian diet; bees love them! Most are too time consuming to gather for human consumption, but consider the cattail, which can be held over a large paper bag and shaken until you have several cups of pollen in just a few minutes. Most definitely worth the trouble.

Add eggs and milk products to your vegetarian menu, and you can build an amazing vocabulary of wild food choices. Our recipes only begin to scratch the surface of possible choices. A vegetable quiche, rich with eggs and milk and flavored with wild onions and greens; a soufflé full of spinachlike lamb's-quarter and protein-rich amaranth seeds; a pot of beans simmered in wild-greens broth and savory with wild garlic and onions—who could ask for more?

Simple Herb Omelet   Serves 4

For an easy and quick dish, try this herb and cheese omelet. It takes its flavor from the wild.

2 T. butter or margarine
4 eggs
¼ C. milk or half-and-half
1 T. fresh wild sage
1 T. fresh wild thyme
1 clove wild garlic
2 T. diced wild onion (include green stalks for eye appeal)

½ C. cheddar, Swiss, or Havarti cheese, diced, or a combination
Salt and pepper to taste; a dash of paprika if you like

NOTE: Diced wild mushrooms, cooked gently beforehand, make an excellent addition to this simple dish.

Melt butter or margarine in a heavy skillet. Mix eggs and milk plus seasonings in a medium-sized bowl. Dice other ingredients finely and stir into the egg mixture. Add cheese.

Pour into the skillet and let it cook over low heat until the eggs are set; this will not be as light and fluffy as the following dish. In fact, if you prefer to convert it to trailside scrambled eggs, simply stir as it cooks.

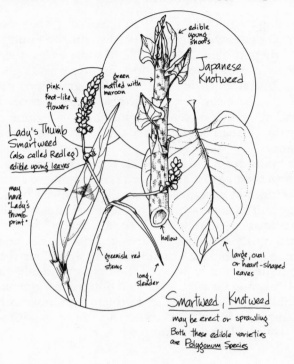

Sorrel Omelet

Serves 4

In summer, when it's too hot to turn on the oven, or when I am too tired to fix something more elaborate, our main dish is often an omelet. Easy to make even on the trail, this recipe takes advantage of whatever wildings are available. My favorite addition is sorrel, for its tart, lemony bite.

6 eggs, separated
½ C. well-washed and drained sorrel leaves (or any other wild green or combination that suits your fancy—this is good with dandelion, chicory, dock, lamb's-quarter, or what have you)
2 T. wild chives, diced (green wild onion tops may be substituted)

½ C. chopped wild onion, ramps, or leeks
2 T. butter or margarine
Salt and pepper to taste
2 T. cottage cheese
Dash of nutmeg (optional)

OTHER WILD ADDITIONS: You may want to try Japanese knotweed, sliced husk-tomatoes, daylily buds, or sliced wild asparagus, as well.

Beat egg yolks separately until they are just stirred. Chop or slice vegetables, except onions, and add to beaten eggs.

Melt 2 T. butter or margarine in a large, heavy skillet (substitute a light olive oil if you prefer) and sauté onions until they are just transparent. Stir into egg/vegetable mixture.

Meanwhile, in a separate bowl, beat egg whites until they become stiff and fold them very gently into egg yolk mixture. Pour gently into the skillet; add cheese and sprinkle lightly with freshly ground nutmeg. Cook over low heat until the eggs are just set—don't overcook or they become tough on the bottom.

NOTE: For a super-deluxe omelet, when done drizzle with white wine or balsamic vinegar for flavor.

Wildflower Omelet Surprise

Serves 6

There is a growing interest in cooking with wildflowers, not only for their beauty but for their delicate flavor and good nutritional value as well. This unexpected omelet would be perfect for a Sunday brunch.

6 eggs, separated
2 T. milk or half-and-half
Dash of nutmeg or cinnamon
1 C. of whatever edible wild-
    flowers are in season (day-
    lilies, dandelions, violets,
    red clover blossoms, elder
    flowers, yucca petals, wild
    rose petals, chicory flowers)
    or any combination for
    color and flavor.

2 T. butter or margarine (or
    light oil)
1 t. powdered sugar

Beat eggs separately, yolks until they are lemon colored, whites until just stiff. Add milk or half-and-half, nutmeg, or cinnamon. Fold yolks and whites together gently; fold in wildflowers.

Melt butter or margarine in your skillet and pour in egg mixture carefully. Cook gently over medium-low heat until eggs are just set. Sprinkle with powdered sugar and garnish each helping with a fresh flower.

Wild Greens and Onion Quiche

Serves 6

This rich and hearty old-country peasant dish has a wonderful blending of eggs, cheese, milk, and foraged vegetables. Add meat if you must, but do try it vegetarian; it's satisfying and delightful either way.

1 T. oil	3 eggs
1 C. chopped wild onions (include green stalks for eye appeal)	2 C. milk, scalded and cooled for a smoother, custardlike texture
1 C. washed and chopped wild greens (fresh, in season, or thawed and well drained if you have stocked up on them in your freezer)	¼ t. salt Pepper to taste
1 9'' piecrust (see page 155 or use a purchased crust)	1 C. shredded cheddar or other cheese (quiche is often made with Swiss cheese; use it if you prefer)

Sauté onions in hot oil; when they are transparent and just beginning to turn golden brown, drop in greens just to wilt.

Arrange onions and greens in the bottom of piecrust.

Beat eggs slightly and mix with cooled milk. Add seasonings. Pour into your pie shell over the chopped onions and greens and top with shredded cheese.

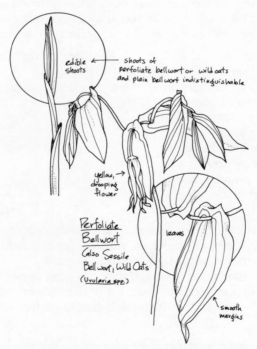

edible shoots

shoots of perfoliate bellwort or wild oats and plain bellwort indistinguishable

yellow, drooping flower

Perfoliate Bellwort
(also Sessile Bellwort, Wild Oats)
(Uvularia spp.)

leaves

smooth margins

Bake at 375° for 35–40 minutes or until set and knife inserted in center comes out clean.

(If you like, make this a seafood quiche; add up to a cup of crayfish, shrimp, or shellfish. Add a sprinkle of nutmeg on top.)

Mushroom Bake (One-Dish Dinner)   *Serves 4*

Try this one when you've been fortunate enough to find a real cache of mushrooms—or one huge, fresh giant puffball. A large beefsteak mushroom might just do it, too.

1   C. bread crumbs (use your own sourdough bread from the next chapter, for extra flavor)
1   C. wild vegetable broth (beef broth may be substituted, if desired)
½   C. wild onions, sliced
2–3 C. chopped wild mushrooms (morels, chanterelles, puffballs, etc.)

2   T. butter or margarine
1   T. fresh wild sage (or substitute 1 t. dried, crumbled sage leaves)
1   T. capers
1   C. mild-flavored cheese, shredded
Salt and pepper to taste

Soak bread crumbs in broth. Sauté onions and mushrooms in butter or margarine until they just begin to brown. Mix all ingredients except cheese; place half the mixture in a well-buttered, shallow baking dish, cover with cheese, then add the rest of the mushroom mixture. Bake at 375° for 45 minutes or until top is golden. This is a delightful vegetarian dish (if you use vegetable broth instead of beef, of course).

You can serve the leftovers the next day by covering and heating the dish or by slicing what's left and frying it quickly in hot oil.

Cheese Risotto   *Serves 4–6*

This is a lovely Italian recipe by way of New England—by way of the nearest fence row or bog.

6 oz. grated cheddar cheese
½ lb. wild and brown rice, cooked
½ C. chopped wild onions
½ C. chopped nuts (pecans, hickory nuts, pine nuts, etc.)

½ C. wild greens stock, page 109, or water
6 T. dry white wine
2 T. oil, margarine or butter
Salt and pepper to taste

Sauté onion in oil, butter or margarine until translucent and just beginning to brown. Add to rice; stir in stock or water and wine and simmer for ten minutes or so, stirring occasionally. Stir in nuts and taste before adding salt and pepper; you may like it as is. Pile into well-greased baking dish and smother with grated cheese; heat in warm oven (300°) until cheese is just melted.

Pasta and Pesto Sauce

Yields 2 C.

If you live where a supply of pine nuts is readily available, gather your own for a lively pesto.

1½ C. fresh basil leaves
½ C. pine nuts
2–3 cloves wild garlic

¾ C. finely grated Parmesan cheese
¾ C. olive oil

Pound the basil leaves in a mortar; some people use parsley here, but basil is traditional and delicious. Add pine nuts and garlic and continue pounding; mixture will be quite thick. Add grated cheese, then slowly add oil, stirring constantly. Use 1–2 T. per serving; refrigerate or freeze the remainder.

Serve over hot pasta (½ C. per serving), or make your own from our recipe, below.

NOTE: This dish is easily made in a blender or food processor.

Homemade Egg/Cattail Noodles

Serves 6–8

I make these rich egg noodles with or without cattail pollen; it adds a beautiful golden color and an indefinable taste.

1 C. white or whole wheat flour or a mixture of both
¼ C. cattail pollen
Salt to taste

1 egg
Hot water just to mix to thick dough consistency

Mix dry ingredients; drop an egg in a well in the middle. Add water, a little at a time, to make a very thick dough. Keep your hands and working surface well floured, and knead till smooth. Let dough rest 30 minutes, then roll out on a floured board or between two sheets of waxed paper.

Roll as thin as you like, then lightly flour the surface. Roll dough up like a jelly roll, then cut through to make slices ¼"–½" wide. Unroll and use immediately or let dry and store in an airtight container. Cook by boiling until tender, about 10 minutes.

Serve with pesto sauce or add to your homemade soups or stews; plan on ½ C. cooked noodles per serving.

Wild Lasagne Florentine

If you like Italian food, you'll love this rich lasagne. I serve it whenever I can find wildings.

½ 8-oz. package of lasagne
    noodles
¼ C. olive oil
1½ C. wild onions, chopped
3 cloves wild garlic, thinly sliced
2 C. mild wild greens (lamb's-
    quarter, dock, chickweed,
    etc.)

1½ C. of Italian tomato sauce
    (or make your own, if
    you've the knack)
1 C. ricotta or low-fat cottage
    cheese
½ C. grated Parmesan cheese
1 C. crumbled mozzarella cheese
2 t. oregano

Prepare lasagne noodles according to package directions. Add a bit of oil to the boiling water to keep the noodles from sticking to each other.

Heat olive oil in a skillet and sauté onions and garlic until tender and golden. Steam greens and cool them to the touch. Drain well.

Grease a large, shallow casserole pan. Layer lasagne noodles on the bottom and add layers of sauce, vegetables, greens, and cheese. Add another layer of noodles, and continue as before, ending with a layer of sauce and cheese alone. Sprinkle each layer with oregano as you go.

Bake at 350° for about 40 minutes or until the top is bubbly and beginning to brown. Since "florentine" means the dish contains spinach, the wild greens stand in here.

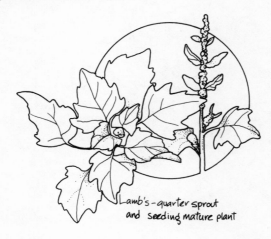

Lamb's-quarter sprout
and seeding mature plant

Greek Lamb's-Quarter Pie

This hearty, rich dish is based on a recipe that calls for spinach and broccoli; I like it even better with wildings.

Unless you are a master at pulling Greek phyllo dough, I suggest you purchase it, either frozen in your grocer's case or fresh from a Middle Eastern deli.

1 C. wild onion, finely
   chopped
3 C. lamb's-quarter, well washed
2 T. olive oil
1 C. feta cheese (substitute
   ricotta or cottage, if you
   must)

2 eggs
2 T. parsley
2 T. chopped wild chives
Salt and pepper to taste
12 phyllo leaves
¼ C. melted butter or margarine

Sauté onions in olive oil and add lamb's-quarter; cover and cook 5 minutes or until lamb's-quarter is wilted and tender. Add cheese, eggs, parsley, wild chives, salt, and pepper. Cool slightly.

Cut phyllo leaves to make 24 sheets; layer the first 12 sheets in a well-greased oblong baking dish, brushing each layer with melted butter or margarine. Add the lamb's-quarter, egg, cheese mixture and top with remaining phyllo, brushing with butter as before. Bake at 350° for 1 hour or until golden.

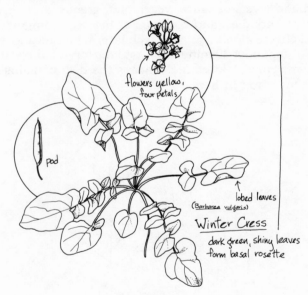

flowers yellow, four petals

pod

lobed leaves
(Barbarea vulgaris)

Winter Cress

dark green, shiny leaves form basal rosette

M'Jeddrah

Serves 6–8

This wonderful dish is Middle Eastern in origin; it is thought, in fact, to have been the original pottage for which Jacob sold his birthright. When I smell it cooking, I'm ready to join him.

¼ C. olive oil	2 C. mild wild greens, such
1 C. brown or mixture of	as young winter cress,
brown and wild rice	dandelion, or chicory
1 C. lentils, soaked in water	3–4 wild onions, chopped
for 4–5 hours	2 cloves wild garlic, diced
2 C. wild onions, sliced	¼ C. chopped wild mint
2½ C. water or stock	Juice of ½ lemon
Salt to taste	Pepper to taste

Put 3 T. olive oil in a heavy skillet and heat. Add rice and stir until it begins to cook (it will become somewhat translucent when coated with butter; continue to cook until it becomes opaque again). Add soaked and drained lentils.

In a separate pan, sauté 2 C. of onions in a small amount of oil; add to the lentils and rice. Add stock and cover; cook 30 minutes over low heat until tender. Salt to taste.

When the hot part of the dish is almost done, make a salad of the greens, chopped wild onions, garlic, and whatever else you may find (try cooked and cooled wild mushrooms or crab apples). Chop mint finely and add to salad.

Dress with olive oil, lemon juice, salt, and pepper; put directly on top of hot rice and lentils if you are adventurous; on the side if you want to play it safe the first time. The contrast is delightful, tart, and filling.

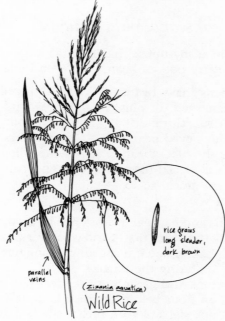

rice grains long slender, dark brown

parallel veins

(Zizania aquatica)
Wild Rice

Wild Rice Casserole

You may have to buy the wild rice for this dish; if it is prohibitively expensive, substitute a commercial wild rice/brown rice mixture, but do keep that wild flavor if possible.

1 C. wild rice or wild rice/ brown rice mix
2½ C. water or wild greens stock (see page 109)
2 eggs
1 C. shredded cheddar cheese
¼ C. grated Parmesan cheese
½ C. ricotta or cottage cheese
Salt and pepper to taste

Dash of nutmeg
½ C. chopped wild onions
1 C. chopped, steamed, and drained wild greens (lamb's-quarter, dock, or one of the other mild-flavored greens is best in this dish)

Cook rice, covered, in water or stock till done—about 40 minutes. Drain off any excess liquid. Mix the eggs, cheeses, and seasonings together. Sauté the onions in a bit of butter, margarine, or oil until just tender and add to the mixture. Stir in rice and chopped greens and bake at 350° for 30–35 minutes or until dish is set.

If you have leftovers, they can be sliced and fried in hot oil the next day for a different but still delicious treat.

Bean Pot Beans and Wild Onions

This is a staple at my house; has been as long as I can remember—I grew up on hearty pots of beans. It's even better the second day.

1 lb. dried beans (navy beans, butter beans, red, or pinto beans—or substitute dried peas or black-eyed peas. My favorite is the black bean, which has a special flavor.)
3 C. wild greens stock (recipe follows) or water

1 C. chopped wild onions
3 cloves wild garlic
1 bay leaf (if you can pick a fresh bay laurel leaf from the wild, all the better!)
Salt and pepper to taste

Boil the beans and bay leaf in stock 3–4 hours or until tender; there's no need to soak the beans first. (And whatever you do, don't soak them overnight with baking soda. It speeds cooking but destroys nutrients—not to mention altering the flavor.)

Sauté the onions and garlic until tender; put into the pot with the beans at least an hour before the dish is done.

Serve with thick slabs of corn bread, homemade sourdough bread, or rich brown bread—for a winter meal it can't be beat!

Wild Mustard
+ Seed Case

Wild Greens Stock

Yields 8 C.

Whatever greens, tubers, rhizomes, or shoots are in season; for this, there is no need to pick the best or most perfectly unblemished plants or to remove tough stems since the wildings will be strained out before using. Do use young, tender greens, however, or the bitterness will be transferred to your stock. You may wish to add amaranth or sunflower seeds and nettle greens to boost the protein content. I like to include plenty of dock and wild onions, whatever the season.

8 C. water   1 t. salt

Throw all the greens or wild vegetables that will fit into a 4-qt. stockpot; add water and salt to draw the juices. Simmer for several hours—I like to put mine on the wood stove and just let it cook half a day, since it isn't costing me any extra fuel to do so.

If everything goes well, you should have a vitamin and mineral rich stock—flavor rich, too. Discard the spent vegetables.

Bean Sandwiches

Serves 4

We like this hearty and flavorful dish for lunches; cold beans may sound bad, but they are delicious. We have this whenever I've cooked a pot of beans.

2 C. *Bean Pot Beans and Wild*   ¼ C. sliced wild onions
   Onions (see recipe, page 108)   Salt and pepper to taste
8 slices bread (wonderful on
   homemade sourdough)

Drain beans well if they are too soupy; reserve bean juice for stock or return to your pot—it's too good to waste. Mash beans with a fork or old-fashioned potato masher. (If you want, try the end of a heavy jar in a wooden bowl.)

Butter the bread well on both slices; spread with the mashed beans and top with sliced fresh onions. Season to taste—this is good with lots of freshly ground pepper.

Red Beans and Wild Rice
Serves 4

This makes rather an elegant version of the old Creole favorite, "hoppin' John."

2 C. red beans, cooked tender
1 C. wild rice, cooked
1 C. chopped wild onions
½ C. wild onion tops (green onion) chopped

1 t. Cajun spice mix (look in your grocer's gourmet section)
Salt and pepper to taste
Tabasco to taste (optional)

Mix cooked beans and rice. Sauté onions and onion tops until just transparent and add to the bean mixture. Stir in Cajun spice mix (I end up using Chef Paul Prudhomme's Poultry Magic mix for almost everything; it has a most pleasing flavor and is not too hot) and salt and pepper.

Bake at 325° for 25 minutes; sprinkle with Tabasco, if desired.

The beans and wild rice together make this a complete protein. (Both the beans and rice swell in cooking; this dish will serve 4 easily.)

Wild Rice and Mushroom Croquettes
Serves 4

Make this for supper, a nice luncheon, or even for breakfast; it's good any time.

2 C. chopped wild mushrooms (morels, puffballs, chanterelles, etc.; remember, it's best not to drink wine or other spirits with wild mushrooms; some will cause a bad reaction when taken with alcohol)
½ C. diced wild onions
2 T. oil to sauté

2 T. flour (or substitute cattail pollen)
½ C. water
1 C. wild rice, cooked
Salt and pepper to taste
1 egg
1 t. diced parsley (or wild mint)
½ C. fine cracker crumbs or bread crumbs
Oil for frying

Sauté mushrooms and onions in 2 T. oil for 10 minutes. Stir in flour or pollen, add water, and stir well; simmer till mixture just begins to thicken, 1–2 minutes, then add rice, parsley, and seasonings. Stir in the egg and cook for perhaps another minute. Make into croquettes when cool and roll in bread or cracker crumbs. Fry in oil until golden brown on both sides.

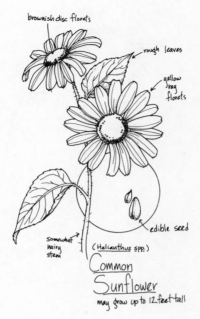

brownish disc florets

rough leaves

yellow ray florets

edible seed

somewhat hairy stem

(Helianthus spp.)

Common Sunflower

may grow up to 12 feet tall

Nut Loaf

Serves 6

This delicious loaf is a good source of vegetable protein and may be made into cakes and fried, on the trail, rather than baked, if you like.

½ C. pecans, shelled
½ C. black walnuts, shelled
½ C. hazelnuts, shelled
⅔ C. sunflower seeds, hulled
2 eggs

1 C. chopped wild onions
½ C. chopped parsley
¼ C. wild mint
½ C. wild rice, cooked
¼ C. grated cheese

Coarsely grind the nuts in your blender (if you're on the trail, chop them as fine as possible; it will be comparable to the blender product). Stir in sunflower seeds.

Beat eggs till lemon colored, stir in chopped onion and nuts. Add parsley and wild mint (choose one of the milder-flavored mints) and the cooked wild rice. Press into a well-greased pan and bake at 325° for 25 minutes; sprinkle with cheese for the last 10 minutes of baking time.

Dock and Onion Soufflé

Serves 4

This makes a lovely side dish, but we use it most often as a meal. With bread and a salad, it's quite filling.

Actually, we use whatever wildings are in season with the basic recipe;

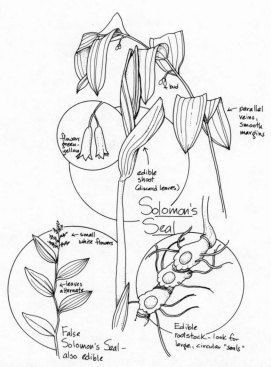

parallel
veins,
smooth
margins

↓ bud

flowers
green-
yellow

edible
shoot
(discard leaves)

Solomon's
Seal

← small
white flowers

←leaves
alternate

False
Solomon's Seal —
also edible

Edible
rootstock — look for
large, circular "seals"

I've made it with asparagus, Jerusalem artichokes, sorrel, lamb's-quarter, chicory—you name it. But I always try to include the onions; it makes the dish.

2 T. melted butter
2 T. flour
1 C. milk
1 C. steamed wild onions
  (steaming makes them
  milder in flavor)
1 C. steamed and drained dock
  (or lamb's-quarter or chicory
  greens, asparagus, Solomon's
  seal, groundnut, salsify, etc.,
  or any combination)

2 t. wild green onion tops,
  chopped
3 eggs, separated
Salt and pepper to taste

Make a roux with the melted butter and flour; stir in milk. Keep stirring until thick and smooth. Add wild onions and other wildings; separate eggs and beat in the yolks. Add seasonings. Whip egg whites until just stiff and fold lightly into the onion mixture. Bake in a well-greased soufflé pan at 325° until just firm, about 40 minutes.

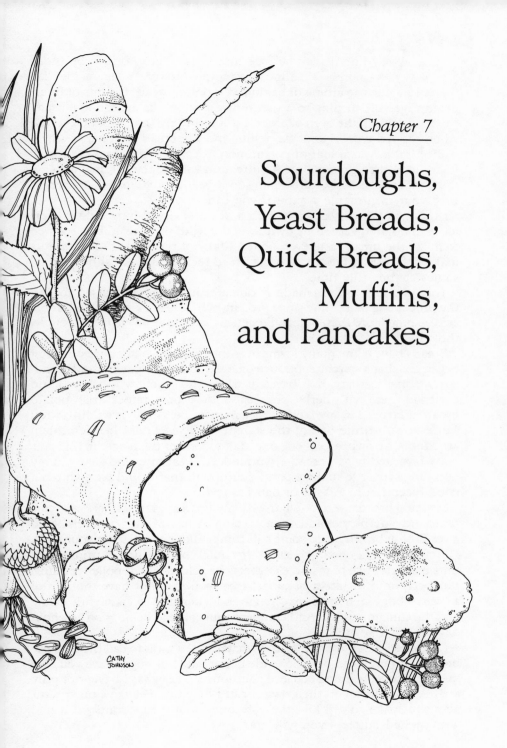

Chapter 7

Sourdoughs, Yeast Breads, Quick Breads, Muffins, and Pancakes

W hile it may be true that "man does not live by bread alone," I'd almost be tempted to try—given recipes like these. Imagine the aroma of baking wild onion bread, the bits of finely diced vegetable turning to a rich brown on top like an edible mosaic. I've made this in the oven of a wood stove; the crisp crust sounds hollow when rapped with a knuckle, telling me the bread is done.

Slice into a warm loaf of persimmon nut bread and enjoy that rich fragrance—then drench it with butter and wild honey. Or imagine anything more deliciously edible than sunny yellow cattail pancakes, served with your own maple syrup—if you can.

I used sunflower seeds in a rich and nutty bread long before I was lucky enough to gather my own from the wild; the free edibles seemed to make the bread taste even better. Many of the wild seeds and nuts make delicious additions to basic bread recipes and boost nutritional values at the same time.

The American Indians made a flour substitute from processed acorns; the processing takes time since protein-rich nuts are also high in tannic acid—some more than others. Processing can be well worth the trouble, though.

Breads have taken many forms over the years since our ancestors first began cooking a starchy substance on a flat rock. Our parents and grandparents made crusty, hot loaves of white and whole wheat bread and enriched them with herbs, cheeses, onions, or potatoes. Irish potato bread, a favorite in my family, is easy to embellish with wildings. You can even substitute one of the starchy wild vegetables like Jerusalem artichokes, arrowhead tubers, or cattail tubers for the potato in this one.

My favorite "wild" bread is wild indeed; I capture wild yeasts in my bubbling starter to make a tangy sourdough that would have gotten a good reception in Alaska or San Francisco.

Steamed breads were popular with my English grandfather; wild currants and elderberries add a special tang. A steamed black acorn bread gives Boston brown bread some stiff competition for a place at your table.

Not all breads need be yeasty; try quick breads and muffins when time is short. I like bran and elderberry or golden cattail-pollen muffins. Blueberry muffins are a breakfast treat you may not have thought of as wild—but blueberries are often found where the soil is slightly acidic and the climate is right. And cranberry quick bread belongs on any holiday table.

Pancakes, hoecakes, flapjacks—whatever you want to call them, these breakfast staples can only be made better with wildings. Have you ever sat down to a steaming stack of sourdough flapjacks? I have; not only are they wonderful on their own, I can't help but feel like a prospector about to strike gold. I love them even without syrup, simply drizzled with melted butter— you will, too.

A more elegant "pancake" is the French crêpe; I make this when I want to demonstrate that gathering wildings is not just the province of hikers, hillbillies, and hippies!

Suggested Wild Ingredients

Wild breads offer a special opportunity to make use of wildings at all seasons of the year. Jerusalem artichokes add a nice nutty flavor to breads any time after a good frost and until the tubers sprout in the spring. Persimmons, also, are just coming into their own after a hard freeze turns them tender and sweet—taste them before that time and you'll feel as if you tasted straight alum!

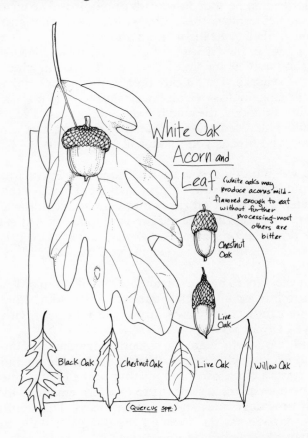

White Oak Acorn and Leaf (white oaks may produce acorns mild-flavored enough to eat without further processing—most others are bitter

Chestnut Oak

Live Oak

Black Oak   Chestnut Oak   Live Oak   Willow Oak

(Quercus spp.)

Acorn breads may be made from midsummer, as the earlier varieties ripen, through late fall—longer, if you've processed and stored the acorn meal.

In the spring, try fresh onion or herb bread. You can add chopped aromatic greens to your recipe for a fine herbed flavor.

Later in the summer, from June through early fall, many of the wild fruits are available for tasty quick breads or muffins. Imagine the subtle, sweet aroma of *Wild Strawberry-Nut Bread* still warm from the oven, with tart cream cheese melting slowly into its sweet crumbs. Elderberries, blueberries, and even cranberries add a special flavor as they come into season—usually midsummer.

Try wild seeds as they ripen late in the summer—amaranth, pepper-grass, lamb's-quarter, sunflower—all of these add an unusual flavor and crunchiness. And cattail pollen, so easy to gather in June and July, makes a delicious addition to almost any recipe—simply replace up to a third of the flour called for with this golden substance.

Even flowers can be added to breads or muffins—I've included a recipe or two using elderblow, the frothy white flowers that strip in seconds from their umbelled heads in June and July.

And, of course, my favorite—the wild yeasts of sourdough—can be captured and used at any time of the year. Be careful when it is hot and humid; the yeasts arrive quickly then and can pack quite a wallop in their robust tang. In deep winter it will take longer to make a starter—like most other wild foods, the cold has slowed the yeast's activity. You may have a milder-flavored winter starter and a strong, tart summer strain. Either way, the breads you make will be delicious.

The history of sourdough goes back to the ancient Egyptians, from whom we have our earliest records of bread making. Russian explorers carried their starter with them on expeditions. In some cultures, sourdough starter was once considered a required gift for a bride; it may have been part of a dowry at one time. Sourdough is tradition, it is continuity, it is romance, it is history—and its magic is available today, in our own kitchens.

It isn't necessary to have a starter given to us by an old Alaskan prospector or to buy a commercial starter or to get some from a friend or relative; we can make our own, from wild yeasts (or with the help of baker's yeast from your grocer).

The wild yeasts, which are the essential ingredients of any starter, are all around us, and when they fall upon a favorable medium they start to work. Yeasts are microscopic fungi that, at the right temperature, react with the carbohydrates in flour to produce fermentation; adding baker's yeast just provides a kick-start to the process. The resulting bubbles of carbon dioxide gas rise through the dough, making the bread (or rolls or pancakes) light and porous.

For the really adventuresome, it's even possible to rely *entirely* on "wild" yeasts. In a kitchen where bread is baked often, this may be

quite satisfactory because "good" yeasts are already abundant in the air. But in most cases it is better to begin with commercial dry yeast; some wild yeasts are gamey in flavor and bitter rather than sour. You will still encourage the growth of wild yeasts if you use dry yeast—they'll just have a better class of forebears.

Making a starter is quite simple and although there are numerous recipes, the basic procedure is the same. The only necessities are yeast, flour, water, salt, and sugar. Here is the recipe I use most often when beginning a new batch of sourdough (which, incidentally, would not be necessary if I didn't forget to "feed" my pot of starter once a week to keep it from dying or to reserve a cup of starter before mixing the bread dough).

Sourdough Starter
Yields 2 C.

1 pkg. active dry yeast (¼ oz.)
½ C. warm water (110°)
2 C. lukewarm water

2 C. sifted all-purpose flour
1 t. salt
1 T. sugar

Dissolve yeast in the warm water in a large bowl. Stir in the lukewarm water, flour, salt, and sugar. Beat until smooth. Cover with cheesecloth held in place with a rubber band. Let stand at room temperature 3–4 days. Stir 3 times daily. Cover at night with a lid.

Using your starter is equally simple, but always remember to keep back at least 1 C. of starter for the pot. This you feed each time with ½ C. of water, ½ C. of flour, and 1 t. sugar. Let stand until bubbly and well fermented for at least 1 day before using again; then store in the refrigerator. If the starter is not used within 10 days, add another teaspoon of sugar.

Sourdough Bread

Makes 2 loaves

This recipe combines dry yeast and sourdough starter for a light and crusty bread, redolent with aromatic, tangy flavor.

1 pkg. active dry yeast (¼ oz.)	2 t. sugar
1½ C. warm water	5–6 C. sifted all-purpose or
1 C. sourdough starter	whole wheat flour
2 t. salt	½ t. soda

In a large bowl, dissolve yeast in warm water. Blend in starter, salt, and sugar. Add 4 C. of flour and beat 3–4 minutes, or until smooth. Cover, let rise in a warm place free of drafts until double in size (about 1½ hours). A good way to do this in winter is to heat the oven for 1 minute, then turn off the heat and put in the bread, leaving it undisturbed until it has risen. Mix soda with 1½ C. flour and stir into dough. Add enough additional flour to make a stiff dough.

Turn out on a floured board and knead for 10 minutes. Divide dough in half. Cover and let stand for 10 minutes. Shape into 2 round or oval loaves. Place on lightly greased baking sheet.

With a sharp knife, make diagonal gashes across the top, then let rise until approximately double (about 1½ hours). Bake in a preheated 400° oven for 40 minutes; brush with butter when done.

You won't believe the taste of this with fresh creamery butter.

Karen's Sourdough Rolls

Makes 1 dozen small rolls

These are really more like muffins; light and fluffy with just a hint of sourdough tang.

1 C. sourdough starter	¼ t. baking powder
¼ C. flour	¼ C. oil
½ t. salt	

Mix all ingredients together and place in a greased muffin tin. Bake 25 minutes at 375°.

Whole Wheat Sourdough French Bread

Makes 2 loaves

This is a richly flavored bread that seems almost a complete meal in itself.

1½ C. warm water	2 t. salt
1 pkg. dry yeast	6 C. whole wheat flour (use
1 C. sourdough starter	white if you prefer)
2 t. sugar or honey	½ t. baking soda

Stir together the warm water, yeast, sourdough starter, sugar or honey, salt, and 4 C. of the flour. Stir until dough feels smooth and elastic,

about 5 minutes. Cover and let rise until double.

Mix baking soda and the remaining flour and add to the dough. Knead for 10 minutes until satiny.

Let rise again until double in size, then punch down and knead again.

Shape into 2 long loaves and place on a lightly oiled baking sheet, slash top with a sharp knife, and let rise again until doubled—about an hour.

Bake at 400° for about 45 minutes, placing a pan of hot water on the lower shelf of the oven (this will help form a crispy, thick crust).

Sourdough Sunflower-Nut Bread

Makes 3 loaves

This loaf is very hearty and full of protein; with a salad and a glass of milk it could be a meal in itself.

1 T. baking yeast	3 T. honey or sugar
2½ C. stock or warm water	2 t. salt
1 C. sourdough starter	6 C. flour (white and whole
1 C. chopped sunflower seeds	wheat mixed in any
2 T. peppergrass seed (optional)	proportions)
1 C. chopped nuts (pecans, walnuts, hickory nuts— whatever you can find)	

Dissolve yeast in the warm stock or water. Add sourdough starter, seeds and nuts, honey, salt, and 3 C. of flour.

Beat until smooth and elastic and allow this traditional ''sponge'' to rise until double.

Add the rest of the flour, kneading until smooth. Let rise in a covered bowl until doubled again.

Shape into 3 loaves, place in well-oiled bread pans, and allow to rise again. Bake at 350° for 45 minutes to an hour; bread is done when it sounds hollow when you knock it with your knuckle.

Sourdough Flapjacks

Serves 4

This batter is very similar to the sourdough rolls, page 118, but, of course, thinner. For a more tart finished product, make the night before and allow it to ''work.''

¾ C. sourdough starter
½ C. flour
¼ C. milk or buttermilk, more
    or less
Dash of salt

¼ C. oil or melted butter or
    margarine
2 t. sugar
¼ t. baking soda

Mix ingredients in a medium bowl. Adjust amount of milk or buttermilk according to how you like your pancakes—I like mine thin and moist rather than fluffy and dry. Use immediately or let it sit overnight in the refrigerator to develop a stronger sourdough flavor and yeast action.

If you have any batter left from breakfast, you may wish to thin it further and use it for crêpes; this batter needs to be about the thickness of heavy cream.

Sourdough Coffee Cake

Serves 12

This recipe used to get raves at church dinners; it gives coffee cake a delightfully different flavor.

1 C. sourdough starter
¼ C. flour
½ t. salt

¼ t. baking powder
¼ C. oil
2 T. sugar

WILD FRUIT TOPPING

Use 2 C. of whatever wild fruits are plentiful or mix and match; try a variety of wild berries together. Later in the year, use chopped crab apples or persimmons. Toss with 2 t. sugar and 2 T. flour.

Mix cake ingredients. Spread dough in a well-greased 9″ square pan and top with fruit. Add topping:

TOPPING

¼ C. butter or margarine
¼ C. sugar or brown sugar

½ C. flour

Mix these ingredients with a fork until crumbly, sprinkle on top of coffee cake, and bake at 375° for 30 minutes.

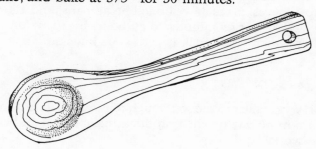

Sourdough Corn Bread

If you have a particularly hearty pot of beans and ham or a nice ''mess'' of mixed greens, you may want to try this somewhat heavy, tasty corn bread. It's best served hot from the oven rather than the next day.

1	C. sourdough starter	2	T. sugar or honey
1	C. yellow cornmeal	¾	C. baking soda
½	C. unbleached white or whole-grain flour	1½	C. evaporated milk or half-and-half
½	t. salt	2	eggs, beaten

Mix everything together in a large bowl and pour into a 9'' x 13'' pan, well greased. Bake at 400° for 30 minutes or until top is golden brown. (If you prefer, use ''corn dodger'' pans, also well greased. Adjust the cooking time downward to 15–20 minutes for the smaller corn dodgers.)

Cheese and Herb Bread

If you like cheese—and lots of flavor—this bread will be a real treat. It needs almost nothing else—even butter—to make it special.

1 pkg. dry yeast	1 t. dried wild pitcher sage
1 C. lukewarm water or stock	1 C. finely shredded sharp cheddar cheese
1 T. sugar	
½ C. wild onions, very finely chopped	½ t. salt
¼ C. wild chives, minced	3 C. unbleached white flour
1 t. dried wild thyme	¼ C. melted butter or margarine

Dissolve the yeast in the lukewarm water or stock; add sugar and allow to sit for 5 minutes. Stir in the rest of the ingredients and knead until silky.

Allow to rise in a warm place until double in bulk. Then punch down, make into a loaf, and put in a well-greased pan. Allow the dough to rise again until almost double. Bake at 375° for 30 minutes or until the loaf sounds hollow when rapped with your knuckle.

This is a fine recipe for using cattail pollen if you have collected it during the summer; simply replace up to a cup of the flour with cattail pollen for a rich, golden flavor.

Whole-Grain Wild Onion Bread (or Buns)

If you choose to make buns instead, bake for a shorter period—these make wonderful Philly beef sandwiches.

2 pkgs. dry yeast
1 C. lukewarm water or stock
¼ C. oil
3 C. whole wheat flour (for a lighter-textured bread, substitute up to half this amount with unbleached white flour)

1 t. sugar
1 t. salt
1 C. chopped wild onions

Dissolve the yeast in the water or stock; add oil, half of the flour, the sugar, and salt and stir until smooth and elastic. Stir in half the chopped onion and the remaining flour.

Let rise until double in bulk; punch down and place in a greased 9'' x 13'' pan or form into rolls and put in a Teflon-lined muffin tin. Let rise again, and top with the rest of the finely chopped onions. Bake at 375° for 25 minutes or until golden brown.

Jerusalem Artichoke Casserole Bread

Serves 8

These earthy-flavored little tubers add a lot of flavor to a dill casserole bread.

1	pkg. dry yeast	1	T. butter
¼	C. warm water	2	t. dill seed
1	C. Jerusalem artichokes, boiled and strained or blended	1	t. salt
		¼	t. soda
		1	unbeaten egg
2	T. sugar	2¼–2½	C. flour
1	T. finely chopped onion		

Dissolve yeast in water and combine remaining ingredients in a mixing bowl. Add flour to form a stiff dough, cover, and let rise until light and double in size. Stir dough down and turn into a greased 1½–2-qt. casserole. Let rise again and bake at 350° for 40–50 minutes.

Not all breads need be yeast or sourdough breads, of course. Quick breads are convenient and fit right in with our hurry-up lifestyles.

Hickory-Nut Bread (Quick)

Makes 2 loaves

Some years the hickory nuts put on a bumper crop and invite us to make this special bread. If you find hazelnuts, black walnuts, or pecans, these may of course be substituted—it will still be a wonderfully aromatic bread, full of nutty flavor.

3 C. whole wheat flour or 2 C.
    whole wheat and 1 C.
    unbleached white flour
¾ C. brown sugar
½ t. salt

4 t. baking powder
2 C. milk
4 T. melted butter or margarine
½ t. almond or other nut flavoring
1 C. nut meats, coarsely chopped

Mix dry ingredients, then add remaining ingredients. Put in 2 well-greased loaf pans and allow to sit for 10 minutes to develop flavor, then bake at 350° for 45–50 minutes.

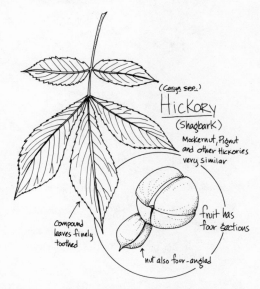

(Carya spp.)
Hickory
(Shagbark)
Mockernut, Pignut and other Hickories very similar

Compound leaves finely toothed

fruit has four sections

nut also four-angled

Persimmon-Hickory Nut Bread

Makes 2 loaves

This recipe is an "antique" from an old cookbook; I've only improved on it by retyping it in modern form.

¾ C. butter or margarine
1 C. sugar
2 eggs, beaten
2 C. flour
1 t. baking soda
1 C. persimmon pulp (force
    fully ripe persimmons
    through a colander to
    remove seeds)

½ C. chopped hickory nuts
½ t. cinnamon
½ t. ginger
½ t. ground cloves

Cream the butter and sugar together, add the eggs. Sift the flour and baking soda together and dump into the first mixture, stirring to form a thick dough. Add remaining ingredients. Spices are optional—the bread is fine without them, if you prefer.

Line 2 loaf pans with waxed paper, and divide the batter between them. Bake at 325° for an hour; bread will be moist and dark like gingerbread, with a flavor all its own.

This, too, is good with a sugar-and-cream-cheese spread with just a touch of lemon juice.

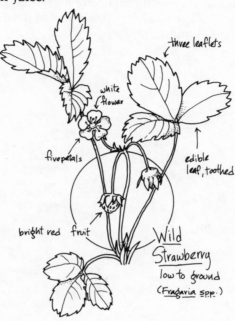

Wild Strawberry-Nut Bread

Makes 8 loaves in pint jars

Serve this pale pink bread for an elegant tea; spread with a bit of cream cheese, it is delicate and piquant.

⅔ C. shortening
2⅔ C. sugar
2 C. wild strawberries, washed and drained
½ C. coarsely chopped nuts (hickory, walnut, pecans, etc.)

⅔ C. water
3⅓ C. flour
½ t. baking soda
1½ t. salt

Cream shortening and sugar; mix in the rest of the ingredients, gently stirring in strawberries last to keep as many whole as possible. Pour into greased widemouthed pint jars, filling them half full of batter. Bake at 325° about 45 minutes. When done, remove from oven one jar at a time, clean the sealing edge, and screw on widemouthed canning jar lids firmly.

These make perfect gifts, with a bow or counted-cross-stitch tops on the jar lids; otherwise, they simply keep well for when you need a special treat. Properly sealed, they will keep for a year.

Apricot-Nut Bread

Makes 1 loaf

This bread is a bit expensive to make; apricots are never cheap, but if you've foraged the nut meats it will help to keep costs down. Believe me, whatever it costs, this bread is worth it!

1 C. dried apricots, soaked in warm water to cover
¼ C. water
2 T. butter or margarine
1 C. sugar
1 egg
2 C. sifted flour

2 t. baking powder
¼ t. baking soda
1 t. salt
½ C. orange juice
⅔ C. coarsely chopped nut meats (pecan, black walnut, hickory, etc.)

Soak the apricots in water until they are soft; cut in ¼'' pieces.
Cream the butter and sugar together and mix in an egg. Add orange juice and stir well.
Sift the flour, baking powder, baking soda, and salt. Add to the previous mixture and stir in apricots and nuts. Bake at 350° for 55–65 minutes in a well-greased loaf pan.

Cranberry Bread

Makes 1 loaf

If you are lucky enough to live in an area of the country where cranberries grow wild, forage your own for this tart and tasty loaf—if not, fresh ones from your grocer will do just fine.

¼ C. butter or margarine
½ C. sugar
1 egg
1½ C. unbleached flour
½ t. salt
1 t. baking soda
¾ C. unsweetened, finely chopped cranberries

¼ C. cranberry juice or the juice that drains from your cranberry pulp
1 C. nut meats (black walnuts, pecans, hickory nuts, etc.)
¾ C. buttermilk, more or less

Cream butter and sugar together and add egg.
Sift flour, salt, and baking soda together and mix with previous mixture. Add cranberries, cranberry juice, and nuts, then stir in buttermilk rapidly until you have a semistiff batter. Place in a greased loaf pan and bake at 350° for 1–1¼ hours.

Bran-Elderberry Muffins

Makes 1½ dozen muffins

The bran muffins I grew up with take on a whole new flavor in elderberry season; we love the wild tang the dark berries give this breakfast treat.

2 T. molasses or sorghum
2 T. shortening
2 T. brown sugar
2 eggs, separated
½ t. baking soda
1 C. flour, whole wheat or
   unbleached white
1 C. bran or bran cereal

2 T. baking powder
½ t. salt
1 C. milk or buttermilk (if you
   use milk, sour it with a
   squeeze of fresh lemon
   juice and let sit 10 minutes)
1 C. washed and drained
   elderberries

Mix molasses or sorghum, shortening, sugar, and egg yolks. Mix baking soda in a bit of warm water. Add the dry ingredients and milk alternately, then fold in well-beaten egg whites—these last should peak but not become dry. Fold in elderberries; bake in greased muffin tins for 15 minutes at 425°—you'll be amazed at how moist and tender they are.

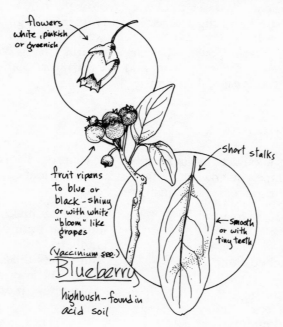

flowers
white, pinkish
or greenish

short stalks

fruit ripens
to blue or
black-shiny
or with white
"bloom" like
grapes

smooth
or with
tiny teeth

(Vaccinium spp.)
Blueberry

highbush—found in
acid soil

Blueberry Muffins

Makes 2 dozen muffins

Depending on where you live—and with whom you're speaking—blueberries may be known locally by a number of names. Some of the most common are whortleberry, huckleberry, or bilberries—they are all very closely related, and you might need to examine the seeds to be able to tell them apart. For the most part, true blueberries have soft seeds while huckleberries have tiny hard seeds. In our recipe, they are virtually interchangeable.

Blueberry muffins are so popular that we no longer think of them as wild foods at all; several of the large companies have put out mixes or frozen versions of this delightful product. Of course, blueberries are now widely cultivated, and you can grow your own or buy them if you can't find the wild variety, but the harder, drier nature of the wildings works well in baking, where the softer domestics tend to fall apart.

1 C. blueberries, washed and drained	1 t. baking powder
	1 egg, slightly beaten
2 C. flour	2 T. oil (or melted butter or
3 T. sugar	margarine)
½ t. salt	¾ C. buttermilk

Flour the berries and toss lightly to keep them from clumping together in your batter.

Sift flour, sugar, salt, and baking powder together in a large bowl. Then add egg, oil, and buttermilk and mix quickly—the secret of successful muffins is not to bruise your batter—it'll be tough if it is overworked.

Gently fold in floured berries and spoon batter into well-greased muffin tins—fill cups half full. Bake at 400° for 15–20 minutes or until set.

Elderberry Muffins

Makes 2 dozen muffins

You can use your dried elderberries to make a delicious alternative to blueberry muffins; in my part of the country, elderberries are much more common than any of the varieties of blueberry.

1 C. dried elderberries	1½ C. water
½ C. sugar	

Prepare your elderberries for muffins by simmering in sweetened water until tender; they are much more flavorful than the fresh berries, oddly enough. They seem to develop flavor and sweetness in the drying process for some reason.

Then, follow the preceding recipe for blueberry muffins, substituting the drained and floured elderberries for fresh blueberries.

Elderblow Muffins

Makes 2 dozen muffins

If you are out and foraging earlier in the season—or if you've a cache of dried elder flowers on hand, try them in your muffins. It's a delicate taste that is hard to identify; your guests will be delighted if your table

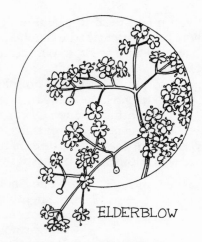

ELDERBLOW

centerpiece is of the same frothy white flowers.

I use a mild muffin batter for these to showcase the elderblow flavor.

1¾ C. unbleached white flour	4 T. melted butter or margarine
½ t. salt	¾ C. milk
3 T. sugar	1 C. elder flowers, stripped
2 t. baking powder	from their umbels
2 eggs	

Sift dry ingredients together. In a separate bowl, beat the eggs and add melted butter and the milk. Quickly mix the liquid and dry ingredients together and fold in elder flowers. Fill well-greased muffin tins half full and bake at 400° about 20 minutes.

Cranberry Muffins

Makes 2 dozen muffins

If you like the tart-sweet taste of cranberries, you'll love these muffins. Try them for a light Thanksgiving-day breakfast.

1¾ C. unbleached white flour	2 eggs
¾ t. salt	¼ C. melted butter or margarine
⅓ C. sugar (if your berries are	¾ C. milk or buttermilk
especially tart, increase	1 C. chopped cranberries
sugar to ½ C.)	Grating of fresh orange rind
2 t. baking powder	

Sift dry ingredients together. Mix eggs and melted butter, then add alternately with milk to the dry ingredients, stirring rapidly. Add cranberries and a grating of orange rind. Fill muffin cups half full. Bake at 400° for 20 minutes.

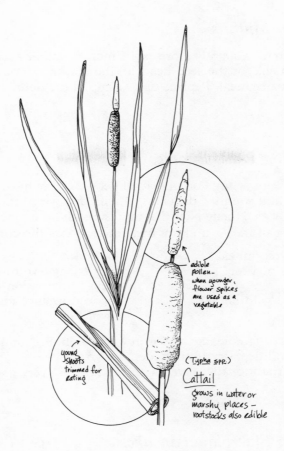

edible
pollen-
when younger,
flower spikes
are used as a
vegetable

young
shoots
trimmed for
eating

(Typha spp.)

Cattail

grows in water or
marshy places –
rootstocks also edible

Corn and Cattail-Pollen Muffins

Makes 1½ dozen muffins

In my family, we often began the day with quick corn muffins; my
mother's recipe only benefits from the addition of buttery colored pollen.

1 C. all-purpose flour (unsifted)
⅓ C. cattail pollen
1 t. salt
2 T. sugar
3 t. baking powder
¾ C. yellow cornmeal

2 beaten eggs
1 C. milk
¼ C. melted butter or margarine
1 C. corn (fresh, cut from the
    cob, or canned)

Sift dry ingredients together (excluding the cornmeal) and mix remaining ingredients only to dampen. Fill muffin cups half full of batter (use
paper muffin cups or grease your muffin pan to prevent sticking). Bake
in a hot oven (400°) for 25 minutes; makes 12 to 18 muffins.

Amaranth Muffins

If you care to try a slightly more exotic muffin, gather amaranth seeds when ripe. Look for the seed heads in the fall, thresh out, and grind to a dark, coarse meal. Replace up to a cup of the flour in any muffin recipe.

Wild Onion Hush Puppies

Makes 1 dozen

When I was very young I often read of people eating hush puppies. At first I thought it sounded delicious—then I discovered they contained onions, and I hated them. Now that my taste buds have grown up—along with the rest of me—I find my first reaction was the correct one!

1 C. yellow cornmeal
1 T. baking powder
½ t. salt
3 T. minced wild onions
1 egg

½ C. milk
Oil for frying—you may wish to use a combination of oil and bacon drippings for extra flavor

Mix the dry ingredients and stir in wild onion, egg, and milk. Form into ovals and deep-fry until golden brown.

These are traditionally served with fried fish—a very good tradition to uphold.

Sour Milk Elderblow Pancakes

Makes 1 dozen 4" cakes

I've combined my brother-in-law's favorite pancakes with elder flowers to make a special breakfast indeed.

1 C. flour
1 t. salt
1 T. sugar
1 t. baking soda
1 C. milk or buttermilk (if you use sweet milk, sour it with a squeeze of lemon or ½ T. mild vinegar—allow to sit 10 minutes or until milk curdles)

1 egg
More milk, if necessary
1 handful of fresh elder blossoms

Mix the dry ingredients together and stir in the buttermilk and egg. To make a rather thin batter, I often add a bit more milk—then stir in elder flowers. Cook as usual on a hot griddle.

NOTE: This same recipe can be used with dried and reconstituted elderberries, blueberries, linden flowers, etc. — or substitute up to ½ C. of the flour with cattail pollen.

Cattail-Pollen Buttermilk Pancakes   *Makes 1 dozen 4'' cakes*

These breakfast griddle cakes are a sunny start for any morning; pollen substitutes for up to half of the flour in almost any recipe. It's similar to the previous recipe with the addition of pollen to turn it golden.

½ C. flour	1 C. buttermilk
½ C. cattail pollen	1 egg
1 t. salt	Milk to make a thin batter
1 T. sugar	consistency
1 t. baking soda	

Mix together flour, cattail pollen, salt, sugar, and baking soda. Stir in buttermilk and an egg; add a bit more buttermilk to make a thin batter. Drop by large spoonfuls on a hot, oiled griddle. Turn when bubbles are visible on the upper surface, and cook until golden brown.

Steamed Acorn Bread   *Makes 3 loaves*

Acorns are a bit time consuming to process; you must remove all the tannic acid or they will be astringent.

BASIC ACORN PREPARATION

Shell out the nut meats and boil for 2 hours to leach excess acids; change the water each time it becomes discolored. Dry to kernels in a slow oven; they will become a rich brown and smell wonderful — and at this point, they are. You may enjoy them just as they are or grind them into a meal to use in muffins, pancakes, or this spicy steamed bread.

1 C. acorn meal	¾ C. dark molasses or sorghum
1 C. yellow cornmeal	1 C. chopped raisins or wild
1 C. unbleached white flour	currants
2 t. baking soda	½ C. sugar-stewed, dried
1 t. salt	elderberries, well drained
2 C. buttermilk or milk soured	
as above (*Sour Milk Elderblow*	
Pancakes recipe, page 130)	

Mix dry ingredients. In a separate bowl, combine the buttermilk, molasses or sorghum, raisins or currants, and elderberries; if you wish, soak the fruits overnight in bourbon or rum.

Mix the liquid and dry ingredients and pour into buttered pudding molds or 1-lb. coffee cans, well greased and lined with greased waxed paper.

Seal tightly with aluminum foil and steam for 3 hours in 1'' of water in a large, covered pot (check occasionally to make sure water level is constant).

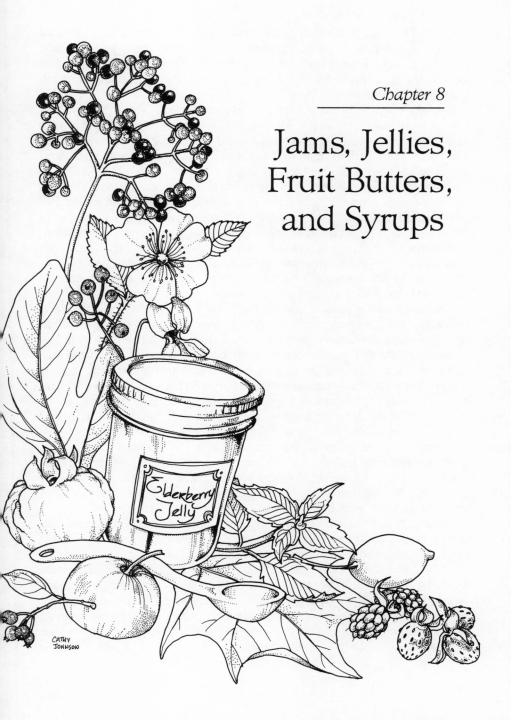

Chapter 8

Jams, Jellies, Fruit Butters, and Syrups

CATHY
JOHNSON

If bread is the staff of life, then surely our jams and jellies and other sweet serendipities are the icing on the cake. They add a festive touch to mealtimes; melting, jewellike colors mixing with the hot butter on a blueberry muffin or giving just the right piquant touch to a roast of venison or pork.

The harvest of wild fruits captured in glowing jars on the pantry shelf tells of the good things in life—it's more than simple survival, it is beauty and sweetness as well. What makes a more welcome gift than homemade elderberry jelly, dark as night and sweet as love? Or perhaps a fire-colored jar of spicy sassafras preserves?

When I was born, World War II was in full swing, and our small town didn't recover economically for a long time after that. I still remember homemade jams and jellies, syrups and preserves—when sugar could be had—that were often what made each meal into a minor celebration. My mother and grandmother collected the wherewithal—the wild fruits and flowers—to flavor our preserves; family and friends often pooled resources of precious sugar to have enough for a "preserving party," and everyone had a share of the bounty.

The flavors were unique and exciting. We had the "normal" flavors, of course, wild grape, elderberry, gooseberry, and wild strawberry, but also the more exotic fare. Sassafras jelly, made from the bark, was my special favorite. My grandmother on my father's side was from England; from her we got recipes for elegant flower jams and jellies that Mother adapted to wildings. I remember the flavors of violet and rose-petal jam, and one year, a finely colored wild-apple-blossom jelly. Wildings made our efforts special; today's ubiquitous grape jelly is lovely, but a wild flavor makes lasting memories.

Today, these things are widely available in any supermarket; ours even carries elderberry jam from the Missouri Ozarks. Every shopping mall boasts a gourmet food store where you can pick up a jar of gooseberry preserves or sassafras jelly; a trip through the Missouri Ozarks is an odyssey of wild-fruit flavors done up in rainbow jars.

Making your own wild fruit preserves—jams, jellies, and syrups—allows you to experiment, mix and match, achieve flavors never available on a grocer's shelf. Elderberries sometimes lack flavor—they can be a bit flat, and many recipes suggest adding lemon juice to punch them up. Why not use another wild fruit, the tart and tasty sumac instead? It accomplishes the same thing but with a special flavor all its own. Mix crab apples and wild mint for another unusual, but delicious, flavor, or try a mixed-berry jam if you don't find enough of one kind—you may come up with your own trademark jelly.

Suggested Wild Ingredients

Unless you begin with the early wildflowers, your jam and jelly making will usually be confined to midsummer through fall; even the tiny wild strawberries with their piquant flavor don't fully ripen—at least around here—until the middle to the end of June. Mayapples make a wonderful marmalade in late July or August.

Look for inky black elderberry umbels in July; there may still be berries as late as September or October, though, so keep looking for them. Sumac is available at roughly the same time and usually nearby, if you plan to make *Elderberry-Sumac Jelly*, page 148.

The young, first-year pads of prickly pear cactus are best for *Prickly Pear Preserves*, page 143—pick them when quite small, 2'' and under, and roast to split the well-needled skin. Be sure to rinse and dry them and check several times for errant needles (see basic preparation information for *nopales* in Chapter 4)—but don't let a bit of a challenge keep you from trying this one. It's good.

Sassafras is available in one form or another through most of the year. The spicy bark of the roots is traditionally used to make the strong tea that acts as a base for this treat, but the twigs and leaves have the same delightful aroma. (Because of the safrole content, a possible carcinogen, sassafras is no longer shipped across state lines.)

Mulberries have an undeserved reputation for being bland and tasteless, as well as a bane on shiny car finishes and a purple nuisance on our sidewalks. And it's true that in a good year a full-grown mulberry tree can produce prodigious amounts of fruit, as popular with the squirrels and birds as they are with me. If you are bothered by an embarrassment of riches in the form of too darned many mulberries, don't curse them—*eat* them. If you pick a few unripe red berries along with the rich black ones, you'll find your preserves plenty tasty enough. Of course, if you have a white mulberry tree nearby, simply include a few green ones for tartness. Use sparingly, as unripe berries, shoots, and leaves may be toxic.

Don't forget the brambles when looking for candidates for the jam jar. Around here, blackberries and raspberries are most common and well worth the scratches and insect bites it takes to harvest them. Even botanists may have trouble distinguishing between the bramble family members, and the plethora of common names does nothing to help those of us without the benefit of a degree in biology. If you have access to a good bramble patch, whether they are locally known as dewberries, salmonberries, buffalo berries, cloudberries, thimbleberries, blackberries, or raspberries, don't worry about a formal introduction—just enjoy them.

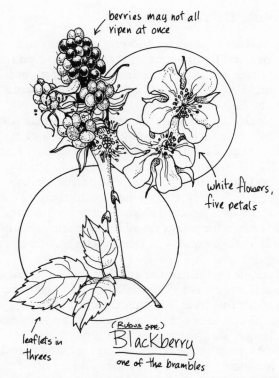

berries may not all ripen at once

white flowers, five petals

leaflets in threes

(Rubus spp.)
Blackberry
one of the brambles

Crab apples are small, compared to our modern, cultivated supermarket giants—but they have a wonderful flavor. Properly prepared, they are no more tedious to deal with than the larger apples, and perhaps less so, since you'd never bother to peel such small fruits. It is easier just to force them through a sieve or to use a jelly bag to collect their pectin-rich juices after cooking them to a mush. They are delicious simmered into a spicy apple butter or mixed with one of the mints for a jelly often served with meats. Their abundant pectin made them useful to our self-sufficient forebears in the days when store-bought pectin was unheard of; jellies made from fruits without sufficient pectin to "set up" were mixed with green crab apples.

Try one of the mints by itself for a delightfully fresh flavor. One of my favorite treats is really quite simple: club crackers buttered with cream cheese and topped with a dollop of wild mint jelly. I like its color just as it is, but if you prefer you can add a bit of green food coloring for the traditional neon green hue.

Why stop with only the abundant wild fruits? Try *Wild Rose Jelly*, page 147, or *Violet Jam*, page 141, for a delicate flavor that will make you think of merry olde England—even if you've never been there! These flower-flavored treats were popular with our Victorian ancestors (and with my

English grandmother). If you have an abundance of multiflora roses or a burgeoning violet bed, try these two flavors. Or experiment with other flowers using our basic recipes (just be sure they are far enough from the pollution of heavy metals from passing cars or herbicide/pesticide sprayings). Linden flowers might be worth a try since they make a pleasant nibble on their own; or those ubiquitous elder flowers, though their mild flavor needs something added for piquancy. And use those rose hips later in the season for jam that's tart-sweet and intriguing.

If you live where blueberries grow wild, you're in luck. Blueberry jam is one of our all-time favorites and unusually easy to prepare; true blueberries have soft seeds that needn't be strained out.

Who could forget the flavor and rich color of fox grape jelly—especially since one's fingers often itch for a time after harvesting these tiny grapes? It's well worth the bother; they are delicious.

Look for chokecherries, ground-cherries, persimmons, and other wild fruits that may grow in your area; it is often an easy matter to substitute one fruit pulp for another called for in a recipe. If you live in Hawaii or Canada or even the midst of the arid regions in our desert Southwest, you may have fruits available that I've never even heard of—don't let that stop you from trying them out. Make sure only that you've confirmed the identity and edibility of your chosen fruit and that it is fully ripe (well, except for an occasional underripe mulberry for tartness) and give it a try.

Making your own preserves—jams, jellies, and the like—is subject to the laws of common sense and safety. Invest in a good book on food preservation, such as *Putting Food By* by Ruth Hertzberg, Beatrice Vaughn, and Janet Greene (also from Stephen Greene Press), and follow directions explicitly.

Always use good quality, sterile canning jars, not used peanut butter jars; you need the strength built into the glass intended for canning purposes to prevent cracking in the processing. Check the rim of each jar for chips and other imperfections that might prevent a good seal between glass and the rubber of the jar lid.

Putting Food By suggests filling jars with boiling hot fruit mixture, allowing ⅛'' headroom in each jar. Then, put on sterilized tops and caps and screw tight; invert each jar for a moment and turn upright immediately. As your jam or jelly cools, a vacuum will be formed to seal the lid tightly in place.

If you are making freezer jellies—that is, the delicate-flavored preserves you never bring to a boil but add prepared pectin to fruit pulp or juice according to package directions—you will need to refrigerate or freeze the jars to assure safety and good keeping qualities. Again, it's important to use good quality canning jars to withstand the rigors of frigid air.

And last, don't forget the sweet syrups given up by the trees. Maple is best known, of course, but did you know that you can make a quite satisfying syrup with the sap from the birch or the sycamore as well? Tapping and boiling off are the same, no matter which sap you've collected—warm days and cold nights make the sap run, but it's best to perform the boiling operation outdoors. It may take up to 40 gallons of sap to make 1 gallon of syrup, and that extra 39 gallons of moisture will seep into your walls and furniture and may even cause your wallpaper to fall in huge festoons. If you must, boil off most of the water outdoors and bring the remainder inside to finish up—a *little* moisture won't hurt our winter-dry houses, but enough is enough.

I prefer to make jams, since it is not only less work (no straining of juices through a jelly bag) but it leaves in the whole, tasty berry and often requires no pectin. For those who dislike seeds in their preserves, you may like jellies better.

Blueberry Jam
Yields 2–6 half-pint jars

Pick a few underripe berries with the blue-black ripe ones for a fuller flavor. I once came by a jar of imported Swedish lingonberries that made a jam very much like this one.

1–3 C. blueberries
¾ C. water, if needed

1 C. sugar to each cup of berries (less, if you like a tart jam)

Wash and drain berries; discard any damaged or rotten berries or stems. Crush lightly (leave a few whole) and simmer till nearly tender. Add sugar and continue cooking until the jam is thick. Put in hot sterilized jars and seal immediately or store in the freezer.

Strawberry Jam
Yields 6 half-pint jars

Wild strawberries are tiny, smaller than your fingernail, but surpassing sweet. If you find a patch of them well in fruit, it's a lucky day indeed. Only once in my life have I found enough of these miniature berries to make jam; the next year a house had been built on the site and my berry patch was sodded over.

I made freezer jam with them, a process that preserves the delightful aroma as well as the delicate flavor; you may like this method for any of your wild fruits.

2 C. strawberries, washed and hulled
4 C. sugar
¾ C. water

½ C. liquid or 1 pkg. powdered pectin
1 sprig of mint per jar, if desired

Crush the strawberries and cover with the sugar. Let them sit to absorb the sweetness while you bring the water and pectin to a boil in a small pan; continue to boil for 1 minute, stirring constantly. Allow to cool slightly, then stir into berries and sugar. Stir well to dissolve any remaining sugar. Ladle into half-pint jars and store in the freezer; this tastes like summer. Add a small sprig of mint to each jar, if you like.

Black Raspberry Jam (or Blackberry, Blueberry, Cloudberry, Dewberry, etc.)

Yields 4–5 half-pint jars

Raspberries are my favorite bramble fruit; they seem sweeter than the wild-flavored blackberry. This recipe can be used with any member of the clan with good results, though.

3 C. berries   1½ C. sugar

Wash berries, then crush. Simmer slowly until cooked, then put through a colander if you wish to remove part of the seeds (they can be *very* seedy). Add sugar, return to heat, and simmer slowly, stirring often, until the mixture is thick. Pour into sterilized jars and seal immediately.

Mixed-Berry Jam

Yields 4–5 half-pint jars

There are times when you can find only a handful of this and that. One year I found blackberries, raspberries, and gooseberries, but only a few of any one kind. The gooseberries had turned a rich purple; most had gone into a green gooseberry pie earlier in the season. In the mood for berry jam, I used my mixed bag of berries with delightful results.

Follow the same recipe as for *Black Raspberry Jam*, above, but use whatever mixed berries you may find—just so the total amounts to 3 C.

Mulberry Jam

Yields 5–7 half-pint jars

The birds have brought us a present. Just by our front porch they planted a lovely volunteer red mulberry tree, and now it feeds us all. The birds and I often just eat the sweet summer fruits out of hand, but when there are plenty, I can make mulberry jam; a lovely way to preserve summer and enjoy it again in December.

2–3 C. fresh mulberries (pick a   ¾ C. sugar for each cup of
     few unripe, still red rather   berries
     than black)   Squeeze of lemon, if desired

Wash berries, drain, and pick them over for any rotten ones or stems. Crush and mix with sugar; bring to a boil and continue to cook, stirring, until jam is thickened. Add lemon juice if your red berries haven't added enough tartness. Ladle into hot sterilized jars and seal immediately or store in the freezer.

Loganberry, Elderberry, or Gooseberry Jam
Yields 7 half-pint jars

This recipe can, of course, be used with any of the low-pectin fruits—or again, mix what you have on hand.

4 C. fruit
1 large or two small apples
  (somewhat green, if you can
  find them)

3 C. sugar
Squeeze of lemon juice for
  flavor, if desired

Wash and drain fruits; discard any stems or leaves. Crush part of the berries, but leave some whole. Add chopped apples and sugar and cook over medium heat, stirring constantly, until thickened. Add lemon juice if you need extra flavor. Jam is finished when a spoonful mounds on a plate. Ladle while still hot into sterilized jars and seal immediately. Homemade sourdough toast can have no finer companion than elderberry jam.

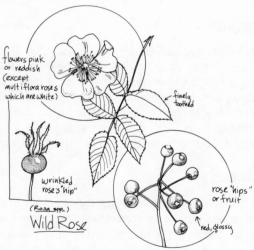

flowers pink or reddish (except multiflora roses which are white)

finely toothed

wrinkled rose's "hip"

rose "hips" or fruit

red, glossy

(Rosa spp.)
Wild Rose

Rose Hip Jam
Yields 4 half-pint jars

This is tart and sunset colored and rich in vitamin C. It looks lovely on a hot biscuit and tastes wonderful as well. Many kinds of rose hips can be used to make this jam; look for larger, fleshier hips if you can find them—some of the red fruits that were the calyxes of wild roses can be quite dry and seedy.

Collect these little jewels in late fall, after a frost has sweetened them.

2 C. rose hips, washed and picked over	Water to cover 2 C. sugar

Simmer rose hips in water until they are tender, then force through a sieve or colander. Add sugar and simmer, stirring often, until thick. Process as usual in hot jars.

Ground-Cherry Jam
Yields 4 half-pint jars

These little parchment-wrapped fruits may look unprepossessing, but they make a very tasty jam. Be sure they are soft and ripe; discard papery husks.

2 C. ground-cherries, washed and drained	2 C. sugar Water to cover

Crush some of the fruits, but leave some whole; just cover with water and simmer till mixture begins to thicken. Add sugar and continue to simmer, stirring often, until a spoonful stands up on a plate without running. Put in hot jars and seal immediately.

Violet Jam
Yields 3 half-pint jars

This is a lovely flower-flavored jam to try on those years when the violets threaten to take over. This delicately flavored treat is for special occasions, not for a hearty breakfast toast; you'll love it for afternoon tea. Violets were once used as a medicinal herb for everything from bronchitis to consumption; I like to think I am protecting myself from ill health—or ill luck—as I enjoy this lavender jam.

Like the wild strawberry jam, this one is not actually cooked, to better preserve the color and flavor of the flowers.

1 C. of violet flowers, packed down (remove stems) Juice of 1 lemon or ½ C. orange juice	½ C. water (more or less) ½ C. liquid pectin or 1 pkg. powdered pectin ¾ C. more water

Put violet blossoms, lemon or orange juice, and ½ C. water in your food processor or blender; blend until it forms a paste. Boil pectin and ¾ C. water for 1 minute, then add to blender. Pack into jars as usual and store in freezer.

Mayapple Marmalade
Yields 10 half-pint jars

Mayapples are also called raccoon berries; we share a fondness for this fine wild fruit with a good friend. In some areas of the country, they're

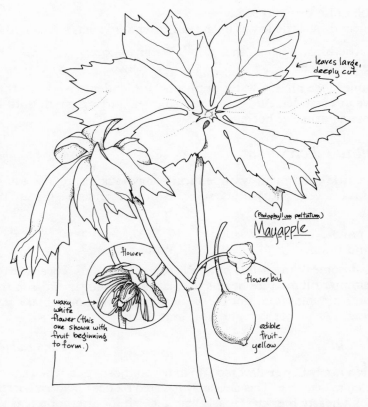

leaves large, deeply cut

(Podophyllum peltatum)
Mayapple

flower

flower bud

waxy white flower (this one shown with fruit beginning to form.)

edible fruit - yellow

known as mandrakes, but they're not the same plant as the European mandrake. They do make a richly flavored jam, however.

This recipe can also be used with maypops or passion fruits if you have enough—our prolifically flowering backyard vine never seems to produce enough fruit to preserve.

I call this marmalade; actually, it's just as much a jam as the other preserves in this section, but the addition of the orange peel gives it a bit of that taste.

4 C. fruits, washed, drained, and chopped
1 C. orange juice
½ C. finely sliced orange peel (discard the bitter white portion)

1 pkg. powdered pectin
6 C. sugar

Prepare fruits and put in a pot with orange juice and peelings. Add pectin, bring to boiling, and stir while fruit pulp thickens. Stir in sugar and boil again for 2 minutes, stirring constantly to keep fruit from sticking. Skim off any foam and ladle into hot sterilized jars. Seal.

Prickly Pear Preserves
(Nopales *Marmalade*)

Yields 8 half-pint jars

Prepare *nopales* as in the basic preparation procedure in Chapter 4. Chop finely.

4 C. nopales, prepared and
   chopped
Water to cover

Juice of 1 lemon
4 C. sugar

Cover prickly pear pulp with water; stir in lemon and sugar. Simmer until mixture thickens, then pack into hot sterilized jars. Enjoy your sweet revenge on this prickly little plant.

Butters are thick, old-fashioned fruit preserves. We commonly think of apple butter—although with its rich, spicy smell, it's hardly what I think of as common. Crab apples make lovely butters, or course—and so do persimmons. The main differences between these and jams is that they take no pectin and they are cooked longer, with spices like cinnamon, cloves, and perhaps ginger.

Crab Apple Butter

Yields 10–12 pint jars

This may be my favorite way of dealing with these sometimes tart and tiny apples. The finished product is brown as a nut, flavorful with apples and spices. It is especially good on hot biscuits or cornbread; a treat my mother taught me.

1   pk. of crab apples, washed
       and drained
Water to just cover (this is even
   better if you substitute cider)
7–8 C. of sugar (white or brown)

1   t. cinnamon
½   t. cloves
¼   t. ginger
¼   t. allspice

Cook the apples in water or cider until they are very tender; strain the whole fruits through a colander or sieve. Add sugar; use less if you are watching calories. (One half–¾ C. of sugar for each cup of apple pulp is enough.) Add spices and continue cooking, slowly, until reduced to a thick, brown, spice-scented consistency. When a rim of liquid no longer forms at the edge of the pan, it is finished. Put in hot sterilized jars and seal.

Persimmon Butter

Yields 9 half-pint jars

After a good, hard frost has sweetened the fruits and made them soft, try persimmon butter for a change.

Persimmons are rich in sugar — nearly 3 times as sweet as apples — so it isn't necessary to add as much granulated sugar to the pot.

6 C. of persimmon pulp (cook slowly with a little water, stirring often, and sieve to make pulp)

1 t. cinnamon
½ t. cloves
¼ t. allspice
¼ t. nutmeg

3 C. sugar (more or less to taste)

1 T. grated orange rind, if desired

Cook persimmon pulp, sugar, and spices until thick and brown. Add orange rind, if desired. Put in hot sterilized jars and seal.

Try other fruits in place of the apples or persimmons, if you like. I've heard of wild grape butter and plum butters as well, made much the same as these.

Jellies are a bit more work to make, since they require pressing the fruit pulp through a fine sieve and, usually, through a jelly bag as well. Some recipes call for pectin, though that increases the requirement for sugar and reduces the fruity flavor — except in the case of freezer jams previously listed. If you doubt your extracted fruit juice contains sufficient pectin to jell properly, use some of the high-pectin fruits in your mixture. These include apples, crab apples, quinces, plums, cranberries, and gooseberries. Low-pectin fruits are those that tend to have a sweeter, more mellow flavor — like strawberries, blueberries, wild cherries, raspberries, blackberries, and wild grapes.

Jelly making requires producing a rich, fruity juice first. Juicy fruits need relatively little water in this process; simply crush the fruits to release the juices, then simmer with only a bit of water added. Drier fruits like cranberries and apples require more water, generally just to cover. Simmer until the fruit is tender and begins to lose its color, then squeeze the fruit through a jelly bag or let it drip through a colander lined with several layers of cheesecloth until all the moisture has dripped through. A clearer, finer jelly can be made by the drip method; squeezing the bag may force some pulp through as well, which can cloud the color.

Crab Apple (or Quince) Jelly   Each 4-C. batch yields 4 half-pint jars

This beautiful jelly is the color of sunset. Try it on hot biscuits or spread on hot sourdough toast in the morning or use it with cream cheese on elegant crackers for tea.

½ pk. crab apples (or substitute quinces), washed and quartered

Water to just cover fruit
1 C. sugar for each cup of juice

Quarter fruits and remove blossom ends. Just cover with water in a heavy pot and simmer until fruit is soft. Let drain through a jelly bag and measure; then, to each cup of juice, add 1 C. sugar. It's best not to cook a larger batch than 4 C. of juice at a time to assure proper jelling. Test for jelling about 10 minutes after your jelly has begun boiling (after adding the sugar) by spooning up a small amount. Let it drop back into the pan; if the jelly drops off in 2 large drops, the jell stage hasn't been reached—return to heat. When the drops run together and fall as a single large drop, the jelly is ready. This may take as little as 10 minutes or as long as 30; use a jelly thermometer if you prefer. Put in hot sterilized jars and seal.

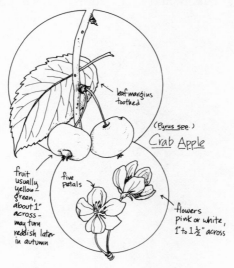

leaf margins toothed

(Pyrus spp.)
Crab Apple

fruit usually yellow-green, about 1" across - may turn reddish later in autumn

five petals

flowers pink or white, 1" to 1½" across

Wild Herb Jelly

Yields 4–5 half-pint jars

Delightful jellies that are good served with game or other meats can be made with wild herbs. Try wild thyme jelly, pitcher sage jelly, gill-over-the-ground jelly, bee balm, or one of the more familiar mints. Begin with the basic *Crab Apple (or Quince) Jelly,* above, steep the fresh washed (and unsprayed) herbs in the jelly until the desired flavor has been reached, then remove. If you wish, leave a small sprig of your chosen herb in each jar to remind you of its flavor.

Fox Grape Jelly

Yields 5–6 half-pint jars

Any of the wild grapes will do for this; I am particularly fond of the taste of fox grapes that are abundant here in Missouri. Gather some of your grapes a bit underripe to increase flavor and pectin content.

4 C. grapes, stemmed and
   washed but not seeded
1 large apple or 2 small ones,
   stemmed and quartered

Water just to cover
1 C. sugar to each cup of juice

Wash grapes and put them in a large pot with the apple quarters. Barely cover with water and boil until fruit is soft. Let it drain through a jelly bag and measure; use only 4 C. at a time for best results. Add sugar and stir until dissolved; return to boiling and start timing from that point. Use the jelly test as before.

For *Spiced Grape Jelly*, excellent with game, add ⅓ C. apple cider vinegar, 1 stick of cinnamon, and 1 t. of cloves, heads removed, before adding sugar.

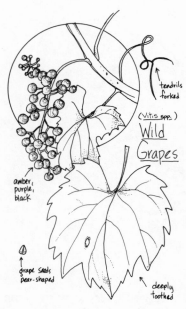

Elderberry Jelly

Yields 8–10 half-pint jars

Elderberries are quite low in pectin and must be mixed with grape or apple juice to jell; I prefer the combination of apple and elderberry for best flavor.

Pick the elderberry umbels when fully ripe and remove most of the stems; it isn't necessary to remove them all. Prepare the elderberry juice as you did the grape juice, above, by just covering the fruit with water in a large pan. Bring to a boil and cook until berries are soft. Strain through a jelly bag. Measure the juice and use immediately or store for later.

3 C. elderberry juice
3 C. apple or grape juice

6 C. sugar

Bring mixed juices to a boil; add sugar and stir until dissolved. Return to the boil and begin timing from that point; depending on the strength of your high-pectin juice, the jelling point may be reached in as little as 10 minutes or as long as 30. Continue to test until a single drop falls from your spoon in a sheet, then put into hot jars immediately. (Jelly that is boiled too long can become rubbery.)

Mulberry Jelly

Yields 8–10 half-pint jars

Like elderberries, mulberries are fairly low in pectin but high in potassium and fruit sugars. Pick some underripe berries and prepare the juice as for elderberries. Mix with apple or grape juice and proceed as above.

Wild Rose Jelly

Yields 10 half-pint jars

This is an old Ozark recipe that uses no still apparatus; it's simple and delicate.

2 qts. wild rose petals	7 lbs. sugar
2½ qts. water	2 C. liquid pectin
½ C. crab apple juice	

Just cover the rose petals with water and bring to a boil; continue to simmer for 15 minutes. Strain through a jelly bag. Add apple juice and enough water to bring the total amount of liquid up to 2 qts. Add sugar and stir to dissolve. Bring to a boil and pour in 2 C. of liquid pectin. Continue to boil briskly for 1 minute, then seal in hot sterilized jars.

Wild Mint Jelly

Yields 5–6 half-pint jars

This jelly is a bit more difficult to prepare, since you will want to preserve all the natural flavor and volatile oils by making a simple still. Use a 3-qt. saucepan with a rounded lid; in the bottom, put 2 C. fresh mint leaves, well crushed; cover with 2 C. boiling water (or process boiling water and leaves in your blender or food processor). Invert the lid on the pan and fill it with ice water. Return the rig to the stove to bring the leaf and water infusion to a simmer, then remove from heat and allow to steep as for tea. Add ice cubes to the cold water on the lid to encourage condensation on the underside of the lid; the steam from the hot mint water will return to the pot and make a strong, aromatic base for your jelly. Run juice through a jelly bag as usual.

4 C. sugar
2 C. mint infusion
¼ C. vinegar

1 pkg. powdered pectin
¾ C. hot water

Dissolve the sugar in the hot mint water. Add vinegar. Bring the powdered pectin to a boil in the water, and continue to boil for exactly 1 minute. Add pectin mixture to the mint water mixture and pour into hot sterilized glasses. Seal.

Try this with any of the wild mint family that catches your fancy. Wild spearmint or peppermint are good, of course, but try wood mint, pennyroyal, or even gill-over-the-ground for a spicy flavor.

When making any of the wild jellies from petals or leaves (mint, rose, honeysuckle, etc.) a still apparatus may be necessary. Otherwise your kitchen will smell wonderful but your jelly may not.

Elderberry-Sumac Jelly

Yields 7–8 half-pint jars

Elderberries are sometimes a bit bland; the addition of the tart sumac juice gives a lively flavor to this jelly. It takes the place of lemon juice, often used to spark this mild-flavored fruit. Prepare elderberry juice as before. Sumac juice is made simply by swishing the reddish, hairy berries in cold water until the water is rose colored. Strain through several thicknesses of cheesecloth to remove all the small hairs.

Again, this is a mixed-juice jelly, since neither elderberries nor sumac has sufficient pectin to jell.

2 C. elderberry juice
2 C. sumac ''ade'' or juice

2 C. apple juice
6 C. sugar

Prepare your juices and strain well to remove all impurities for a lovely, clear jelly. Bring to a boil and add sugar; stir to dissolve and bring to a rolling boil again. Continue to stir as it boils for 10 minutes, then begin to check it with the jelly test. Put in hot jars and seal immediately.

Sumac

Sassafras
Bark

Sassafras Jelly

Yields 4–5 half-pint jars

Sassafras jelly is quite simple to make from a strong infusion or tea; no distilling is necessary.

In spite of the warnings from the American Medical Association about the wisdom of including sassafras in the diet, it continues to be one of my favorite wild foods. I use it so seldom I don't worry about possible side effects (any more than I do with nutmeg, which has the same active ingredient, safrole, that the AMA is concerned with).

2½ C. sugar
3 C. strong sassafras tea
1 pkg. powdered pectin or
    ½ C. liquid

1 T. fresh-squeezed lemon juice

Dissolve sugar in tea, and bring to a boil. Add lemon juice and pectin and boil again for about 5 minutes. Put up in hot jars as usual.

Syrups are extremely easy to make in most cases; they require no lengthy boiling or jelling processes, but they add immeasurably to your enjoyment of homemade pancakes or ice creams. Those syrups made from the sap of trees do require preparation and time; those made from fruits or simple infusions are quick and delicious.

Sassafras Syrup

Yield depends on desired thickness

Again, my favorite old sassafras makes a delightful syrup; the spicy, slightly woody flavor is elusive but good.

1 C. sugar

2 C. strong sassafras tea

Jams, Jellies, and Syrups / 149

Stir sugar into hot tea until it dissolves; bring to a boil and heat until mixture thickens to your liking. Put in hot sterilized jars or bottles.

Elderberry Syrup
Yield depends on desired thickness

Try this on pancakes or ice cream—it's good either way.

2 C. elderberry juice (extract as   1 C. sugar
    for jelly)

Boil elderberry juice and sugar together until the mixture reaches the desired thickness. Bottle or use immediately over pancakes or ice cream.

Wild Thyme Syrup
Yields 2 half-pint jars

This syrup has a strong herb flavor and is said to be good for coughs and colds. Perhaps it's the honey in this one that soothes a raw throat.

1 C. strong thyme tea   1 C. honey

Heat tea and honey together until just simmering; taste mixture to be sure it doesn't become bitter or too strong. Bottle as usual. Try a spoonful or two for a winter cough or try it on hot biscuits.

Strawberry/Raspberry/Chokecherry/ Gooseberry/Blueberry Syrup
Yield depends on desired thickness

This syrup may be made with any or all of the above fruits; mixed, it is wonderfully subtle, but any one of them straight will make a treat for your breakfast table.

2 C. mashed fruit   2 C. sugar (you may substitute
1 C. water   part honey, but the flavor of
                          the fruit will be altered)

Simmer fruit and water together until the mixture is strongly fruit flavored. Put through a jelly bag if you want a smooth syrup, or use as is for "chunky style" if you have been careful to remove stems or leaves.

Add sugar and stir to dissolve. Continue to cook over low heat until mixture reaches desired thickness; you may reduce by as much as half. Bottle or serve immediately.

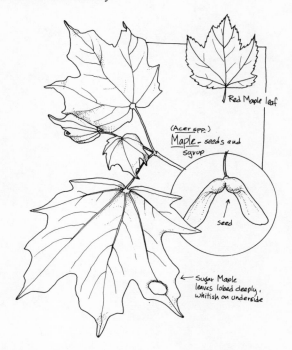

Red Maple leaf

(Acer spp.)
<u>Maple</u> - seeds and
syrup

seed

← Sugar Maple
leaves lobed deeply,
whitish on underside

Maple/Birch/Sycamore Syrup   40 gallons of sap yield 1 gallon of syrup

There is no recipe, per se, for syrup boiled down from tree sap; it's simply a matter of waiting for warmer (above 40°) days and nights below freezing to make the sap begin to rise. Then, tap the trees with clean spiles or tubes; point the hole somewhat upward to encourage draining. Use a large bucket under each spile or hung directly from them; a running tree can produce an amazing amount of sap. Check your buckets often. You may want to cover them with a lid or foil to keep insects or dirt from falling into the bucket.

Use large flat pans to boil in, to encourage rapid evaporation, and keep a hot fire going underneath. Stir constantly as the mixture begins to thicken to avoid sticking or burning; after all the work of collecting sap, you don't want to lose it! As it begins to turn golden rather than thin and watery, check it for taste (one of the best and traditional ways to do this is to drop the hot syrup on a handy bowl of clean snow—and then enjoy it). When syrup reaches its desired thickness and sweetness, bottle as usual to keep it from getting moldy or sour.

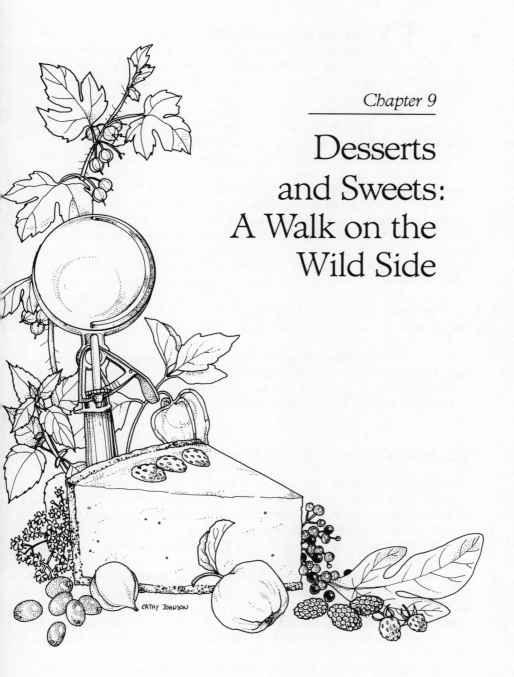

Chapter 9

Desserts
and Sweets:
A Walk on the
Wild Side

CATHY JOHNSON

Desserts are celebration and reward, consolation, consummation, and all-around general spirit lifters—diet books and cholesterol counts notwithstanding. But with fresh wild ingredients, your walk on the wild side can't help but be *somewhat* more healthful, especially if you walk (or jog!) to the woods and fields to do your foraging.

Some of these recipes are old family favorites—I grew up with *Apple/Elderberry Pie* and scarcely knew you could make an apple pie without those tiny dark fruits to add their wild surprise.

The recipes in this chapter run the gamut from light and healthful to sinfully rich, from simple to prepare to elaborate productions. Tart-sweet or spicy or chocolate-nutty, these are meant for sharing.

Imagine a candle-lit evening in front of the fireplace; you've just finished a wonderful meal and are about to share a chocolate fondue. The sweet brown richness is warm and thick; you've collected ripe and juicy wild fruits to dip into the chocolate, one by one, and pop into your mouth. The flavor explodes with exotic fruit tastes and chocolate sweetness. What could be better to share with someone you care about?

Or how about a pie? To top off a meal or to tote to a church social—or to provide the festive finis for a holiday feast—make a southern pecan pie or a traditional mincemeat, bubbly, thick, and hot with venison and fruit and spices.

Desserts make wonderful gifts. At Christmas, a special birthday, at any kind of celebration at all, make and share our wild sweets. Made with wildings you've gathered yourself, you are giving much more than a plate of fudge or a fancy jar of pralines—you're giving of yourself as well.

Suggested Wild Ingredients

Any of the wild fruits that went into jams or jellies in chapter 8 may find their way happily to the dessert course. Elderberries lend themselves to pies, coffee cakes, and fritters, adding their wild tang to old favorites.

Try a traditional gooseberry pie, tart with pale green berries gathered early in the season, or wait until their striated berries hang sweet and purple from their bramble canes.

A cooling summer treat is in store when you make chocolate mint ice cream with the wild mints you've gathered by a boggy meadow or in the woods. Each time you make it, it can be a new experience as you try the various kinds of mint available. Or perhaps a fresh wild strawberry ice cream is more to your taste; look for these tiny berries in June or July.

Wild strawberries may also find their way into elegant crêpes; if you find a trove of these small treasures, freeze a few for a cold winter afternoon when you especially need a breath of summer.

Cranberry coffee cake is a special treat in the fall and winter for brunch with friends; if you live in the Northeast you will be able to gather these berries in the wild. These wildings are sweeter and riper than many machine-picked berries that must be transported overland without bruising. You won't believe the difference in flavor.

If you like chocolate, try our *Cranberry Chocolate Torte* for a special dessert—the combination is fantastic.

All of the wild nuts add their oily richness to your fall or winter desserts. Try *Hickory Nut Pie* or *Black Walnut Fudge*—or my special Christmas treat, hazelnut-studded rum balls. Any of the nuts freeze well; they keep as fresh and sweet as when you gathered them. You can make fruitcakes or brownies any time you like. In fact, most of the wild fruits can also be preserved, dried, or frozen for a year-round celebration of the dessert course.

Don't forget the fancy fruit fritters when you're planning dessert—crab apples in the fall, elder flowers or elderberry fritters in late spring and summer, or blueberry fritters dusted with powdered sugar make a simple but sumptuous finish to your meal.

Cheesecakes are my husband's favorites; try them topped with wild strawberries, cherries, or blueberries.

A persimmon cake is rich and dark and spicy, a wonderful late-fall treat. If you've preserved the pulp you can make this special dessert at any time of the year. Wild nuts and cream cheese icing make this one really festive.

But perhaps the most festive of all is a rich Christmas steamed pudding that you make ahead of time, when the fruits and nuts are fresh and ripe. Store it for the months before the holidays wrapped in cheesecloth and pour brandy, whiskey, or rum over it from time to time. If someone tries to tell you they don't like old, dried-out fruitcakes, get them to try at least a bite of this one—it will change their minds in a hurry.

Pies are among our favorite desserts; they're always festive and usually fairly simple to prepare—*if* you're good at piecrusts. They are definitely not my forte, but this recipe seems to work nearly every time. It's a simple flour-paste shell, and I've yet to go too far wrong with it. However, when I don't have the time or inclination to roll out a crust, I have no hesitation about buying a frozen or refrigerated one.

Piecrust
2 9" crusts

2 C. flour (I use unbleached white)
1 t. salt
¼ C. water
⅔ C. chilled shortening

Sift together flour and salt; measure out ⅓ C. of this mixture and stir water into it. Make a smooth paste. Cut shortening into the rest of the

flour until it resembles a bowlful of small peas, then stir the flour paste in; knead with your hands until the dough forms a ball, but don't over-work. Too much handling will make your crust tough.

Apple/Elderberry Pie

Serves 6

If you can find large enough crab apples to make all that peeling worth-while, the flavor will be quite special. If not, use good tart pie apples, like Jonathans.

Enough apples, when peeled and sliced, to form a mound in the pie pan (depending on the size of the apples, this can be anywhere from 6 or 7 to 20)

½–1 C. elderberries, pulled from their stems, washed and drained

½–1 C. sugar, depending on how tart the apples are (½ C. is usually plenty)

2 T. flour
1 t. cinnamon
½ t. nutmeg
½ t. allspice
¼ t. powdered cloves
1 t. crumbled, dried basil (if desired)

Butter or margarine

Cut up apples to fill pie pan; to assure plenty of fruit, I slice enough to mound the pan high. Dump them into a bowl and line your pie pan with crust. Do not prick the crust, or your juices will leak between the crust and the pan, effectively gluing your pie in place.

Add elderberries, sugar, flour, and spices, and stir gently until the apple pieces are lightly coated with flour. Return to pie pan. Dot with butter or margarine. Top with piecrust or make *Crumb Topping*.

CRUMB TOPPING

½ C. flour
½ C. sugar
2 T. butter or margarine

½ t. cinnamon
¼ t. allspice

Mix everything together until crumbly. Distribute over the top of the pie.

Bake at 375° for 45 minutes or until apples are done and pie is bubbly around the edges. Crust should be golden but not too brown. (If you have to cook the fruit longer and your crust is already as brown as you want it, protect it with a cap of aluminum foil for the remainder of the cooking time.

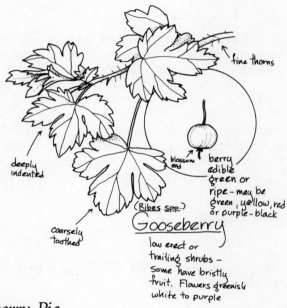

fine thorns

deeply
indented

coarsely
toothed

blossom
end

berry
edible
green or
ripe—may be
green, yellow, red
or purple-black

(Ribes spp.)
Gooseberry
low erect or
trailing shrubs —
some have bristly
fruit. Flowers greenish
white to purple

Gooseberry Pie   *Serves 6*

Prepare crust for a two-crust pie.

2-3 C. fresh gooseberries, washed and well drained. Remove any stems. Use soft green berries for the traditional tart pie or wait until they've ripened to a lovely deep purple for a different flavor.

3   T. flour

2   C. sugar (add more, if necessary—these are *tart*. You can use less, of course, if you prefer, or if part or all of your berries are purple-ripe.)

1   t. cinnamon (optional)

2   T. butter

Mix fruit, flour, sugar, and cinnamon, if desired; pour into pie shell and dot with butter. Cover with second crust or make a fancy lattice crust if you prefer. Bake at 425° for 35–40 minutes.

Pecan Pie
Serves 6–8 (it is rich)

In the South, this same recipe without the nuts would be called Chess Pie—it's delicious either way.

Prepare an unbaked pie shell; bake it about half done, 6–8 minutes or so, at 450°.

4 T. butter or margarine	1½ C. broken pecans
1 C. brown sugar	2 t. vanilla or 1 T. rum
3 eggs	½ t. salt
½ C. light molasses or sorghum	

Cream butter and sugar; add the eggs. Mix in the rest of the ingredients and pour into the partially baked pie shell; bake about 40 minutes. The nuts will rise to the top.

Hickory Nut Pie
Serves 6–8

This recipe is almost exactly like the one for pecan pie, and of course you may interchange them. But for the special flavor of wild hickory nuts, I like to use a slightly milder-flavored filling. Use white sugar instead of brown and 1½ t. vanilla. You may want to substitute light corn syrup for the molasses, as well.

Blueberry/Cherry/Raspberry/ Mulberry Deep-Dish Pie
Serves 6–8

When I was growing up we called this a cobbler; but whatever name you call it, it is rich and wonderful.

3 C. fruit (mix or match)	Dash of salt
1½ C. sugar (more or less, depending on how sweet or sour your fruits are)	1 t. cinnamon
	2 T. butter or margarine

Bring this mixture to a boil and top it with a slightly sweetened dough. Use a packaged biscuit mix or to make your own dough:

1 C. flour	1 T. sugar
1¼ t. baking powder	⅛ C. butter or margarine
½ t. salt	⅓ C. milk

Sift the dry ingredients together; cut in butter or margarine and add the milk. Stir lightly to avoid overworking the dough. Pat thin and place on top of the hot fruit. Bake at 425° for a half an hour or until dough is golden brown.

Sour Cream Wild Cherry Pie
Serves 6–8

Pick, pit, wash, and drain 2 C. of wild cherries for this very special pie.

Prepare a graham cracker crust or buy one at your grocer's. (To prepare, crush 2 C. of graham crackers, add ¼ C. melted butter or margarine, and 2 T. sugar. Mix well and press into a pie pan. Bake 8 minutes at 325° to set crust.)

3 eggs
2 C. prepared cherries

¾ C. sour cream
¾ C. sugar

Beat eggs well and add remaining ingredients. Pour into graham cracker crust and bake at 325° until the custard sets—about an hour (to test, insert a knife into the custard; if it comes out clean, the pie is done).

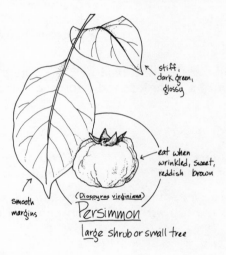

stiff, dark green, glossy

eat when wrinkled, sweet, reddish brown

smooth margins

(Diospyros virginiana)
Persimmon
large shrub or small tree

Persimmon Pie
Serves 6

In a good year, persimmons hang heavy on the bare trees after a hard freeze has made them wrinkled and sweet. They're too good to resist for a late-fall pie.

2 C. pitted, cooked persimmon
   pulp
1 C. sugar (more or less—persimmons are normally very
   sweet once fully ripe—and
   you wouldn't want to eat
   them at *all* if they weren't)

1 C. evaporated milk
1 t. cinnamon
1 t. allspice
2 eggs
1 prepared piecrust

Put all ingredients except the eggs in your blender or food processor (or mix with a hand mixer). Blend until smooth, then add eggs and blend only for a second or two.

Pour into pie shell and bake at 425° for 30–40 minutes or until filling is set. Serve with whipped cream. Some think this pie tastes best cold and even better the second day.

Persimmon Cake

Serves 8–10

I hope you will have had good luck in finding and preserving a good supply of persimmon pulp; it's handy for all kinds of things, especially this rich and spicy persimmon cake.

1 C. persimmon pulp
½ C. sugar
1 egg
1 C. flour
1 t. baking powder
2 T. butter
½ t. baking soda

½ C. seedless raisins
½ C. chopped walnuts, pecans, or hickory nuts
1 t. cinnamon
½ t. allspice
¼ t. ground cloves

Mix everything together and bake at 375° in two 9'' cake pans for 40 minutes or until a knife inserted into cake comes out clean.
Frost with:

CREAM CHEESE ICING

3 oz. cream cheese
1½ T. milk or half-and-half

¾ C. powdered sugar
1 t. vanilla or rum

Mix cream cheese and milk until smooth and soft; add sugar and vanilla. Frost cake and top with ¼ C. finely chopped pecans or hickory nuts.

Elderblow Fritters

Serves 6–8

These are quite easy to prepare and appear more fancy than they really are; your guests will enjoy them and so will you.

1½ C. flour (I use unbleached white)
Dash of salt
2 t. baking powder
1 egg
½–¾ C. milk
Fat for deep frying; try peanut oil to reduce smoking

Elderberry flowers, still attached to their umbels but broken into heads about 3'' across
¼ C. powdered sugar
½ t. cinnamon (optional)

Mix up the batter; meanwhile, heat fat to *almost* smoking. Dip each "head" of elderberry flowers in the batter, holding it by the stem; shake to remove the excess. Drop into hot oil and fry until just golden. Dust with powdered sugar flavored, if you like, with a bit of cinnamon.

Blueberry Fritters (or Apple, Raspberry, or Strawberry, etc.)

Serves 4-6

This is the more traditional form of fritter; something very similar to this is made with domestic apples at Stephenson's Apple Farm, a wonderful restaurant in Harry Truman's hometown of Independence. Everyone asks for more!

1 C. flour	2 egg yolks
Dash of salt	1 T. melted butter or margarine
1 T. sugar	⅔ C. milk
1 C. fruit (if larger fruit like crab apples, quarter, core or seed, and chop)	2 egg whites

Sift dry ingredients together; drain fruit well. Mix egg yolks, butter, and milk; stir into dry mixture. Whip egg whites until fluffy but not dry and fold them into the dough. Add fruit. Deep-fry until golden brown; dust with powdered sugar, if desired.

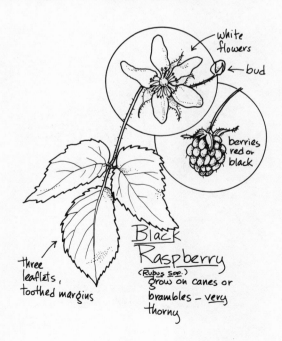

white flowers

← bud

berries red or black

Black Raspberry

(*Rubus spp.*) grow on canes or brambles — **very** thorny

three leaflets, toothed margins

Wild-Fruit Cloud

This is a cool summer dessert, easy to make and easy to take.

1 C. whipping cream
¼ C. sugar
¼ C. sour cream
Dash of cinnamon (optional)
1 T. crème de menthe (optional)
    (Choose one or the other
    but not both cinnamon and
    crème de menthe.)

2 C. wild fruits, mixed or one
    kind only

Whip cream until it forms peaks; add sugar slowly and continue to beat. Fold in sour cream and cinnamon or crème de menthe (if you prefer, Grand Marnier may be substituted for the crème de menthe). Alternate layers of cream with layers of fruit in a parfait glass. Garnish with a slice of orange if you've used Grand Marnier or a mint leaf if you've chosen crème de menthe.

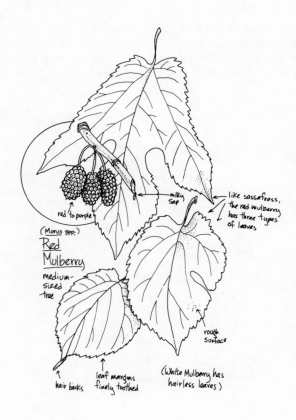

milky sap

red to purple

like sassafrass, the red mulberry has three types of leaves

(Morus spp.)
Red Mulberry
medium-sized tree

rough surface

hair backs

leaf margins finely toothed

(White Mulberry has hairless leaves)

Mulberries and Cream

This one couldn't be simpler and in fact needs no recipe—I sometimes think it's the best way to enjoy mulberries—or most other wild fruits.

2 C. fruit (washed, picked over, drained—if you are using fruit other than mulberries, seed or chop accordingly)

4 T. sugar
2 C. half-and-half or cream

Clean and prepare fruit, sprinkle with sugar, and pour the cream over; allow to sit a few minutes until the cream begins to color.

Wild Strawberries and May Wine

Another wild treat that proves elegant needn't mean elaborate. This is a good one for lovers to share; you could substitute champagne for the May wine, but I love the sweet woodruff flavor of the delicate German wine.

4 C. wild strawberries; wash and drain but leave the hull on

½ C. May wine or champagne
½ C. sugar, brown sugar, or powdered sugar

Grasp each tiny strawberry by the green calyx or hull and dip it first in wine, then in sugar. Pop them in your mouth and enjoy!

Hickory Nut Rum Balls

Around the holidays I get a great craving for these little nut-studded treats. If you prefer, chop pecans, black walnuts, or hazelnuts or mix and match.

A friend from Kentucky makes these with bourbon, and they're just as good; they make delightful gifts for adults only—they're strong enough to make you a bit silly.

¼ C. butter or margarine
1 C. crushed vanilla wafers
2 T. cocoa
1 C. powdered sugar

1 C. chopped hickory nuts
¼ C. rum or bourbon
1½ T. light corn syrup (optional)

Melt butter or margarine; crush vanilla wafers. Mix all ingredients together; if the mix is too thin, add a few more crushed cookies or a bit more powdered sugar; refrigerate until you can make teaspoon- to tablespoon-sized balls. Roll between your palms and then roll each in powdered sugar. These will keep for weeks—or forever, perhaps—but I've never been able to wait that long.

Hickory Nut Brownies

These are extremely rich and totally satisfying for the chocolate junkie. Use pecans or black walnuts if you can't find hickory nuts.

1 C. butter or margarine	⅓ C. cocoa
2 C. sugar	1 T. vanilla
4 eggs, slightly beaten	1 C. coarsely chopped nuts
1½ C. sifted flour	

Cream shortening and sugar together until fluffy. Add eggs. Sift together flour and cocoa, add to creamed mixture, and blend carefully. Add vanilla and nuts. Bake in a greased and floured 9½'' x 13'' pan at 350° for 35 minutes.

To add even more richness, you may cover the hot brownies with a layer of miniature marshmallows; return to the oven until marshmallows are melted but not brown—about 10 minutes. Cool before icing with:

ICING FOR HICKORY NUT BROWNIES (Optional)

½ C. butter or margarine	⅓ C. cocoa, sifted after
1 t. vanilla	measuring
½ C. evaporated milk	½ C. chopped hickory nuts,
4 C. powdered sugar, sifted	pecans, or black walnuts

Combine all ingredients with the exception of the nut meats. Beat with an electric mixer until fluffy; fold in nuts and spread over the top of the brownies.

Black Walnut Fudge

If you are a fan of fudge, it can only be improved by the addition of these rich, oily nuts. They are a bit of a pain to hull; more than one nut picker has had to deal with walnut-stained fingers for days on end. My father used to throw the nuts he gathered in the driveway and then drive the car over them for a few days; this broke open the staining thick green hull and allowed the nutshells themselves to air-dry for a while—we had much less staining once they had had a chance to weather.

1 C. half-and-half or evaporated milk	2 oz. grated baking chocolate
	4 T. butter or margarine
2 C. sugar	2 T. vanilla
Dash of salt	1 C. chopped nuts

Bring milk just to a boil; remove from heat and stir in the sugar, salt, and chocolate to dissolve. Return to heat and boil for 2–3 minutes, covered, then uncover and cook to the soft-ball stage (238° on a candy thermometer). Cool to 110° and stir in butter or margarine and vanilla.

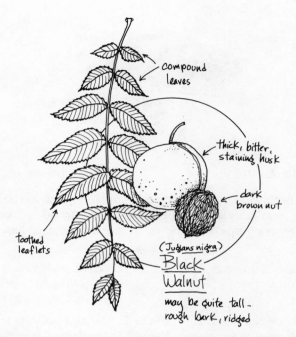

compound
leaves

thick, bitter,
staining husk

dark
brown nut

toothed
leaflets

(Juglans nigra)
Black
Walnut

may be quite tall -
rough bark, ridged

Add nut meats and stir quickly. Pour into a 10'' x 15'' buttered pan and cut before it is fully cooled for neater results, or cool slightly, knead, and form into fudge balls.

Maple Candy

Serves 6–8

If you've made your own maple or birch syrup from the last chapter, or if you have a handy source, this candy is simplicity itself to make—it's nothing more than maple syrup, boiled down a bit further.

My cousins used to have this candy often when they were young; it is supposed to be slightly crisp outside and creamy inside, but whenever they'd give me some to take home, I'd age it to a nicely hard stage and enjoy sucking on the maple sweetness for hours. You can do the same, if you wish.

2 C. maple syrup   1 t. vanilla

Bring syrup to the boil over low heat and continue cooking till it reaches 233° on your candy thermometer. Allow it to cool naturally to 110° (don't speed up cooling by submersing the pan bottom in cool water), then add the vanilla and beat until the mixture is light and fluffy. Form into patties or balls or press into candy molds—we always had little maple soldiers and teddy bears when I was young. For soft candy, keep in tightly covered container. Allow to dry for hard candy.

HOREHOUND CANDY

Horehound Candy

Yields 2 qts. of cracked candy

In earlier times, horehound candy was considered an extremely useful medicine to treat coughs and colds. I simply learned to like the flavor when I was growing up. Who knows? Perhaps I coughed less than other children!

1   qt. horehound leaves
6   C. boiling water
4   C. sugar

1¼ C. dark molasses, sorghum, or cane syrup
1   T. butter or margarine

Make a strong tea or infusion of the leaves and boiling water; allow to steep for 5 minutes or more. Strain out the leaves and measure out 2 qts. of liquid. Add the remaining ingredients and bring to the hard-crack stage on your candy thermometer—300°–310°. Skim off the foam that rises to the top and pour into a well-buttered cookie sheet with a 1'' rim. Score as the mixture cools to break into uniform pieces, or break after it cools fully.

I once made a horehound tea with a plant I found in my garden when we moved to the farm; I didn't know horehound would make you sweat, and I spent a nervous few moments wondering if I had poisoned myself before I confirmed identification. The moral of that story is—be *sure* you know what you are picking! I could have been sorry as well as sweaty.

Sassafras Candy

Yields 2 qts. of cracked candy

This candy is practically a staple in the Missouri Ozarks where I spent much of my childhood; its spicy flavor and sunset color still please me.

2   C. sassafras bark or root
6   C. boiling water
4   C. sugar

1¼ C. light corn syrup
1   T. butter or margarine

Like the horehound candy above, make a strong tea with the sassafras bark and boiling water. It should be deep reddish brown—add more bark if necessary. Strain out bark pieces and add remaining ingredients to the liquid. Bring to hard-crack stage (300°–310°) and pour out into a well-buttered cookie sheet with a rim. Score while cooling or allow to cool thoroughly and crack with a knife.

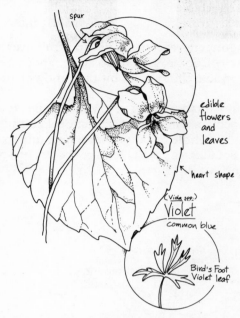

Glazed Wildflowers (or Mint Leaves)

Serves 6–8

These are elegant little sweetmeats that are best eaten the same day; they don't keep well. What you choose to glaze depends on what you are able to find, but do make sure you are choosing an edible flower or leaf. I am fond of rose petals, violets, borage, comfrey, or linden flowers. You could also try elderblow.

1   egg white
1–2 t. cold water
2   C. flowers or leaves, rinsed
     and dried gently

1   C. granulated sugar

   Beat the egg white gently, not to cause foam but simply to stir; add water, continuing to stir gently. Dip each flower or leaf in this mixture, then sprinkle all over with sugar. Let dry thoroughly and put in a well-sealed container to keep them from reabsorbing moisture from the atmosphere.

Chocolate Fondue

Serves 4

Fondues are fun for one, fun for two, and fun for a party; why not forage your wild ingredients and have a special gathering?

6 oz. chocolate—bittersweet is
   my favorite, but you may
   prefer milk chocolate
1 T. butter or margarine

1 C. water
½ C. sugar
1 t. vanilla
4 C. wild fruits

Combine all ingredients except vanilla and fruit over a medium heat; chocolate will melt. Cook to the syrup stage, about 5–8 minutes; if it is too thick for fondue, thin with a bit of brandy or rum—or water, if you prefer.

Wash and drain fruits well; pat dry with a paper towel if necessary to make sure chocolate will adhere. Put chocolate sauce in the top of a fondue pan with a candle or other gentle heat underneath; dip fruits in one at a time. Smaller fruits may require the use of a toothpick rather than a fondue fork to dip them.

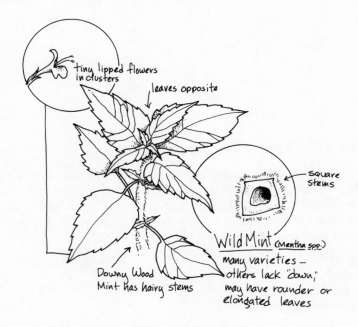

tiny lipped flowers in clusters

leaves opposite

square stems

Wild Mint (Mentha spp.)
many varieties—others lack "down," may have rounder or elongated leaves

Downy Wood Mint has hairy stems

Chocolate Mint Ice Cream

Serves 4–6

If you have access to an old-fashioned ice-cream machine you have the makings for a wild-foods treat that is a summer classic. The hand-cranked models will make concocting the frosty cream a social affair, as more hands make the turning light—but even an electric model or one that fits in your fridge will turn out a respectable ice cream.

Follow the directions with your freezer for the mechanics of turning the soupy mixture into ice cream, but enjoy our recipe for a different treat.

1 C. mint leaves, finely diced	2 egg yolks
3 C. cream	Dash of salt
¾ C. sugar	1 C. chocolate, finely grated
1 C. cream	2 t. vanilla

Soak mint leaves in 3 C. cream for 2 hours or overnight. Heat sugar and 1 C. of cream to just warm to dissolve the sugar granules. Add salt. Cool and stir in egg yolks. Add the minted cream, chocolate, and vanilla. Freeze according to ice-cream machine manufacturer's directions.

Wild Strawberry Ice Cream (or Raspberry, Mulberry, Blueberry, etc.)

Serves 6–8

Try this for a fruity, creamy dessert you won't soon forget.

1 qt. berries, hulled, washed, and drained	2 C. cream or half-and-half
1 C. sugar	2 C. whipping cream

Crush the berries with the sugar and allow flavors to blend while chilling. Add cream or half-and-half and whipping cream and freeze as usual. This is a very simple recipe; it needs nothing else to make it delicious.

Wild Strawberry Crêpes

Serves 4

Again, you may substitute any of the other wild fruits or berries you may find for this; it would even be good with persimmon pulp in late fall. I often use blueberries instead of the harder-to-find strawberries.

This can substitute for a delightful Sunday-morning breakfast; it's filling and not even too fattening.

CRÊPES

1 C. milk	2 eggs
¾ C. flour	2 t. butter or margarine

Combine milk, flour, and eggs in a blender container; grease a nonstick skillet or griddle with the butter and drop the thin batter ¼ C. at a time into the skillet, swirling to cover the bottom of the pan. Cook until lightly browned; turn and brown other side. Repeat 7 more times, keeping crêpes warm on a plate.

FILLING

1⅔ C. cottage cheese or ricotta
1 egg
2 T. sugar
1 T. butter or margarine

½ C. wild strawberries (or other fruit)
Dash of cinnamon

Blend cottage or ricotta cheese with egg and sugar; fold in strawberries and cinnamon. Spoon into each crêpe and fold sides in; roll to enclose the filling. Place seam side down in skillet and brown lightly in butter or margarine.

Top with sauce made from yogurt, sugar, vanilla, and berries.

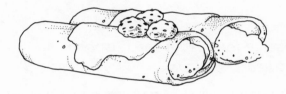

SAUCE

½ C. plain yogurt
1 t. sugar

1 t. vanilla
½ C. berries

Stir sugar and vanilla into plain yogurt until smooth. Fold in berries gently.

Wild Strawberry Cheesecake (or Blueberry, Raspberry, Mulberry, etc.)

Serves 6

Any cheesecake lover will appreciate this recipe; my husband eats huge slices of it at a time. The special flavor of our foraged wildings only adds to his appreciation.

1 lb. cream cheese
3 eggs, well beaten
1 C. sugar
½ C. flour
2 C. sour cream

1 t. fresh lemon juice
Grating of fresh lemon rind
Dash of salt
Prepare or buy 1 graham cracker crust

Mix cream cheese, eggs, salt, and sugar until fluffy. Add flour and mix well; fold in sour cream, lemon juice, and grated lemon rind.

Pour into the graham cracker shell and bake at 350° for 45 minutes. As it nears completion make:

WILD STRAWBERRY GLAZE FOR CHEESECAKE

1 C. wild berries, washed and hulled
½ C. sugar

1 t. vanilla, cognac, or Grand Marnier

Crush berries and mix with sugar; heat gently until the mixture begins to thicken; add vanilla, cognac, or Grand Marnier and stir. Pour over the top of cheesecake while the glaze is still warm. Garnish with a few whole berries.

VARIATIONS

Use any of the other fruits for the glaze; the recipe remains the same. Or add chopped pecans, pine nuts, etc., to the cheese mixture or, finely chopped, to the crust. Cheesecake has always been wonderfully versatile; in this recipe you may also substitute cottage cheese or ricotta for the cream cheese; blend until smooth in your food processor or blender.

Cranberry-Chocolate Torte

Serves 8–10

This elegant dessert wouldn't be out of place at a state dinner party— who's to know you foraged the berries in the bog down the hill? If you can't find wild ones, substitute those from your grocer's.

½ C. water
¾ C. sugar
½ C. chopped pecans, hickory nuts, or walnuts
¼ C. flour
7 oz. dark sweet chocolate, chopped

½ C. butter or margarine
3 large eggs, separated
¾ C. sugar
2 C. cranberries
¼ t. vanilla

In a saucepan, combine cranberries, water, and sugar; cook until mixture thickens. Cool. In another bowl, combine chopped nuts and flour. Melt chocolate and butter in the top of a double boiler until well blended. Set aside.

Beat egg yolks and sugar until thick and light. Add flour and nut mixture to egg yolks and beat on low until just blended. Add the chocolate/butter mixture and stir gently. Stir in cranberries and vanilla by hand. Beat egg whites until fluffy but not dry; fold into cranberry batter.

Pour into a greased and floured 9'' springform pan and bake at 350° for 50–60 minutes. Remove from oven and cool in the pan before trying to remove. Serve with hard sauce (page 173) or *Cranberry Glaze*:

½ C. wild berry jelly   Finely chopped nuts
2 T. cranberry juice

Heat jelly and juice in a small saucepan until jelly melts. Pour over torte; sprinkle with nuts.

Cranberry Coffee Cake
Serves 6–8

This is good with huckleberries, gooseberries, chokecherries, strawberries, or whatever you can find. This is a quick-bread recipe and, as such, should be served warm—it doesn't weather as well as a sourdough or yeast coffee cake.

1½ C. flour   ⅔ C. milk
Dash of salt   ¾ t. grated lemon rind
2 t. baking powder   ¾ C. chopped nuts (optional)
½ C. sugar   1 C. berries
1 egg

Sift flour, salt, and baking powder together. Cream sugar, butter, and egg; add milk. Mix with the dry ingredients and add lemon rind and nuts.

Chop or crush berries and mix with a bit of sugar if they are too tart.

Pour half the batter into a greased pan and top with berries; then add the rest of the batter. Bake at 375° for 25 minutes. Cover with crumb topping, from *Apple/Elderberry Pie*, page 156.

Steamed Christmas Pudding
Serves 6–8

Actually, this is good at any time of the year; it was just a special favorite of my father's at Christmas. I enjoy it more when things are not so hectic. It's an old recipe of my grandmother's brought up-to-date.

1 C. beef suet   1 t. cinnamon
1 C. brown sugar   2 C. chopped and cored crab
3 eggs   apples
1 C. milk   1 C. chopped hickory nuts,
3 T. rum   pecans, walnuts, etc.
1½ C. bread crumbs   ½ C. dried elderberries, recon-
2 t. baking powder   stituted in water (optional)
1 t. ground ginger or 2 t.   2 T. grated orange rind
  ground wild gingerroot

Cream beef suet and sugar together; add eggs. Stir in milk and rum, then add bread crumbs and baking powder. Add ginger, cinnamon, apples, nuts, elderberries, and orange rind. Pour into a well-greased mold or large 3-lb. coffee can and steam for 4 hours. Serve with hard sauce (see below).

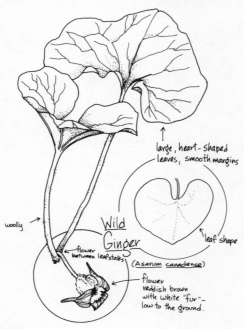

large, heart-shaped leaves, smooth margins

woolly →

Wild
Ginger

leaf shape

flower between leafstalks

(Asarum canadense)

flower reddish brown with white "fur"— low to the ground.

TO STEAM PUDDINGS

Grease mold or pan well, and sprinkle with sugar. Fill only ⅔ full. Put a cooling rack or trivet in the bottom of a heavy pan with a lid and add 1'' of water. Rest the pudding mold or pan on the trivet. Cover the pot and bring to a boil; reduce heat for the rest of the cooking. Check occasionally to make sure the water doesn't boil away.

Serve immediately or store for later, wrapped in cheesecloth and returned to their pans; pour rum or bourbon over the cake until cheesecloth is well soaked. Repeat every few weeks. (Store in the refrigerator or freezer if you prefer.)

HARD SAUCE

1 C. powdered sugar
4 T. butter
Dash of salt
1 T. rum, brandy, bourbon,
    coffee, or lemon juice

Spice with cinnamon, cloves,
    nutmeg, allspice, etc., if desired
1 egg

Beat sugar into butter and add remaining ingredients.

Chapter 10

Beverages:
Hot and Cold
and
Wild All Over

CATHY
JOHNSON

The idea of wild beverages is not so unique—or so wild—as you may think. The fine restaurants of the South have been serving coffee rich with the flavor of dark-roasted chicory for many generations; you can buy the same coffee in your local supermarket.

And who hasn't dropped a sprig of mint into a tall julep—or a cool glass of iced tea, for that matter? Why not let the mint *be* the tea? It's wonderfully cooling on a hot day.

In the Missouri Ozarks and in adjoining mountainous areas, sassafras tea has long been the beverage of choice, especially in the spring, when the spicy elixir is said to thin the blood.

Mormon tea is so called because when these pioneers made their way West looking for religious freedom, they found a tasty wild tea as well. My great-grandmother made many a cup.

Dandelion wine was a great favorite long before Ray Bradbury wrote a book by that name in 1957. My first experience with the homemade version was like drinking bottled sunshine; mellow and golden and laughing. Many of our more established and recognized wines started less elegantly as down-to-earth fermented wild grape juices. Through the centuries, vintners have learned the secrets of taming these wild strains to produce the proper flavor, the proper mix—but a carefully made and well-aged fox grape wine from your own cellar is hard to beat. There's more in that bottle than the tangible elements of fruit and sugar and yeast—there is your own enjoyment of the day you spent foraging in the wild and your care and concern throughout the fermenting and bottling process.

Hot or cold herb or fruit punches are a special treat for a party; serve them with pride and enjoy the conversation; they're great icebreakers.

In the sixties and seventies, more of us became concerned with the effects of caffeine and tannic acid in conventional coffees and teas. It seemed that each year that passed a new herbal tea company appeared to address that concern, and by the eighties the giants of the industry were also producing herbal tea blends. We learned to appreciate rose hip tea, the clovers, and comfrey—and the full, robust flavor of coffee substitutes. Even those of us who still need that morning blast of cof-

COMFREY

fee—and I am one—like a rich and spicy hot drink for later in the day; a drink we won't have to pay for with coffee nerves or insomnia.

Why settle only for what you can buy on the shelf? It's an easy matter to make your own herbal teas; a bit more of a production to concoct coffee substitutes or additives—but it's well worth it. We know our beverages are fresh and pure—we had the pleasure of collecting and processing them ourselves.

An elderly woman from the old country that I once knew brought me a jar of her own "house tea." She had perfected her recipe and picked all the ingredients from wildings that grew by her long country driveway. Through the blue glass of the antique jar I can still see dried red clover blossoms, raspberry leaves, rose petals, rosemary leaves, crumbled bits of comfrey, and who knows what else? Kept tightly sealed and in a dark place, the fragrance is still rich and full, as is the flavor. Why not concoct your own house tea from those flavors that particularly please you? I love the scent of bergamot and pennyroyal, the flavors of wild basil, rose petals, and wood mint—these and many others go into my house tea.

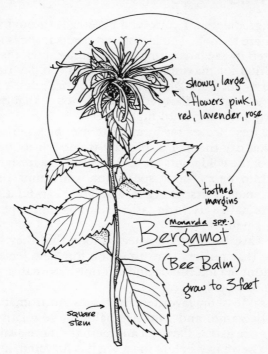

showy, large flowers pink, red, lavender, rose

toothed margins

(Monarda spp.)
Bergamot
(Bee Balm)
grow to 3 feet

square stem

Many of these wild ingredients were also considered beneficial to health and beauty at one time. Comfrey is known by a variety of names, reflecting its long history of use; "the healing herb" is only one. It was also known as "boneset," "bone heal," and "knit bones"; direct links to

its medicinal past. Sassafras was used as a spring tonic, sage to aid digestion, and wild thyme to soothe a cough and comfort bronchitis.

Mr. Koss, an elderly immigrant from Poland whom I met while out
gathering wildings, once told me that his complexion had stayed smooth
and young from a lifelong habit of drinking chickweed tea. And whatever
the cause, his cheeks were indeed as smooth and pink as a baby's.

Whatever their healing properties, these flavors are pleasant enough
to include in your teapot. But do take care; many of our pharmaceuticals
are still extracted from powerful medicinal herbs or have been synthe-
sized from their active ingredients. Foxglove or digitalis is a lovely flowering plant and an indispensable medicine for those who need it for heart
troubles — it is definitely *not* for the teapot, since strength of dosage is
critical. Too much can kill. With the exception of sassafras, I have included only the innocuous and flavorful wild herbs and left the more
powerful medicinals alone.

Suggested Wild Ingredients

You can find ingredients for your wild beverages throughout the year,
if you know where to look. The leaves and petals for teas and punches
are best collected in the late spring and summer; pick them when the
dew has just dried for maximum flavor. But if the day has been long
and you're thirsty for a tall glass of iced mint tea, don't let that stop
you — most of the mints are flavored strongly enough that they'll be delicious from early morning until night.

If you collect fresh leaves for immediate use, pick perhaps ½ C. for
each glass; if you dry them, 1 T. per cup is enough to put in the pot.

Look for any of the wild mints for tea or to add to a fresh fruity punch;
pennyroyal, catnip, peppermint, spearmint, wood mint, bee balm, etc.
Crush a leaf to smell it first to see if it's a good candidate; some mint
family members have very little taste or aroma and others have only
a rank, weedy smell.

Some plants have been used for tea so long that they have taken a
common name that reflects that use; look for New Jersey tea or the
evergreen labrador tea in Canada and our northern states; Mormon tea
in the arid regions of the West.

Oswego tea is one of my favorites; the leaves are aromatic and wildly
minty. Purple bergamot and wild bee balm, close relatives all in the
monarda family, are just as flavorful and perhaps more available to you.

Pick leaves for beverages before the plant has flowered; after that time
some aromatic and volatile oils may be lost to reproduction. Hang in
a hot, dry place to dry — an attic is perfect — or lay them out in a single
layer on clean newspapers. When the leaves are crisp to the touch, crumble and store in airtight containers.

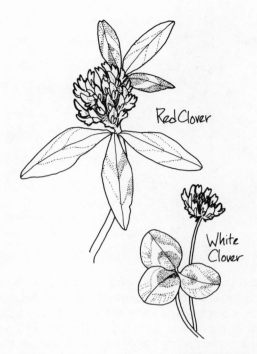

Red Clover

White Clover

Flowers and petals may be preserved in the same way; when I've found a bumper crop of rose petals or clover heads, I spread them out on newspapers in the attic as I did the leaves and allow them to dry thoroughly. You can accomplish the same thing in your oven if it has a pilot light or a very low setting for an electric oven—or use a commercially available dehydrating unit. Some people even have good results drying leaves or petals in a microwave oven; experiment to find the shortest time necessary to achieve complete dryness. If you are using artificial drying means rather than the heat of your attic, the important thing is to maintain a relatively low temperature. Above 150°–200°, flavor is sacrificed as oils are driven off into the air. Your kitchen may *smell* wonderful but your teas will lack flavor.

You may find clovers in your own yard; they have become an integral part of the suburban lawn. Any of the flowering clovers make good beverages: red, yellow, and white sweet clovers; alsike; or crimson. (They can even be ground into a healthful flour additive when thoroughly dried.) Use only fresh, whole blossoms, though—deteriorating sweet clovers develop anticoagulants.

Violets, linden flowers, wild chamomile, and elderblow or flowers may be found throughout the spring and summer, blooming more or less in succession (although chamomile may bloom from May through October).

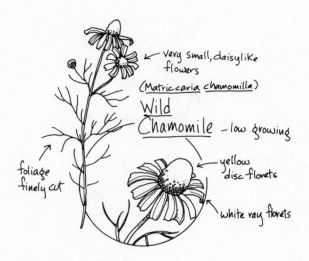

very small, daisylike flowers

(Matriccaria chamomilla)

Wild
Chamomile — low growing

foliage finely cut

yellow disc florets

white ray florets

Barks, roots, and twigs are often used as beverages. Sassafras grows in the southern states; slippery elm grows from New England westward to the Dakotas; and birch lends its wintergreen flavor in our northern states (in mountainous areas as far south as northern Georgia). Gather the twigs only where the plants are plentiful, or gather the inner bark of prunings or the roots of those trees or shrubs that will be cut anyway; harvesting bark indiscriminately can harm or even kill the parent plant.

Fruits make delightful teas, punches, or juice drinks. Look for the hairy red-brown berries of the staghorn or the smooth sumac, but avoid the white berry clusters of the poison sumac. Rose hips are a fruit, too, and may be harvested any time after they turn red and globelike. This is a large family that includes the wrinkled rose, sweetbrier, and multiflora rose. Some rose hips become sweeter after a frost or freeze has nipped them, and others may stay on the bushes nearly till spring. They are an important food source for winter-hungry wildlife, though, so unless they are particularly abundant I'd take only enough for an occasional cup.

In full summer, look for the bramble fruits like blackberry, raspberry, and cloudberries; others to harvest include elderberries, mulberries, grapes, strawberries, and blueberries. Cranberries fruit from August through October; some, like the rose hips, may remain on the plants throughout the winter months. Crush or chop these fruits with water and sweeten to taste for cold fruit juices or punches, hot or cold. These same fruits may be used to make a variety of wild wines, as can some of the flowers (elderblow, dandelion).

Coffee substitutes or additives are available throughout the year. In late summer or fall, sunflower seeds are free for the gathering. Any time of the year is right for the root ''coffees,'' although they may be easier to find in the more temperate seasons. Even in deep winter, chicory and dandelion have small, ground-hugging rosettes of leaves to give away their position; if they are not covered with snow, they should be easy to discover and identify.

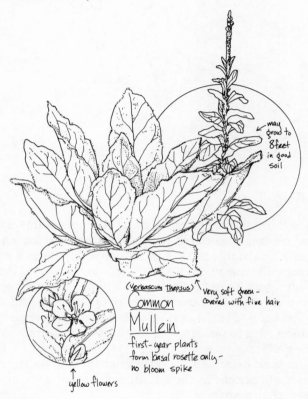

may grow to 8 feet in good soil

(Verbascum thapsus)
Very soft green - covered with fine hair

Common Mullein

first-year plants form basal rosette only - no bloom spike

yellow flowers

Leaf Teas

Teas made from the leaves of wildings follow approximately the same recipe, and that is based as much on your personal taste as on any formal decree. For dried leaves, use from 1 t. to 1 T. per cup of hot water; put directly into your teapot or in a tea ball; cover with boiling water and allow to steep to desired strength. Serve hot or cold; with lemon or milk and sugar if desired.

For fresh leaves, increase the amount used to up to ¾ C. per cup of hot water.

Plants commonly used for leaf teas are raspberry, blackberry, violet, strawberry, chickweed, nettle, wild basil, pitcher sage, any of the bergamots, catnip, mint, comfrey, horehound, gill-over-the-ground, Mormon tea, labrador tea, New Jersey tea, and sweet goldenrod.

Mix or match as you wish; my favorite mixture is comfrey and mint.

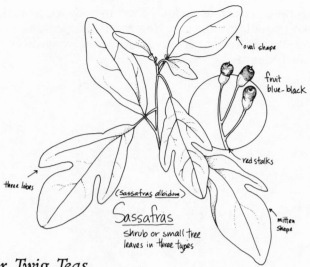

oval shape

fruit
blue-black

red stalks

three lobes

(Sassafras albidum)

Sassafras
shrub or small tree
leaves in three types

mitten
shape

Bark or Twig Teas

These include the sassafras, sweet birch, and slippery elms. The tender inner bark of roots is considered the prime candidate for tea, but you can make quite a palatable brew with tender young twigs. Crush them slightly to release the maximum flavor. Twigs should be used fresh; about a small handful per cup of boiling water will do it. Bark may be used immediately or dried for later use. A tablespoon full of the dried product will make a good cup of tea. Again, sweeten to taste; some people like to add a cinnamon stick to sassafras tea, but I love its natural spiciness—it needs nothing more.

Slippery elm is an extremely mild tea once used to soothe colds and sore throats; it will benefit by the addition of a bit of mint—or perhaps you could use that cinnamon stick here.

Flower Teas

Many of our wildflowers make pleasant additions to the teapot. Clover is said to be quite helpful, but its bland flavor benefits from a bit of mint. Rose petals, fresh or dried, make a delightfully fragrant drink; steep gently for best results, and never boil. Whether you are using rose petals, clover, elderblow, violets, or wild chamomile—or a wildflower tea of your own choosing (bergamot blossoms are fine, too)—use 1 T. of the dried product or ½ C. of fresh for each cup of hot water.

Fruit Teas or Juices

One of my favorite wildings is the staghorn sumac; it grows lustily all over Missouri and most of the rest of the country as well. When I was growing up I was told this was the poison sumac and avoided it as I did poison ivy. Years later I discovered it is the white-berried sumac that causes contact dermatitis (itching) and that the furry red-brown berries of staghorn and smooth sumac make a wonderful wild drink. Of course if I had known my Indian great-great-grandmother, she could have told me that long ago; the tart drink was a great favorite with the original occupants of this country, who dried the sumac heads for year-round use.

Bruise sumac berries (leave them right on their heads) in a large pot of water—hot or cold, it doesn't matter. When the water is pleasantly sunset colored, remove the stalks and stems that are left and carefully strain out any remaining berries and hairs—you will want to use several layers of cheesecloth or muslin. The tart juice may be sweetened with honey or sugar, spiced with cinnamon and nutmeg, mellowed with a bit of milk, and served hot or cold. The malic acid in sumac berries—the same principle that makes green apples so tart—makes a wonderful lemony drink.

Rose hips work well as a hot or cold tea or punch, as well; crush and steep as always.

Cranberries, as I have mentioned elsewhere, have a special place in my heart—you can make two products at the same time, always handy when you are busy. I chop cranberries for breads, salads, or sauces by dumping them into the blender. Then I add cold water and push the "chop" button. Voilà—seconds later I have finely chopped berries and a delicious (if tart) juice for drinking. It's delightfully pink and refreshing, but it does need rather copious amounts of sugar to make it palatable—at least since I am forced to buy my rather unripe berries at the local supermarket. I drain the berries over a generous bowl where I collect my "free" cranberry tea.

Some recipes call for cooking the cranberries for a more mellow flavor; see our section on punches for such a process.

Other fruit juices or teas are just as simply made; wild strawberries, raspberries, grapes, and elderberries can all make delightful and refreshing drinks. Simply mash or crush the berries and strain to make your juice. (Or blend them if they are not too seedy—large seeds might tend to be broken up by the blender's blades—not always a good idea since cherry pits contain a poison and other seeds are unpleasantly rough.) Sweeten if necessary.

House Tea

What goes to make up your house tea—and therefore your own unique recipe—depends largely on where you live, the seasons in which you are collecting, and your own tastes. If you are fond of mint, you'll go heavy on the minty notes. If you find a cache of roses, you may add a strong flower flavor to your tea; later in the season, that same cache will give your tea a tart rose hip flavor and a lovely carmine color. You may find very few heads of yellow sweet clover but lots of elder flowers. It may be that from year to year your house tea will change; one year you may be too busy to even get out of the house to forage in the summer and you may miss out on the plants that flower then. Don't worry—whatever goes into your blend will be delicious as long as you choose flavors that please you and go well with each other.

My own house tea generally contains these things:

2-3	handfuls of raspberry leaves	1	C. comfrey leaves
2-3	heads of elderblow (flowers)	1	C. red clover heads
1	handful of whatever wild mint I can find—usually downy wood mint	¼	C. bergamot leaves and flower heads
1	C. rose petals	¼	C. wild basil

All ingredients are picked as they are at their height of flavor and dried; a house tea is an ongoing affair, like a potpourri or a rumtopf—I keep adding to it as the months pass and plants appear or blossom. Again, 1 heaping T. makes a cup of tea.

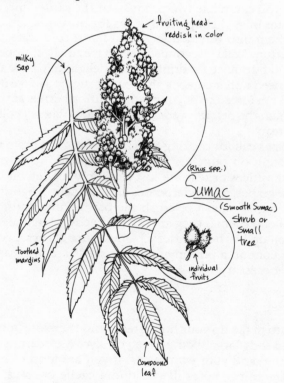

fruiting head—reddish in color

milky sap

(Rhus spp.)

Sumac

(Smooth Sumac)
Shrub or small tree

toothed margins

individual fruits

compound leaf

Sumac-ade Punch

Serves 8–10

Try this for a summer party; the mixed flavors are quite delicious.

8 C. sumac-ade, made as for
    juice or tea
Sugar to taste—at least a cup
2 T. bergamot leaves

2 cinnamon sticks
Grating of wild gingerroot
Slices of lemon to garnish

Heat all ingredients together gently to encourage blending. Adjust proportions of sugar if need be. Serve hot or chill and garnish with lemon slices.

Hot Cranberry Punch

Serves 8–10

This is made by a friend, Ginger Donohue, who often serves it around the holidays.

1 qt. cranberries
2 qts. water
2 C. sugar
1 stick cinnamon

1 t. cloves
2 C. water
1 C. orange juice
2 T. lemon juice, freshly squeezed

Cook cranberries and 2 qts. of water together; mash berries and strain. Boil sugar and spices in 2 C. water and remove the spices. Mix orange juice and lemon juice and add to other ingredients. Serve hot with vodka or other spirits, if desired.

Pineapple Punch

Serves 14–16

Another punch that is good hot or cold, I first had this at a potluck luncheon at the home of an herbalist.

1   46-oz. can of pineapple juice
5   sprigs fresh or 1 T. dried
      rosemary
½ C. sugar
2   C. sassafras tea (optional)
1   t. dried bergamot leaves

2   T. gill-over-the-ground leaves
     (optional)
1½ C. lemon juice
2   C. water
1   16-oz. bottle ginger ale
3   sprigs fresh mint, if available

Bring 2 C. of the pineapple juice to a boil and add rosemary; steep 5 minutes. Add sugar, sassafras tea, and remaining ingredients. Chill or serve hot in an electric pot, if desired; garnish with mint and lemon slices.

Rosemary is quite a strong herb; use too much and you will overpower the more delicate flavors.

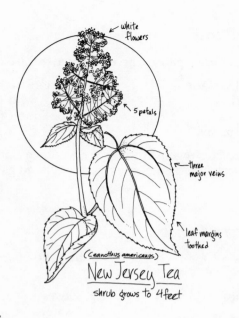

← white
flowers

← 5 petals

← three
major veins

← leaf margins
toothed

(Ceanothus americanus)

New Jersey Tea

shrub grows to 4 feet

Wild Wassail

Serves 14–18

Another hot holiday punch that could be served chilled in a big punch bowl in midsummer, if you like.

1 qt. hot strong oriental or herb tea (New Jersey tea is the wilding said to taste closest to the imported orientals)

1 qt. apple cider or juice (this is good with juice made from wild crab apples)

1 qt. cranberry juice (see recipe, page 183)

1 C. sugar

2 C. orange juice

3 cinnamon sticks, broken

Small handful of cloves

Combine all ingredients and bring to a boil. Add punch to your punch, if you like, with rum, vodka, or a white wine. Slice an orange and float on top.

Wild Coffees

Wild sunflower seeds—or domestic ones, for that matter—have been used for coffee additives or substitutes for generations. Hull them and roast them in a medium oven until dark brown, then grind to your desired fineness. Use 1 T. per cupful of water and brew your favorite way—I perk mine.

The root "coffees" are a bit more trouble to make than the seed-based brews, but they are admirable substitutes. Dig dandelion or chicory roots;

look for the largest plants you can find. Scrub well or peel, slice in ⅛"-thick slices, and roast in a 350° oven until dark brown. Grind and add to your store-bought coffee for that old New Orleans taste or use alone for their own unique flavor.

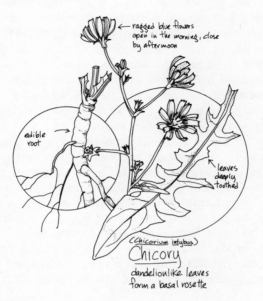

← ragged blue flowers open in the morning, close by afternoon

edible root →

leaves deeply toothed

(Chicorium intybus)
Chicory
dandelionlike leaves form a basal rosette

Spiced "Coffee"

Serves 6–8

2 C. water
1 star anise
1 small piece wild gingerroot
1 T. sassafras bark
1 stick cinnamon

1 T. roasted barley, ground
1 T. roasted malt, ground
1 t. allspice (whole)
4 C. hot wild "coffee"

Bring water to a boil; steep anise, gingerroot, sassafras, cinnamon, barley, malt, and allspice for 10 minutes or so; strain out solids and add to hot "coffee." Proportions may vary according to number of people to be served.

Serve with sugar and cream or spike with Irish whiskey and whipped cream for a wild Irish coffee.

Wild Wines

"Wine maketh glad the heart," the psalmist said, and a day spent gathering a gallon or two of butter yellow dandelion heads — and the reward reaped at the end of the simple, if slow, wine-making process — makes for a merry heart as well.

Many wild plants have been used in wine making. Elderberries (and elder flowers, called elderblow), crab apples, cranberries, raspberries, blackberries, strawberries, rose petals, and even herbs like coltsfoot and mint have found their way into home-vintner's bottles.

A variety of wild grapes are popular with home wine makers, from scuppernong to fox grapes. Someone has said the whitish "bloom" on grapes teaches them what they are to do—the bloom is made up of wild yeasts and the grapes will ferment on their own. Most wild fruits or flowers, however, need the addition of yeast and of sugar or honey for the yeast to feed on to become wine. This interaction between yeast and sugars is what actually produces the alcoholic content of the wine.

The process of wine making can be as sophisticated as you care to make it. Any good wine shop can acquaint you with air locks, wine yeasts, and hydrometers and will probably have a range of books on the subject as well. A plastic air lock will ensure that gases produced in the fermentation process can escape, but no air can reenter the fermentation chamber. (This may produce vinegar rather than wine; fruit vinegars are still a useful and delicious product, though, so don't be too quick to throw out all your work. Taste it first to see if it wouldn't add a special touch to salads or sweet-and-sour dishes.)

"Fining" materials clear the wine and a hydrometer will determine the wine's sugar content, telling you when to decant and bottle the new wine. Commercial wine yeast is said to produce a slightly higher alcoholic content.

When you add your "must" (fruit juice, flower heads, etc.) to the yeast and sugars, there will be a great deal of bubbling as the wine works and carbon dioxide is released. Usually the slowing of bubbles to 1 per minute is the sign that the first step is finished and the air lock, if you have used one, may be removed. Then it is time to lightly cork the jug and let the wine mellow in a cool place. After a month or so you may want to rack the wine, that is, to siphon it into sterilized bottles, being careful not to disturb the sediment that has settled to the bottom. Store your homemade wine with the bottles on their sides so that the corks will remain moist and tight.

I've included recipes only for those wild-wine ingredients familiar to novice and expert alike, but there are many others that have been successfully used by our forebears, including the original occupants, the American Indians. Coltsfoot, the mints, sage and other herbs, wild cherries, agave, mesquite and saguaro, and even the tart gooseberry have found their way into the must.

You may prefer the simpler methods used by our forebears; my recipes reflect that simplicity. A clean crock, supplemented by a gallon jar or two, measuring cups, yeast, and sugar are all you really need to produce a serviceable and hospitable brew. (That and the blessings from the Department of the Treasury's Bureau of Alcohol, Tobacco and Firearms.

Obtain two copies of their wine-maker's form, fill them out, and return them for permission to make up to 200 gals. of wine a year. There is no cost for this permit.)

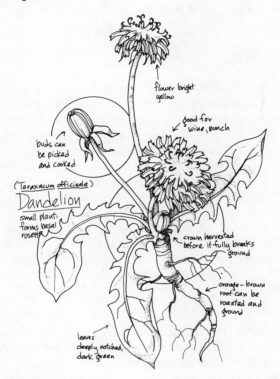

flower bright yellow

good for wine, punch

buds can be picked and cooked

(Taraxacum *officinale*)
Dandelion
small plant, forms basal rosette

crown harvested before it fully breaks ground

orange-brown root can be roasted and ground

leaves deeply notched, dark green

Dandelion Wine

Yields 1 gal.

Dandelion is a favorite among the wild wines, like summer sunshine captured in a bottle. It contains all the cheerfulness of these small yellow flowers and seems a fitting revenge on the ubiquitous pests of lawn and garden.

Pick a gal. of dandelion flowers on a dry morning, when strength and flavor are at their best. Just pluck the heads from the stems—further trimming is unnecessary. Put them in a 2-gal. crock and pour a gal. of boiling water over them. Cover and let stand for 3 days. Strain through cheesecloth and squeeze the last of the juice from the flowers. Put the liquid in a large pot, add a small piece of gingerroot (½'' or less), and the rind and juice of 3 oranges and 1 lemon. Add 3 lbs. of sugar and simmer for 20 minutes. Return to the crock and let cool to lukewarm, then add 1 T. of yeast spread on a piece of rye toast to float on top of the liquid.

Cover and keep in a warm place 6–7 days, strain out the solids, and pour the new wine into a clean gallon jug, corking it loosely with cotton. Store in a dark cool place for 3 weeks, decant into sterilized bottles, cork it, and forget it—at least until Christmas. Longer aging will improve the flavor, of course, so if you can wait for a sample it is well worth your patience.

Elderberry Wine

Yields 6 qts.

Like dandelions, elderberry is a wonderfully useful plant. It will give you two kinds of wine for your cellar, a rich, dark wine from the berries and a delightful, pale yellow from the flower or elderblow. The plant is easiest to spot along roadsides in July and August, when the heads are heavy with blackish purple berries.

Remove the larger stems from a gal. of elderberries, add a gal. of water, and bring to a boil for ½ hour. Cool to lukewarm and strain out the berries. Add enough water that you have previously boiled and cooled to make 6 qts. of liquid. Add 6 C. of sugar, 2 thinly sliced lemons, 1 lb. of raisins, and 1 T. of dry yeast dissolved in a cup of warm water.

Let the wine "work" in a clean crock for 2 weeks, well covered. Strain and siphon into sterilized bottles. Cork lightly. When the cork no longer pops up, drive it home and let your elderberry wine age for a year.

Elderblow Wine

Yields 3 gals.

Raisins are used in this recipe to add character and flavor. Elderblow wine is delicious cold; use champagne glasses for a festive touch.

Put ½ gal. of elder flowers (easy to harvest since they grow in large, composite flower heads called umbels; the smaller stems need not be removed) and 10 C. of sugar in a 3-gal. crock and fill to not quite full with water you have boiled and cooled to lukewarm. Add 1 T. of yeast. Cover lightly and let stand for 9 days. Put 1 lb. of raisins in each of 3 clean 1-gal. jars and strain the wine into them in equal amounts. Cap loosely and store in a cool dark place for 6 months. Carefully decant into sterilized bottles, cork tightly, and try to forget it for another year.

Wild Strawberry Wine

Yields 1 gal.

Strawberry wine has the delicate and elusive taste of early summer sealed in its ruby depths. It has very little in common with commercial strawberry wine beyond the name itself, and best results are obtained by using tiny wild strawberries. Domestic berries may be substituted if you are unable to find enough of the wild variety—or can't resist eating them all out-of-hand.

Mash 4 qts. of berries in a crock and cover with boiling water. Let set for 24 hours to extract the full flavor. Squeeze the pulp through cheesecloth to strain out seeds and solids.

Add 2½ lbs. of sugar to the juice and simmer for 10 minutes. When cool, return to the crock and add enough boiling water to make 1 gal. Add 1 T. of yeast. Ferment for 2 weeks, lightly covered. Skim, strain, and bottle in sterilized bottles for 3 weeks. Cork lightly. When the bubbles have slowed almost to a stop, drive home the corks gently and store as long as possible. A year is considered the minimum, so wine making may be seen as an exercise in both patience and faith.

Blackberry Wine   *Yields 6 qts.*

This is a natural for a mulled-wine warmer on cold winter days—the finished product is heated gently (never boiled) and sweetened to taste, flavored with 5 or 6 cinnamon sticks and perhaps an allspice berry or two.

The wine itself is, again, simple to make—if time consuming. Mash 6 qts. of berries and add 6 qts. of water. Boil gently for 10 minutes and let cool. Strain the juice through cheesecloth and add 2 C. of sugar for each qt. of juice. Pour into your large crock and float 1 T. of yeast spread on rye toast on top. Cover and store for 1 week, then carefully pour off into gallon jugs and work with cotton. Keep in a cool place until fermentation stops. Carefully decant into sterilized bottles and seal. Store until New Year's, at least. Then try it mulled and spicy on a snowy night.

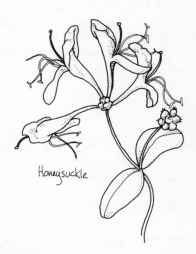

Honeysuckle

Honeysuckle Wine   *Yields 1 gal.*

Honeysuckle makes a rich, amber wine—a small glass is usually sufficient. (For a more delicate wine, substitute rose petals for honeysuckle flowers.)

Pick 1 gal. of flowers, then cover them with a gal. of boiling water.

Let simmer for 15 minutes, then cool and strain. Add enough boiling water to the liquid to make 1 gal., if you have lost volume in the heating process. Stir in 2½ lbs. of sugar, 2 C. of white raisins, 2 thinly sliced lemons, and 1 T. of yeast dissolved in a cup of warm water. Add a small piece of gingerroot—about ½'' long.

Pour into a clean crock and let ferment, lightly covered, for 2 weeks. This may be stirred daily. Strain into sterilized bottles and cork. Store in a cool dark place, checking the corks occasionally—when they no longer pop back up when gently depressed, drive them home. Seal the top with paraffin, if desired.

Mead

Yields 1½ gals.

Mead was a popular drink with our ancestors and deserves a revival. Some writers call it honey wine, although it is a bit different in character from a true wine.

Add 1 gal. of water to 4 lbs. of honey and boil slowly until well mixed, then skim and cool. Add 1 15-oz. box of raisins, 6 cloves, 2 sticks of cinnamon, and the juice and peel of 1 lemon and 1 orange. Add 1 T. of yeast dissolved in a cup of warm water to provide the "ferment."

Pour into a clean crock and keep in a warm place, lightly covered, for 3 weeks, stirring daily. Strain out the solids and store in sterilized glass jars, lightly corked. When all fermentation has ceased and bubbles no longer rise to the surface, decant into sterilized bottles and seal.

Wild Beers

Many of the "beers" are only mildly alcoholic and really considered soft drinks by the Miller-time crowd. But in the old days, root beer was really made from roots collected from the forests and fields; and more than drugstore cowboys bellied up to the bar to order a frosty sarsaparilla. Lesser known, perhaps, are the birch and persimmon brews familiar to our forebears.

Beer making requires some special procedures; heavy glass bottles are used to store your home brew and a special bottle capper is used to cap the fizzy drink. Keep your brew in a basement or other low-traffic area, and put the bottles in large cardboard boxes or surround the area with a screened enclosure—bottles of homemade beer have been known to burst and fling shards of glass in all directions. With the boxes or screens, at least the damage is confined to a controlled area and pieces of glass aren't flying by just as you go down to stoke the furnace.

Sarsaparilla

Yields 5 gals.

I like the more flavorful brew made from mixing ingredients, but you can make this with sarsaparilla root alone, if you prefer.

1 qt. of sarsaparilla roots or
    1 qt. mixed of sarsaparilla,
    spikenard, and sassafras
    roots
Boiling water to cover
4 lbs. sugar

5 T. vanilla, if you have used
    only sarsaparilla
1 gal. of warm water
1 T. yeast
1 t. sugar
Water to make 5 gals.

Bring roots to a boil with the water to cover; simmer all day or overnight in a covered kettle, making sure the water doesn't boil away. Cool and strain into a large crock. Add sugar and vanilla; add 1 gal. of water and stir well. Dissolve yeast and 1 t. of sugar in a little warm water; add to the crock and add enough warm water to make 5 gals. Stir well and let stand 2–3 hours. Siphon into strong, heavy returnable bottles and cap tightly. Store bottles on their sides at room temperature, about 70°, for 4 days.

Carefully remove bottles to a cool dark place, stand them up, and let them alone for about a week; they will settle and clear as well as develop flavor. Chill and enjoy.

Persimmon Beer

Yields 5 gals.

For Dan at our wood stove company, I include this recipe for persimmon beer—he has lots of the late autumn fruits and a fondness for brew.

10 lbs. wheat bran   Boiling water to fill a 5-gal. crock
1 gal. of very ripe persimmon   1 T. dry yeast
      pulp

Mix bran and pulp together and bake in "corn" pones (small, longish cakes) until very brown and firm throughout. Break it up and grind it with your food processor, blender, or a food grinder equipped with a coarse blade. Put this into a 5-gal. crock and cover with boiling water nearly up to the rim of the crock.

Allow to cool to lukewarm, then mix yeast with a bit of the brew and return to the crock. Cover with a clean cloth and let it brew; after a week (give or take a day or two) it will calm down. When it stops working, bottle it in heavy glass bottles and cap it tightly. Keep in a cool dark place for about 3 weeks.

Birch Beer   *Yields 5 gals.*

If you have a good source of birch trees (*Betula lenta*), you'll enjoy this fine, wintergreen-flavored drink.

1 gal. of honey   4 qts. of fresh twigs, cut fine
4 gals. of birch sap (tap as for   1 T. of yeast
      birch or maple syrup in the
      early spring)

Boil honey and birch sap together in a large pot; pour over birch twigs in the bottom of a 5-gal. crock. Cool and strain out birch twigs, then return the liquid to the crock. Dissolve yeast in a little warm water and stir into the contents of the crock.

Cover with a clean cloth and allow to ferment until the cloudiness begins to settle; depending on the weather, this will probably take about a week. Siphon off carefully into strong glass bottles; disturb as little of the sediment as possible. Cap tightly and store in a cool dark place. This will taste wonderful on a hot day; chill it well to serve.

Gilly Ale   *Yields 8 gals.*

My ancestors from the old country would have enjoyed this light malt beer made from one of my favorite wildings, gill-over-the-ground. My aunt assured me when I took a start of her gill that I'd be sorry as it took over the backyard. I haven't been; I love it in teas and other drinks, in salads, and in the stew pot—it has an interesting spicy flavor that makes walking in the yard a real pleasure, as my feet crush the small scalloped leaves and send that fragrance upwards.

1	pt. fresh gill-over-the-ground (or ground ivy) leaves, washed and drained	4	lemons, thinly sliced

1   pt. fresh gill-over-the-ground   4   lemons, thinly sliced
       (or ground ivy) leaves,   1   3-lb. can of malt
       washed and drained   1   T. dry yeast
Water to cover   2   gals. of warm water
4½ lbs. sugar   Water to make 8 gals.

Boil leaves in water to cover for 10–15 minutes. Strain to a 10-gal. crock. Add water, sugar, lemons, and malt; stir well. Add yeast which has been dissolved in a little warm water. Allow to ferment for 5–7 days, at room temperature.

When the bubbles have almost stopped (if you use a hydrometer, the reading will be 1.005), bottle in heavy glass bottles and cap tightly. Store upright for 6 weeks in a cool dark place where the bottles are not likely to be disturbed. Chill well before serving; you may have to develop a taste for this one.

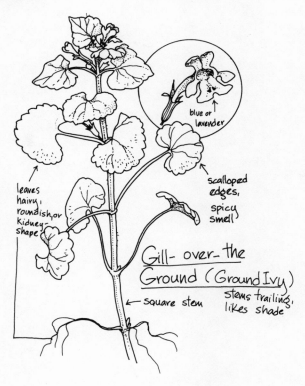

blue or lavender

leaves hairy, roundish, or kidney shape

scalloped edges, spicy smell

Gill- over- the Ground (Ground Ivy)

stems trailing, likes shade

← square stem

A Concise Chart
to Common Wild Edibles

The following is a list of commonly available wild foods. This chart cannot stand in for a field guide, of course; it is simply intended to act as a cook's introduction to some of the most common edibles. Look here to find the Latin name of what you have collected and cross-reference with a more complete source to confirm your identification. Use the chart also to find season, listed as Sp. (spring), Su. (summer), F. (fall), and W. (winter). Some wildings may have more than one edible part or season to collect; the chart will reflect that as well.

You will find here, too, any cautions found in my research; these reflect the latest information at press time and were checked both with available field guides and with Dr. James Duke, botanist with the USDA. But of course, ordinary caution should be the rule here, as well—taste a bit at first to check for allergic reactions or other signs of discomfort. Certain sensitive individuals may contract dermatitis from wild plants that will have no effect on others. Those sensitive to colchicine may experience gastric distress when sampling daylily roots or tubers. And of course, we all must be careful to collect in unpolluted areas, where chemical herbicides and pesticides are not in use, where automobile exhaust has not settled on plants, or downstream from a water treatment chemical plant.

Common Name	Latin	Where Found
Acorn	*Quercus spp.*	Mixed hardwood forest, throughout U.S.
Amaranth	*Amaranthus spp.*	Backyards, gardens, fencerows, waste ground
Arrowhead	*Sagittaria spp.*	Low water, ponds, lakes, bogs, swamps
Asparagus	*Asparagus officinalis*	Fencerows, old farmsteads, abandoned gardens
Basswood	*Tilia americana*	Mixed hardwood forest
Bellwort	*Uvularia spp.*	Moist woods, north-facing hillsides
Bergamot	*Monarda spp.*	Moist woods, weedy patches, near water
Birch	*Betula spp.*	Mixed woods
Blackberry	*Rubus spp.*	Sunny thickets, edge of woods
Black Haw	*Viburnum prunifolium*	Open woods, weedy patches, along roadsides
Black Raspberry	*Rubus spp.*	Edge of woods, old fields, country roads
Black Walnut	*Juglans nigra*	Rich woods, valleys, open woods
Blueberry	*Vaccinium spp., Gaylussacia spp.*	Acid soils, bogs, open woods, thickets

Season	Parts Used	Cautions
Su., F.	Kernels	Except for the mild white oaks, tannic acid makes acorns impossible to eat without processing; tannic acid toxic in large doses.
Sp. F.	Leaves Seeds	None found.
Late Su., F., W.	Tubers	Do not confuse with toxic atamasco lily (*Zephyranthes atamasco*).
Early S.	Shoots	None found.
Sp. Su.	Buds Flowers, fruits	None found.
Early Sp.	Shoots (discard leaves).	Be sure of identification, gather only where abundant.
Sp.–F.	Leaves Flowers	None found.
Late W., Sp. Anytime	Sap Twigs and inner bark for tea or ground as flour substitute.	None found.
Sp., S.	Peeled shoots, berries, leaves	None found, but do *dry* leaves for tea.
Late Su., F.	Fruits	None found.
Sp., Su.	Peeled shoots, berries, leaves	None found, but do *dry* leaves for tea.
F.	Nut meats (hulls used to dye cloth).	None found.
Su., F.	Fruits	None for blueberries, but do not confuse with cathartic buckthorn.

Common Name	Latin	Where Found
Butternut	*Juglans cinerea*	Mixed hardwood forest
Catbrier	*Smilax spp.*	Woodlands, edges of woods, along roads
Cattail	*Typha latifolia*	Edges of ponds, lakes, low-water areas, moist roadsides
Chamomile, wild	*Matricaria chamomilla*	Roadsides, old fields, waste places
Chanterelle Mushroom	*Cantharellus spp.*	Mixed hardwood and coniferous forests
Chickweed	*Stellaria spp., Cerastium spp.*	Disturbed ground, waste places, gardens, yards, roadsides
Chicory	*Cichorium intybus*	Waste places, roadsides, uncut fields
Chive, wild	Various *Allium spp.*	Sunny places, waste places, lawns, gardens
Comfrey	*Symphytum officinale*	Waste places, old fields, gardens
Crab Apple, other wild apples	*Pyrus spp.*	Thickets, old fields, edge of woods
Cranberry	*Vaccinium spp.*	Acid or peaty bogs, rocky regions, depending on spp.

Season	Parts Used	Cautions
F.	Nut meats (American Indians made syrup from sap and ground nuts for flour).	None found.
Early Sp.–late Su.	Tender tips	None found; do not eat thorny parts.
Various parts, year-round	Rootstocks, young shoots, pollen, fruiting heads or buds, young bloom spike	None found.
Sp.–F.	Ripe flower heads	None, but wait to collect until flower heads are easily identified.
Late Sp.–late F.	Fruiting body	Check for chanterelles' strong fruity aroma.
Early Sp.–early Su.	Stems, leaves, flowers	Harvest only where chemical fertilizers or herbicides are not in use.
Early Sp. F.–early Sp.	Leaves Rootstocks	None found.
Early Sp.–late F.	Leaves	None found, but do check for hollow leaves and characteristic odor.
Early Sp.	Leaves, flowers	Do not use root as a medicinal or leaves as *primary* potherb; found to contain alkaloids of the pyrrolizicine group (leaves in lesser concentrations); hepatotoxic and possibly hepatocarcinogenic. At this writing, no *human* illness ever found to be caused by eating comfrey.
Late Su.–early W.	Ripe fruits	None found.
Late Su.–early W.	Ripe fruits	None found.

Common Name	Latin	Where Found
Dandelion	*Taraxacum officinale*	Lawns, gardens, road-sides, parks
Dayflower	*Commelina spp.*	Rich woods, waste places, edges of yards, gardens
Daylily	*Hemerocallis fulva*	Roadsides, old gardens
Dock	*Rumex spp.*	Waste places, disturbed ground, fencerows
Elderberry	*Sambucus canadensis*	Thickets, roadsides, fencerows
Fern	*Pteridium* and *Pteretis spp.*	Moist woods, wet or swampy areas, stream banks; bracken fern even found in dry or burned-over areas
Garlic, wild	*Allium spp.*	Open woods, yards, prairies, waste places
Gill-over-the-Ground	*Glechoma hederacea*	Lawns, gardens, road-sides, parks

Season	Parts Used	Cautions
Various parts, year-round	Crowns, buds, leaves, roots	Gather only where chemical fertilizers or herbicides are not in use.
Sp.–early Su.	Leaves, stems	None found.
Various parts, year-round	Tubers, shoots, buds, flowers	Roots or tubers may be laxative to people sensitive to colchicine.
Early Sp.–early Su.; Late Su.	Leaves Seeds	Oxalic acid in leaves of some spp. may be harmful if overindulged.
Early Su., Su.	Flowers, buds Ripe fruits *only* (do *not* use leaves or canes).	Identify carefully; use only black or blue elderberry—red elderberry is poisonous; avoid stems or canes if you are sensitive to dermatitis.
Early Sp.	Young shoots, called fiddleheads	Do not use after they are taller than 6''–8''; confirm identification—do not confuse with water hemlock or poison hemlock, which also have delicate foliage but no "fiddlehead." Studies in Europe, where bracken fern is eaten often, show it may be carcinogenic in large quantities.
Early Sp. Su. F., W.	Young leaves Flowers and bulblets Bulbs	Check for strong garlic odor; do not use if it is not present.
Early Sp.–F.	Leaves, tender stems, flowers	None found.

Common Name	Latin	Where Found
Ginger, wild	*Asarum canadense*	Open woods, ravines, base of cliffs
Goldenrod	*Solidago odora*	Roadsides, waste places, old gardens
Gooseberry (and Currant)	*Ribes spp.*	Some spp. prefer dry, rocky areas, others like damp areas.
Grape, wild	*Vitis spp.*	Open woods, thickets, stream banks, fencerows, roadsides
Ground-Cherry (Husk-Tomato)	*Physalis spp.*	Open dry ground, waste places, roadsides, sandy areas
Groundnut	*Apios americana*	Thickets, rich soils, stream banks, open woods
Hickory	*Carya spp.*	Various habitats, from riverbanks to dry upland slopes
Jerusalem Artichoke	*Helianthus tuberosus*	Waste ground, roadsides, damp ground, prairies
Lamb's-quarter	*Chenopodium album*	Waste ground, disturbed ground, abandoned gardens, farmyards
Leek, wild, or Ramp	*Allium tricoccum*	Rich moist soil, mixed hardwood forest
Locust, Black	*Robinia pseudoacacia*	Thickets, dry or rocky woods

Season	Parts Used	Cautions
F., W.	Rootstocks, as seasoning or candy	On protected species lists in many states; best to harvest edible roots after flower production is past.
Su., F.	Leaves and flowers for tea	None found.
Su.–early F.	Fruits	Be sure berries are tender before harvesting for "green" gooseberries; watch out for prickles.
Late Su., F.	Fruits, (young, tender leaves may be harvested in early Sp.).	Do not confuse with poisonous Canada moonseed, which has bitter, ill-tasting black fruit with flat, crescent-shaped seeds.
Su.–F.	Fully ripe fruits (yellow, reddish, or purplish, *soft*)	Leaves and unripe fruits contain toxins.
Year-round	Tubers	None found.
F.	Nut meats	None found.
Early Sp.	Sap for syrup	
F.–early Sp.	Tubers	None found.
Sp.–F.	Leaves, shoots	None found.
Late Su.–F.	Seeds	
Sp.	Leaves	Check for distinctive onion smell.
Year-round	Bulbs	
Su.	White flowers *only*	Use only the flower of black locust; *all* other parts toxic.

Common Name	Latin	Where Found
Locust, Honey	*Gleditsia triacanthos*	Roadsides, mixed hardwood forests, fields
Lotus	*Nelumbo lutea*	Quiet water, ponds, lakes
Maple	*Acer spp.*	Moist woods, base of bluffs, upland glades, streamsides
Mayapple	*Podophyllum peltatum*	Moist woods, dry thickets, open woods
Milkweed	*Asclepias syriaca*	Old fields, wet meadows, prairies, open woods, roadsides
Mint	*Various spp.— Mentha, Monarda, Nepeta cataria, Pycnanthemum spp.*	According to spp., in damp or rocky soil, old fields, thickets, woods, clearings
Morel Mushroom	*Morchella spp.*	Old-growth forest, abandoned orchards, fencerows
Mormon Tea	*Ephedra spp.*	Arid, rocky regions, Southwest desert, western U.S.
Mulberry	*Morus spp.*	Rich woods, old fields, roadsides, edges of streams

Season	Parts Used	Cautions
Su.	Pulp of unripe pods	Do not confuse with fat, stubby pods of Kentucky coffee tree, which are toxic unripe.
Early Sp. F. F.–Sp.	Leaves Seeds Tubers	Harvest in unpolluted waters.
Late W. Early Sp. Sp.–Su.	Sap Inner bark Fruits	None found.
Late Su.	Ripe fruits *only*	Use only soft, ripe fruits; all other parts are toxic.
Early Sp. Early Su. Su.	Young shoots Unopened buds Flowers, young, tender pods	Process all parts in several changes of *boiling* water to remove bitter, milky sap. (Raw sap may be toxic if ingested. Do not use related butterfly weed.)
Sp.–F.	Leaves, stems, flowers	None found, but be aware that the furry medicinal horehound will make you sweat.
Sp.	Fruiting body	Confirm identification; use only fresh, firm specimens. Do not confuse with *Gyromitra spp.* and *Verpa spp.*, convoluted-capped (not pitted, like morels) mushrooms known as false morels.
Year-round	Stems, twigs, leaves for tea; seeds as a bitter gruel	None found.
Sp. Su.	Young shoots, cooked Ripe fruits	Unripe fruit and raw shoots may be hallucenogenic.

Common Name	Latin	Where Found
Mullein	*Verbascum thapsus*	Widespread; waste places, edges of gardens, abandoned fields, roadsides
Mustard	*Brassica spp.*, *Cruciferae* Alien Garlic Mustard is *Alliaria officinalis*	Waste places, fields, roadsides, thickets
Nettle	*Urtica spp.*, *Laportea canadensis* (Wood Nettle)	Open woodlands, thickets, roadsides, edges of fields or gardens
New Jersey Tea	*Ceanothus americanus*	Prairies, open woods, thickets, roadsides
Pawpaw	*Asimina triloba*	Mixed forests, along streams, ravines
Pecan	*Carya illinoensis*	Mixed hardwood forests
Peppergrass	*Lepidium spp.*	Waste places, yards, fields, roadsides
Persimmon	*Diospyros virginiana*	Rocky or dry woods, old fields, prairies
Plantain	*Plantago spp.*	Yards, gardens, waste places

Season	Parts Used	Cautions
Sp.–F.	Dried leaves as tea	Mullein may have a digitalic action; use sparingly.
Early Sp. Su.	Young leaves Flower buds, young seedpods, seeds	Strong flavor may cause gastric distress if overindulged.
Early Sp.	Young leaves, shoots as cooked vegetable	Wear gloves to pick; stinging hairs cause temporary discomfort (cooking neutralizes sting).
Su.	Dried leaves	None found, but this plant is on endangered species lists in many states; check before you pick.
F.	Ripe fruits	Sensitive individuals may have allergic reactions from eating or touching pawpaws.
F.–early W. Early Sp.	Nut meats Sap for syrup	None found.
Sp. Su.	Young leaves Seedpods, seeds	None found.
Sp. Early W.	Leaves for tea Fully ripe fruits	Wait to collect until after hard frost; unripe fruit will cause your mouth to pucker like alum.
Early Sp. Sp.–F.	Young leaves for greens Mature leaves for tea	None found.

Common Name	Latin	Where Found
Pokeweed	*Phytolacca americana*	Old fields, waste places, roadsides
Prickly Pear Cactus	*Opuntia humifusa*	Variable habitats, mostly dry and rocky
Puffball Mushroom (Giant)	*Calvatia gigantea*	Open places, disturbed grounds, old fields, barnyards
Purslane	*Portulaca oleracea*	Waste places, old fields, gardens
Redbud	*Cercis canadensis*	Thickets, moist or rocky woods, near streams
Rose, wild	*Rosa spp.*	Edges of woods, open woods, clearings, pastures, roadsides, sand dunes, seashores
Sage, wild	*Salvia spp.*	Abandoned farms, gardens, prairies

Season	Parts Used	Cautions
Early Sp.	Young shoots *only*	Use poke before it is 8'' tall. Mature plant, leaves, berries, root all contain phytolaccin, a powerful cathartic and emetic that could be fatal in concentrations. Recent research shows poke juice may cause genetic alterations; wear gloves to collect; use only occasionally. You may wish to forgo poke if you are pregnant.
Sp.–early Su. Late Su.–F.	Pads and flowers Fruits and seeds	Handle with gloves to avoid small, hairlike bristles.
Late Su.–F.	Fruiting body	Cut open lengthwise to make sure there are no caps or gills not yet emerged; flesh of an edible puffball should be featureless and pure white. If it has begun to turn yellow it will be bitter.
Sp.–early W.	Leaves, stems, seeds	None found.
Sp.–early Su.	Buds, flowers, tender pods	None found.
Sp.–early Su. Late Su.–W.	Petals, leaves Rose "hips" or calyxes	None found.
Sp., Su.	Leaves, for tea or flavoring agent	None found but should be used sparingly.

Common Name	Latin	Where Found
Sassafras	*Sassafras albidum*	Open woodlands
Shaggymane Mushroom (Inky Cap)	*Coprinus comatus*	Lawns, gardens, waste places, roadsides
Shepherd's Purse	*Capsella bursa-pastoris*	Waste places, old fields, roadsides
Smartweed (Lady's Thumb and Japanese Knotweed most palatable)	*Polygonum spp.*	Waste places, old gardens, streamsides
Solomon's Seal	*Polygonatum spp.*	Thickets, woods, upland areas
Sorrel, Sheep	*Rumex spp.*	Waste places, yards, gardens
Sorrel, Wood	*Oxalis spp.*	Yards, gardens, waste places, woods
Strawberry, wild	*Fragaria spp.*	Old fields, open places, openings in woods, rocky places

Season	Parts Used	Cautions
Su. W., year-round	Leaves Bark (flavor best in February or March)	Safrole in the plant has been found to cause cancer in laboratory animals; use in moderation.
F.	Fruiting body	Use only when young and firm; shaggymanes contain a self-digesting enzyme that turns older mushrooms black and fluid; do not ingest with alcohol.
Early Sp. Su.	Leaves Seeds	None found.
Early Sp., Su.	Leaves	None found, but some species of *Polygonum* too acrid to be palatable.
Early Sp.	Young shoots Rootstocks	Do not confuse root- stocks with those of mayapple; look for characteristic circular "seals" on large nodes. (On endangered species list of some states; check before harvesting.)
Sp., Su.	Tender leaves	Oxalic acid in this plant inhibits absorption of calcium. Use sparingly.
Sp., Su.	Leaves, seedpods	Like sheep sorrel, wood sorrel contains oxalic acid and should be eaten only occasion- ally or as a flavoring agent.
Sp. Su.	Leaves Berries	None found.

Common Name	Latin	Where Found
Sulphur Shelf Mushroom (Chicken of the Woods)	*Polyporus sulphureus*	Dead or dying trees, injured wood
Sumac	*Rhus spp.*	Edges of woods, old fields, roadsides
Sunflower	*Helianthus spp.*	Prairies, old fields, roadsides, open places
Tree Ear Mushroom	*Auricularia auricula-judae*	Deciduous woods
Violet	*Viola spp.*	Open woods, sunny areas, rocky lands, wetlands (habitat depends largely on species)
Watercress	*Nasturtium officinale*	Cold streams, springs
Wild Rice	*Zizania aquatica*	Northeastern rivers, shallow water, lakes
Winter Cress	*Barbarea vulgaris*	Roadsides, disturbed ground, waste places, old fields, moist woods

Season	Parts Used	Cautions
Late Su.–F.	Fruiting body	None found, but do confirm identification.
Su.–F., W. in some instances	Hairy red berries, as a beverage	Do not use or touch white-berried sumac (*Rhus vernix*), which causes poison ivy-like symptoms.
Late Su.–F.	Seeds	Seeds must be well chewed if raw; may cause gastric distress otherwise.
Year-round	Fruiting body	None found.
Sp., Su., F.	Leaves, flowers	None found.
Year-round	Leaves, tender stems	Collect from unpolluted streams or soak in water containing a water-purification tablet.
Late Su.–F.	Ripe seeds	Be sure to collect this wild grass seed only where legal; in some areas only those of American Indian descent may harvest. Watch also for ergot, a pinkish or purplish fungus growth that causes grains to grow grotesquely: toxic. Collect elsewhere.
Early Sp. Sp.	Leaves Flower buds	None found.

Edible Plants

There are many more edible plants than I had room or opportunity to use in this book. Some were excluded for reasons of space or unfamiliarity, others because they are locally rare (like spring beauty) or becoming endangered; still others because of limited usefulness or questionable flavor. Some plants are *edible*, and if I were starving I certainly would use them as survival rations. But this book is intended to be a *pleasurable* outing; only those plants and recipes were included that are particularly good. You will find many of these plants on this more inclusive listing.

CAUTION: Do not assume that because a plant is listed here—or in any other field guide—that all parts of the plant are edible, or in all seasons. Look each one up in the field guide section or in another book before harvesting for consumption to confirm edible parts. Like the common garden rhubarb, some perfectly delightful edibles may have parts that are poisonous to humans.

Alfalfa *Medicago sativa*
Alpine Bistort or Alpine Smartweed *Polygonum viviparum*
Amaranth *Amaranthus spp.*
Angelica *Angelica atropurpurea*
Anise-root *Osmorhiza longistylis*
Arbutus, Trailing *Epigaea repens*
Arrow Arum *Peltandra virginica*
Arrowhead (Sessile-fruited, Broad-leaved, Grass-leaved)
    Sagittaria spp.
Artichoke, Jerusalem *Helianthus tuberosus*
Asparagus *Asparagus officinalis*
Aster, Large-leaved *Aster macrophyllus*
Avens, Water *Geum rivale*
Balsam Fir *Abies balsamea*
Barberry *Berberis vulgaris*
Basswood, American *Tilia americana*
Bayberry *Myrica spp.*
Beach Pea *Lathyrus japonicus*

Bean, Wild *Phaseolus polystachios*
Bearberry, Kinnikinik *Arctostaphylos uva-ursi*
Bedstraw *Galium spp.*
Bee Balm *Monarda didyma*
Beech, American *Fagus grandifolia*
Bellflower, Creeping *Campanula rapunculoides*
Bellwort *Uvularia spp.*
Bergamot (Purple, Wild) *Monarda spp.*
Birch, Black *Betula lenta*; Yellow, *Betula lutea*
Bitter Cress, Pennsylvania *Cardamine pensylvanica*
Blackberry *Rubus spp.*
Black Haw *Viburnum prunifolium* (Raisin, wild)
Bladder Campion *Silene cucubalus*
Blueberry *Vaccinium spp.*
Bracken *Pteridium aquilinum*
Brooklime, American *Veronica americana*
Broomrape, Lesser *Orobanche minor*
Bulrush, Great *Scirpus spp.*
Bunchberry *Cornus canadensis*
Burdock *Arctium spp.*
Burnet, European Great *Sanguisorba officinalis*
Butternut *Juglans cinerea*
Calamus *Acorus calamus*
Camass, Eastern, Wild Hyacinth *Camassia scilloides*
Caraway *Carum carvi*
Carrion-flower *Smilax herbacea*
Catbrier *Smilax spp.*
Catnip *Nepeta cataria* (see mints)
Cattail *Typha spp.*
Chamomile *Matriccaria chamomilla*
Checkerberry, Wintergreen *Gaultheria procumbens*
Cheese, Common Mallow *Malva neglecta*
Cherry (Black, Choke, Fire, Pin, Wild) *Prunus spp.*
Chervil, Wild; Honewort *Cryptotaenia canadensis*
Chestnut *Castanea dentata*
Chicken of the Woods (mushroom), Sulphur Shelf *Polyporus
    sulphureus*
Chickweed (Common, Mouse-ear, Star) *Stellaria spp.,
    Cerastium spp.*
Chicory *Cichorium intybus*
Chinquapin (Eastern, Ozark) *Castanea spp.*
Chive, Wild *Allium spp.*
Chokeberry *Pyrus spp.*
Chufa, Yellow Nut-grass *Cyperus esculentus*
Cicely, Sweet *Osmorhiza claytoni*
Cleaver (Goose Grass Bedstraw) *Galium aparine*

Clover *Trifolium spp.*
Coltsfoot *Tussilago farfara*
Comfrey *Symphytum officinale*
Corn-salad *Valerianella olitoria*
Cow-cress, Field Peppergrass *Lepidium campestre*
Crab Apple *Pyrus spp.*
Cranberry *Vaccinium spp.*
Cress, Spring *Cardamine bulbosa*
Cress, Winter *Barbarea vulgaris*
Cucumber-root, Indian *Medeola virginiana*
Currant *Ribes spp.*
Daisy, Ox-eye *Chrysanthemum leucanthemum*
Dandelion *Taraxacum officinale*
Dayflower *Commelina spp.*
Daylily *Hemerocallis spp.*
Deerberry *Gaylussacia spp.*
Dewberry *Rubus spp.*
Dittany *Conila origanoides*
Dock (Curled, Yellow) *Rumex crispus*
Dogtooth Violet *Erythronium americanum*
Dulse *Rhodymenia palmata*
Elderberry, Common *Sambucus candensis*
Elecampane *Inula helenium*
Elm, Slippery *Ulmus rubra*
False Solomon's Seal *Smilacina racemosa*
Ferns *Pteridium* and *Pteretis spp.*
Feverwort, Tinker's Weed *Triosteum perfoliatum*
Fir, Balsam *Abies balsamea*
Fireweed *Epilobium angustifolium*
Garlic, Wild *Allium spp.*
Gill-over-the-Ground, Ground Ivy *Glechoma hederacea*
Ginger, Wild *Asarum canadense*
Ginseng *Panax quinquefolius*
Glasswort *Salicornia spp.*
Goat's-beard, Yellow *Tragopogon pratensis*
Golden Club *Orontium aquaticum*
Goldenrod, Sweet *Solidago odora*
Gooseberry *Ribes spp.*
Grape, Wild *Vitis spp.*
Greenbrier, Catbrier *Smilax spp.*
Ground-Cherry *Physalis spp.*
Groundnut *Apios americana*
Hackberry, American *Celtis occidentalis*
Harbinger-of-Spring *Erigenia bulbosa*
Hawthorn *Crataegus spp.*
Hazelnut *Corylus spp.*

Hickory *Carya spp.*
Hobblebush *Viburnum spp.*
Hog-Peanut *Amphicarpa bracteata*
Honey Locust *Gleditsia triacanthos*
Horsemint, European *Monarda spp.* (See Bergamot)
Huckleberry *Vaccinium spp.*
Husk-Tomato (same as Ground-Cherry) *Physalis spp.*
Hyssop, Giant Blue *Agastache foeniculum*
Iceland Moss *Cetraria islandica*
Jack-in-the-Pulpit *Arisaema atrorubens*
Japanese Knotweed *Polygonum cuspidatum* (see Smartweed)
Jewelweed *Impatiens spp.*
Juneberry *Amelanchier spp.*
Juniper, Ground *Juniperus communis* var. *depressa*
Kelp *Alaria esculenta*
Kinnikinik, Bearberry *Arctostaphylos uva-ursi*
Kudzu *Pueraria lobata*
Labrador Tea *Ledum groenlandicium*
Lady's Thumb, Redleg *Polygonum persicaria*
Lamb's-Quarter *Chenopodium album*
Larch, American; Tamarack *Larix laricina*
Leek, Wild *Allium tricoccum*
Lettuce (Hairy, Prickly, Wild Blue) *Lactuca spp.*
Lily, Bullhead *Nuphar variegatum*
Lily, Canada *Lilium canadense*
Lily, Day *Hemerocallis spp.*
Lily, Trout *Erythronium americanum* (see Dogtooth Violet)
Lily, Water *Nymphaea spp.*
Lily, Turk's Cap *Lilium superbum*
Live-Forever, Orpine *Sedum purpureum*
Lotus, American, Nelumbo *Nelumbo lutea*
Mallow, Common *Malva neglecta*
Maples *Acer spp.*
Mayapple *Podophyllum peltatum*
Maypop, Passionflower *Passiflora incarnata*
Mexican Tea *Chenopodium ambrosioides*
Milkweed, Common *Asclepias syriaca*
Mint (various species) *Mentha spp.*
Morel (mushroom) *Morchella esculenta*, related spp.
Mormon Tea *Ephedra spp.*
Moss, Irish *Chondrus crispus*
Moss, Reindeer *Cladonia rangiferina*
Mulberry *Morus spp.*
Mullein, Common *Verbascum thapsus*
Mushroom, various edible, spp.
Mustard (Black, Field, Wild) *Brassica spp.*

Nannyberry *Viburnum spp.*
Nettle *Urtica spp.*, *Laportea canadensis*
New Jersey Tea *Ceanothus americanus*
Nut Grass, Chufa *Cyperus esculentus*
Oak-acorn (various species) *Quercus spp.*
Oat, Wild, related to Bellwort *Uvularia sessilifolia*
Onion, Wild *Allium spp.*
Orache *Atriplex patula*
Oswego Tea (same as Bee Balm) *Monarda spp.*
Oyster Plant *Tragopogon porrifolius*
Parsnip (Cow, Water, Wild) *Heracleum maximum*, *Sium sauve*,
    Pastinaca sativa
Partridgeberry *Mitchella repens*
Passion Flower (same as Maypop) *Passiflora incarnata*
Pasture Brake, Bracken Fern *Pteridium aquilinum*
Pawpaw *Asimina triloba*
Pecan *Carya illinoensis*
Pennycress, Field *Thlaspi arvense*
Pennyroyal, American *Hedeoma pulegioides*
Peppergrass *Lepidium spp.*
Persimmon *Diospyros virginiana*
Pickerelweed *Pontederia cordata*
Pigweed (Lamb's-Quarter) *Chenopodium album*
Pine, White *Pinus strobus*
Pineapple Weed *Matricaria matricarioides*
Plantain *Plantago spp.*
Plum (Beach, Wild) *Prunus spp.*
Pokeweed *Phytolacca americana*
Potato-vine, Wild *Ipomoea pandurata*
Prickly Pear Cactus *Opuntia humifusa*
Primrose, Common Evening *Oenothera biennis*
Puffball, Giant (mushroom) *Calvatia gigantea*
Purslane *Portulaca oleracea*
Queen Anne's Lace *Daucus carota*
Raisin, Wild (Black Haw) *Viburnum spp.*
Ramp *Allium spp.*
Raspberry *Rubus spp.*
Redbay *Persea borbonia*
Redbud *Cercis canadensis*
Reed *Phragmites communis*
Reindeer Moss *Cladonia rangiferina*
Rice, Wild *Zizania aquatica*
Rock Tripe *Umbilicaria spp.* and *Gyrophora spp.*
Rose *Rosa spp.*
Sage *Salvia spp.*
Salsify (Oyster Plant) *Tragopogon porrifolius*

Sarsaparilla *Aralia racemosa*
Sassafras *Sassafras albidum*
Saxifrage *Saxifraga spp.*
Sea Lettuce *Ulva lactuca*
Sea-Purslane *Sesuvium maritimum*
Sea-Rocket *Cakile edentula*
Serviceberry *Amelanchier spp.*
Shaggymane (mushroom) *Coprinus comatus*
Shepherd's Purse *Capsella bursa-pastoris*
Silverweed *Potentilla anserina*
Smartweed, Alpine *Polygonum viviparum*
Solomon's Seal *Polygonatum spp.*
Sorrel (Sheep, Garden) *Rumex spp.*
Sorrel, Wood *Oxalis spp.*
Sow Thistle *Sonchus spp.*
Spatterdock *Nuphar advena*
Spicebush *Lindera benzoin*
Spiderwort *Tradescantia virginiana*
Spikenard *Aralia racemosa*
Spring Beauty *Claytonia spp.*
Spruce (Black, Red) *Picea spp.*
Storksbill *Erodium cicutarium*
Strawberry, Wild *Fragaria spp.*
Sulphur Shelf (mushroom) Chicken-of-the-Woods *Polyporus sulphureus*
Sumac (Dwarf, Smooth, Staghorn) *Rhus spp.*
Sunflower, Common *Helianthus spp.*
Sweetbrier *Rosa eleganteria*
Sweet Cicely *Osmorhiza claytoni*
Sweet Flag *Acorus calamus*
Sweet Gum *Liquidambar styraciflua*
Sycamore *Plantanus occidentalis*
Tamarack, American Larch *Larix laricina*
Tansy, Common *Tanacetum vulgare*
Thimbleberry *Rubus parviflorus*
Thistle (Bull, Common) *Cirsium spp.*
Toothwort *Dentaria spp.*
Touch-Me-Not (Jewelweed — Pale, Spotted) *Impatiens spp.*
Trailing Arbutus *Epigaea repens*
Trillium *Trillium spp.*
Vervain, Blue *Verbena hastata*
Viola *Viola spp.*
Violet *Viola spp.*
Wake-Robin (Red Trillium) *Trillium erectum*
Walnut *Juglans spp.*
Wapatoo (Arrowhead) *Sagittaria latifolia*

Watercress *Nasturtium officinale*
Willow *Salix spp.*
Winter Cress *Barbarea vulgaris*
Wintergreen, Checkerberry *Gaultheria procumbens*
Wood-nettle *Laportea canadensis*
Wound wort *Stachys palustris*
Yucca *Yucca filamentosa*

Poisonous Plants

It pays to know and recognize the poisonous plants you may encounter in gathering wild edibles. Throughout I have included cautions when parts of edible plants may be poisonous or if the edible species resembles a non-edible one, but there are other plants you will need to avoid. It is beyond the scope of this book to include them all in the field guide section, but here is a partial listing. Some may cause gastric distress or even death; others are known to produce contact dermatitis. Those marked with an (×) are poisonous to eat; a (★) denotes plants that can cause skin irritation. Those with edible parts that are also included in this book are identified with a (•). It is a good idea to look these plants up in a field guide for botanically accurate drawings or color photographs to make sure you know the plants to avoid.

A good rule of thumb in dealing with wild edibles is—it isn't necessary to know all the poisonous varieties. Just be sure you know which plants are *edible* before you pick them.

This list was compiled from several sources, and includes only the most common of the poisonous plants, ones I felt you might be most likely to encounter. Check with a more complete source such as *Poisonous Plants, A Color Field Guide* by Lucia Woodward (New York: Hippocrene Books, Inc., 1985) for any questionable plants you may find.

As in any outdoor endeavor, it's best to know what you are doing before plunging into unfamiliar territory. Many of our domestic vegetables have their toxic parts as well as their edible parts, or seasons in which you should not eat them—spinach, potatoes, tomatoes, and rhubarb, for instance. The same is true of wildings. Again, use a good field guide with accurate drawings or color photographs to aid in identification or go with an expert. In this book I have included drawings of some of the more easily recognized wildings, but they are intended more as decorative art than as diagnostic tools.

Use only those parts recommended for eating, and make *sure* you know what it is you are harvesting. Dr. James Duke, botanist with the USDA, recommends novice foragers avoid the carrot family and wild mushrooms, until you know your way around the outdoors.

Remember, just because something looks edible—even if it closely resembles a plant you know to be safe, and even if animals or insects seem to be dining with impunity—don't assume it is in fact safe for human consumption. Check before you eat.

Individual food allergies or sensitivities may cause gastric distress even if a plant is commonly recognized as edible. Go slowly, to start out. Identify correctly, prepare as suggested—and try only a little to begin with. Even a well-known edible like wild mustard can produce an upset stomach if eaten the first time in excessive amounts. I found out the hard way! Someone allergic to domestic strawberries may expect the same symptoms with the small wild varieties.

People with sensitive skin should avoid members of the *Rhus* clan, of course—poison ivy, poison oak, and the rest. Nettles may cause excessive discomfort, as may some of the spurges and the common wild parsnip.

Gather wild foods, incidentally, only where you know chemical herbicides or pesticides are not in use. Gather nothing from polluted waters. Aside from surface contamination of leaves, plants have the ability to concentrate nitrates in their tissues.

Tempting as some of the healthy, edible weeds that grow by the highway may seem, it's best to leave them alone as well. Heavy metals and asbestos deposits from automobile exhaust and brake linings may be present in quantities detrimental to your health near a heavily traveled roadway. Railway and power line rights-of-way are often sprayed with herbicides.

  × Amanita (mushroom) *Amanita muscaria*
  × American Yew *Taxus candensis*
  × Autumn Crocus *Colchicum autumnale*
  × Azalea *Rhododendron spp.*
  × Baneberry *Actaea spp.*
  × Belladonna (Nightshade) *Atropa belladonna*
  × Black Henbane *Hyoscyamus niger*
 • × Black Locust *Robinia pseudoacacia*
  × Bloodroot *Sanguinaria canadensis*
  × Blue Flag *Iris spp.*
  × Buckthorn *Rhamnus spp.*
  × Buttercup *Ranunculus spp.*
  × Butterfly Weed *Asclepias tuberosa*
  × Canada Moonseed *Menispermum canadense*
  × Castor Bean *Ricinus communis*
  × Chinaberry *Melia azedarach*
  × Chinese Lantern *Physalis spp.*
  × Destroying Angel (mushroom) *Amanita spp.*
  × Ergot *Claviceps spp.*
  × False Hellebore *Veratrum viride*
  × Fool's Parsley *Aethusa cynapium*
  × Foxglove *Digitalis*

× Goat's Rue *Tephrosia virginiana*
× Horse Chestnut (Buckeye) *Aesculus hippocastanum*
× Jimsonweed *Datura stramonium*
× Laburnum *Laburnum anagyroides*
× Larkspur *Delphinium spp.*
× Lobelia *Lobelia spp.*
× Lupine *Lupinus spp.*
× Mistletoe *Phoradendron flavescens*
× Monkshood *Aconitum spp.*
× Morning Glory *Ipomoea spp.*
•× Mulberry, Red, White, *Morus spp.*, *Rubra*
•★ Nettle *Urtica spp.*
· × Nightshade *Atropha belladonna, Solanum spp.*
× Poison Hemlock *Conium maculatum*
★ Poison Ivy *Rhus radicans*
★ Poison Oak *Rhus toxicodendron*
★ Poison Sumac *Rhus vernix*
•× Poke, Pokeweed *Phytolacca americana*
× Red Elderberry *Sambucus racemosa*
× Rhododendron *Rhododendron spp.*
× Scotch Broom *Cytisus scoparius*
× Spindle Berry (Wahoo) *Euonymus europaeus*
× Spurge *Euphorbia spp.*
× Water Hemlock *Cicuta spp.*
•× Wild Cherry *Prunus spp.*
× Wild Indigo *Baptista tinctoria*
× Wood Anemone *Anemone nemorosa*
× Yew *Taxus baccata*

A Casual Bibliography

I find a bibliography more interesting—as well as more useful—when I am given a bit of information about the books suggested rather than a simple listing, so I will follow my own advice here.

Wild Food Cookbooks and Field Guides

Over the years, there have been a number of books on wild edibles. Euell Gibbons may be the most famous devotee of the forager's craft, but he is certainly not the first—nor the last. Many authors have provided us with information and a fascinating trek through the edible outdoors in the form of field guides and wild foods cookbooks; a very few books are a combination of the two.

One early field guide is *Edible Wild Plants of Eastern North America*, by Merritt Lyndon Fernald and Alfred Charles Kinsey (New York: Harper and Row, 1943 and 1958). This is one book that is nearly always mentioned in the bibliography of any wild foods book; it is excellent, though I wish it had more drawings and photographs of the edible plants discussed.

A Naturalist's Guide to Cooking with Wild Plants by Connie and Arnold Krochmal (New York: New York Times Book Co., 1974) is much more a cookbook than a field guide. It does have a wide range of recipes for many of the easiest-to-identify plants.

A good, portable book for pocket or pack is *Nature Bound, A Pocket Field Guide* by Ron Dawson (Boise, Ida.: OMNIgraphics, Ltd., 1985). The photographs are excellent, although of necessity a book of this size leaves out a few of my favorite wildings. The section on poisonous plants is worth the price of the book.

Euell Gibbons books are classics, and with good reason. The love Mr. Gibbons felt for the outdoors shines through the descriptions of foraging trips, making the reader feel as if he is walking alongside the master. The recipes are wonderful in most cases, and the graphics generally good. Look for *Stalking the Wild Asparagus* (New York: David McKay Co., 1970), and *Stalking the Blue-Eyed Scallop* from the same publisher, (1974). If your interest runs to recipes for medicinals as well, you'll like *Stalking the Healthful Herbs* (New

York: David McKay Co., 1966). (Don't overlook this book; there are a number of useful and delightful food recipes.)

Oliver Perry Medsger's *Edible Wild Plants* (New York: MacMillan Co., 1966) is very complete and should be available through your library.

One of my favorite "oldies but goodies" is *Eat the Weeds*, by Ben Charles Harris (New York: Keats, 1973 in paperback).

Using Wayside Plants by Nelson Coon (New York: Hearthside Press Incorporated, 1957, 1960, 1969) incorporates recipes with information about medicinals, dye plants, scrubbing reeds, plant fibers, and more.

Arranged by flower color for easy identification in the field, *Wild Edibles of Missouri* by Jan Phillips (Jefferson City, Mo.: The Conservation Commission of the State of Missouri, 1979) also has some quite good recipes in the back of the book. Don't be put off by the title; many of these wildings are available throughout much of the Midwest.

Billy Joe Tatum's Wild Foods Field Guide and Cookbook has a number of wild edibles in its listings, and good-sounding recipes arranged by plant source in the back of the book. (New York: Workman Publishing, 1976. Paperback.)

The most gorgeous entry to date is *Wild Foods* by Roger Phillips (Boston: Little, Brown, and Co., 1986). Mr. Phillips is a superb photographer who not only included photos of the wild plant foods discussed, he shot graphics of the recipes, as well. A very tempting book!

Two books provide a fascinating look at the Native Americans' use of wild plants: *Native Harvest, Recipes and Botanicals of the American Indian* by Barrie Kavasch (New York: Random House, 1979) and a new entry from Kelly Kindscher, *Edible Wild Plants of the Prairie* (Lawrence, Kan.: University Press of Kansas, 1987).

You may not have thought of the all-time classic cookbook, *The Joy of Cooking* by Irma S. Rombauer and Marion Rombauer Becker (New York: Bobbs-Merril Co., Inc., 1975) as a wild foods cookbook, but look through the index if you've found a plant or animal you want to experiment with; in many cases you'll find an excellent choice there. They don't call this "the all-purpose cookbook" for nothing. If you have a favorite general cookbook, check in the index, or experiment: substitute wildings for domestic ingredients.

Unfortunately, most wild foods cookbooks neglect the meat course, assuming your interest in wildings extends only to the plant kingdom. If this is not so, if you prefer to go completely wild, your choices (until this book) were somewhat slim. The best in my collection is a rather chatty, down-home little volume called *Cy Littlebee's Guide to Cooking Fish and Game* (Jefferson City, Mo.: The Conservation Commission of the State of Missouri, 1983 [eleventh printing]). This is the book that lists skunk among its possible ingredients, so you see it is amazingly complete. The book also contains a number of recipes for using wild plants; it's quite useful. *The Joy of Cooking* (see above) also addresses the wild meat course.

As we have said, you needn't be a hunter to use these recipes; a friend may give you a haunch of venison, and many of the items suggested in the meat course chapter are available in specialty markets—or even your local supermarket. Mine often boasts buffalo meat in various forms. Visit a fish market for frog legs or crayfish as well as many of the varieties of fish.

The best of the wild food field guides is one of the Peterson Field Guide Series, *A Field Guide to Edible Wild Plants* by Lee Allen Peterson (Boston: Houghton Mifflin Co., 1977). Many of the excellent diagrammatic drawings are from the earlier field guide in the series by Roger Tory Peterson, *A Field Guide to Wildflowers*, from the same publisher; additional species were drawn by the author, the elder Peterson's son. This is an excellent and extremely complete book, and although it lacks recipes it gives much-needed information about edible parts, season of availability, and basic preparation. I wouldn't be without it.

General Field Guides

Perhaps you only want to supplement this book with a general-purpose field guide. There are many good ones on the market, listing everything from wildflowers and weeds to mushrooms, from ferns to mussels and clams.

The Peterson Field Guide Series is always excellent and I would look there first. There are guides to birds and mammals, shells, ferns, trees and shrubs, and reptiles and amphibians that would be of interest to the serious wild foods forager.

Look also at the Audubon Society field guides for plants and flowers, mushrooms, mammals, and birds. Their color photographs are unsurpassed. (All from Alfred A. Knopf, New York.)

Among the most useful of field guides are the *Field Guide to the Wildflowers* by Roger Tory Peterson, mentioned above (Boston: Houghton Mifflin Co., 1968), and the *Audubon Society Field Guide to North American Wildflowers* (New York: Alfred A. Knopf, 1979). Van Nostrand Reinhold's *Wildflowers and Weeds* by Booth Courtenay and James H. Zimmerman is arranged according to plant family; the photos are excellent. (New York: Van Nostrand Reinhold, 1972.)

If you are planning to forage for wild mushrooms, a book with good, clear, color photos is a must. Look at the Audubon Society field guide series book, or check out *Simon & Shuster's Guide to Mushrooms* by Giovanni Pacioni. (New York: Simon & Shuster, 1981.) Not only are the photographs excellent in this book, but information on edibility (and palatability!) is included as well, making this a good choice to take to the field.

Edible trees and shrubs may be found among the 500 entries in *Trees of North America and Europe* by Roger Phillips, the same excellent photographer who brought us the *Wild Foods* book mentioned earlier. Identification of edible species should be easy using this one. (New York: Random House, 1978.)

If birds will be a part of your diet, *A Field Guide to the Birds* by Roger Tory Peterson (Boston: Houghton Mifflin, 1980) would be a help, or find a book on game birds. Be sure you have identified correctly, and that the bird you are after is in season and on the game bird list.

If you need help in identifying members of the animal kingdom, I can suggest no better book than *The Wild Mammals of Missouri*, by Charles W. and

Elizabeth R. Schwartz (Columbia, Mo.: University of Missouri Press, 1981). It is beautifully illustrated with Mr. Schwartz's drawings and tells all you need to know about many of our common mammals and their habits. Don't be put off by the title; most of the mammals are widespread.

For a more manageable size in a field guide, try *The Audubon Society Field Guide to North American Mammals* (New York: Alfred A. Knopf, 1980).

Check with your local conservation commission for books they may have on game fish, birds, or mammals; many of the states put out beautiful volumes that are full of information pertinent to your area.

Poisonous Plants

Although I feel it is *most* important to recognize the edible species of plants and their seasons, it is also good to acquaint yourself with plants to steer clear of. Some resemble the edible varieties, others may grow nearby, and some simply look as if they should be edible. Don't be tempted to try such a plant without proper identification. I want to remind you that even if squirrels or insects seem to be dining with impunity it is no guarantee that the plant is safe for humans. Look up *Poisonous Plants, A Color Field Guide*, by Lucia Woodward (New York: Hippocrene Books Inc., 1985), or two by John M. Kingsbury, *Poisonous Plants of the United States and Canada* (Englewood Cliffs, N.J.: Prentice-Hall, 1964) or *Deadly Harvest: A Guide to Common Poisonous Plants* (New York: Holt, Rinehart and Winston, 1965).

Index

236 / *Index*